teach® yourself

quick fix
spanish grammar
keith chambers

For over 60 years, more than
50 million people have learnt over
750 subjects the **teach yourself**
way, with impressive results.

be where you want to be
with **teach yourself**

The publisher has used its best endeavours to ensure that the URLs for external websites referred to in this book are correct and active at the time of going to press. However, the publisher and the author have no responsibility for the websites and can make no guarantee that a site will remain live or that the content will remain relevant, decent or appropriate.

For UK order enquiries: please contact Bookpoint Ltd, 130 Milton Park, Abingdon, Oxon, OX14 4SB. Telephone: +44 (0) 1235 827720. Fax: +44 (0) 1235 400454. Lines are open 09.00–17.00, Monday to Saturday, with a 24-hour message answering service. Details about our titles and how to order are available at www.teachyourself.co.uk

For USA order enquiries: please contact McGraw-Hill Customer Services, PO Box 545, Blacklick, OH 43004-0545, USA. Telephone: 1-800-722-4726. Fax: 1-614-755-5645.

For Canada order enquiries: please contact McGraw-Hill Ryerson Ltd, 300 Water St, Whitby, Ontario, L1N 9B6, Canada. Telephone: 905 430 5000. Fax: 905 430 5020.

Long renowned as the authoritative source for self-guided learning – with more than 50 million copies sold worldwide – the **teach yourself** series includes over 500 titles in the fields of languages, crafts, hobbies, business, computing and education.

British Library Cataloguing in Publication Data: a catalogue record for this title is available from the British Library.

Library of Congress Catalog Card Number: on file.

First published in UK 1999 by Hodder Education, 338 Euston Road, London, NW1 3BH.

First published in US 1999 by The McGraw-Hill Companies, Inc.

This edition published 2006.

The **teach yourself** name is a registered trade mark of Hodder Headline.

Typeset by Transet Limited, Coventry, England.
Printed in Great Britain for Hodder Education, a division of Hodder Headline, 338 Euston Road, London, NW1 3BH, by Cox & Wyman Ltd, Reading, Berkshire.

Hodder Headline's policy is to use papers that are natural, renewable and recyclable products and made from wood grown in sustainable forests. The logging and manufacturing processes are expected to conform to the environmental regulations of the country of origin.

Impression number   10 9 8 7 6 5 4 3 2 1
Year   2010 2009 2008 2007 2006

iii

contents

introduction

This basic grammar is designed as a handy reference work for someone who has recently started Spanish and who would like the opportunity to practise some of the important points of the language in a systematic way.

The book is divided into units, each summarising a specific grammatical point on one page and with related exercises opposite. Answers are provided at the end of the book for you to check your progress.

Most learners find that regular but limited, targeted practice is the most helpful way to get on with a language and make real progress. Use the contents page to identify a point you particularly want to revise and set yourself a specific goal to practise as time allows. You need not complete a whole unit in one go, neither do you necessarily have to work through the book in rigid order.

Grammatical points have been split up in logical bite-sized pieces.

The sign ⚠ warns of special danger to English-speaking learners.

Explanations have deliberately been kept as simple as possible and err on the side of general correctness so far as the beginner is concerned; however, to help learners gain an insight to how the language works and for further study, I have also included some examples of more advanced use.

My thanks go to my students past and present who have experienced and helped to refine the contents of this basic grammar. I hope you too will find it useful and informative.

Keith Chambers

1 The rules of spelling

Spanish spelling is very straightforward. The rules are logical and universally applied.

A The Spanish alphabet contains the following letters; their names (i.e. the way they are pronounced individually) are given in brackets.

A (a) B (be) C (ce) CH (che) D (de) E (e) F (efe) G (ge)
H (ache) I (i) J (jota) K (ka) L (ele) LL (elle) M (eme)
N (ene) Ñ (eñe) O (o) P (pe) Q (cu) R (ere) S (ese)
T (te) U (u) V (uve) W (uve doble) X (equis) Y (i griega)
Z (zeta)

K and **w** are rarely used and are found in words borrowed from other languages: **kilo** (= *kilogram*), **whisky**, etc. In older dictionaries, the letters **ch**, **ll** and **ñ** follow **c**, **l** and **n** as separate entries. Few words actually start with **ñ**.

B Spanish avoids double consonants except with four exceptions, which you can remember by applying the CaRoLiNe rule.

- **cc** as in **diccionario** (*dictionary*), **acción** (*action*), **acceso** (*access*), where the **c** has two different sounds;
- **rr** as in **terrible**, **horror**, **Inglaterra** (*England*), where the **r** sound has double strength;
- **ll** as in **millón** (*million*), **guerrilla**, **llama** (*flame*), where the **ll** is a different sound from **l**;
- **nn** (much less common) as in **innecesario** (*unnecessary*), **innegable** (*undeniable*), where an existing word starting with **n** has added a prefix.

C **Z** is not permitted before **e** or **i**; **c** is used instead: **cebra** (*zebra*); **cero** (*zero*)

D Where you want to write a **kw** sound, use **cu**: **cuestión**.

Where you want to write a **k** sound in front of **e** or **i**, use **qu**: **tranquilo** (*quiet*), **quiosco** (*kiosk*), **querer** (*to want*); otherwise use **c**: **catorce** (*fourteen*).

To write a **g** sound (as in *go*), use **gu** in front of **e** or **i**: **guerra** (*war*), **Miguel** (*Michael*), **espaguetis** (*spaghetti*); otherwise use **g** as in English: **gol** (*goal*).

A **g** on its own in front of **e** or **i** sounds like a Spanish **j** (i.e. a strongly aspirated **h**): **general**, **Gibraltar**, **genuino**, **gitano** (*gypsy*).

A very few words have a **gw** sound in front of **e** or **i**: in this case, the spelling is **gü**: **cigüeña** (*stork*). In front of **a** or **o**; use **gu** with no dots: **guante** (*glove*).

1 Exercises

1 Spell out these place names in Spanish.

  a Madrid
  b Sevilla
  c Granada
  d Barcelona
  e Toledo
  f Sitges
  g Aranjuez

2 Change these words into their Spanish versions.

  a professor
  b possible
  c zero
  d million
  e gorilla

3 What are the English equivalents of these Spanish words?

  a ecuador
  b elepé
  c güisqui
  d tren
  e énfasis
  f símbolo

4 How does Spanish spell these words?

  a sweater
  b football
  c kiosk
  d shampoo
  e chauffeur
  f tennis
  g goal
  h zebra

5 Now that you have had a chance to practise, write down the names of the letters of the Spanish alphabet in full.

A B C CH D E F G H I J K L LL M N Ñ
O P Q R S T U V W X Y Z

2 The use of the written accent

*Spanish needs to spell some words with an accent.
Fortunately, the rules are fairly simple and logical.*

The accent mark (´), always placed over the stressed vowel, is used in four main circumstances.

A To distinguish two words of different meaning: **si** (*if*), **sí** (*yes*); **mi** (*my*), **mí** (*me* after a preposition); **tu** (*your*), **tú** (*you*); **como** (*like*), **cómo** (*how*).

B To distinguish a question word from a relative pronoun: **dónde** (*where?*), **qué** (*what?*), **cuándo** (when?), **por qué** (why?), **quién** (who?).

⚠ Cómo (*how*) always has an accent.

C To distinguish pronouns from similarly spelt adjectives: **este libro** (*this book*), **éste es mi libro** (*this (one) is my book*).

D To indicate some irregularity in stress (probably the most important use).

- Spanish words are normally stressed on the final syllable, unless the word ends in a vowel, **s** or **n**, where the stress falls on the last-but-one syllable.

  usted, Madrid, azul, Gibraltar BUT casa, Inglaterra, cinco, comen

- Any exception is indicated with an accent.

  habitación, fútbol, física, veintidós, inglés

- Bearing this in mind, note what happens when endings are added to certain types of words.

  inglés (*English (m.)*) → inglesa (*English (f.)*);
  habitación (*room*) → habitaciones (*rooms*);
  volumen (*volume*) → volúmenes (*volumes*).

- Sometimes other changes occur to fit in with the spelling rules.

  lápiz (*pencil*) → lápices (*pencils*)
  actriz (*actress*) → actrices (*actresses*)
  un libro (*one book*) → veintiún libros (*21 books*)

2 Exercises

1 Write down the Spanish for these words, paying attention to the need for an accent.

a yes   c my   e you   g like

b if   d me   f your   h how

2 Write down the Spanish for these words. Remember an accent mark is needed if they ask a question.

a Where?   c How?   e Why?

b When?   d What?   f Who?

3 Say each word out loud and underline the stressed vowel.

a Madrid   f casa

b Barcelona   g hospital

c Pedro   h universidad

d Elena   i ocupado

e España   j hablar

4 The following words sound very much like English but have an accent mark missing. Say each word out loud and write the accent mark on the correct vowel.

a lamina   f cafe

b Dali   g futbol

c Peru   h medico

d Bogota   i video

e limite   j record

5 Make the necessary spelling or accent changes to the second word in each pair.

a feroz/ferozes

b francesa/frances

c posiciones/posicion

d resumen/resumenes

e sigo/siges

f hice/hico

g Paco/Pacita

3 Nouns and articles: gender

Nouns in Spanish are either masculine or feminine.
The gender is frequently obvious from the spelling.

A Most nouns which end in -o, are masculine. The word for *the* *(the definite article)* with a masculine noun in the singular is **el**.

el libro (*the book*); el colegio (*the (high) school*); el niño (*the child*); el chico (*the boy, lad*); el vino (*the wine*); el periódico (*the newspaper*)

B Nouns which denote males are usually masculine.

el hombre (*the man*); el padre (*the father*); el estudiante (*the (male) student*); el profesor (*the (male) teacher*); el director (*the (male) director*); el cantante (*the (male) singer*); el ladrón (*the (male) robber*); el señor (*the gentleman*)

C Nouns ending in -a are usually feminine. The definite article with a feminine singular noun is **la**.

la casa (*the house*); la cerveza (*the beer*); la chica (*the girl*); la niña (*the (female) child*); la señora (*the lady*)

D Nouns which denote females are usually feminine.

la mujer (*the woman*); la madre (*the mother*); la cantante (*the (female) singer*); la directora (*the (female) director*)

E Nouns which end in -e may be masculine or feminine, so you will need to learn the gender.

- Common masculine nouns ending in -e include:

  el café (*the coffee, café*); el cine (*the cinema*); el aceite (*the oil*)

- Nouns ending in **-aje** are masculine.

  el garaje (*the garage*); el peaje (*toll (on motorway, etc.)*)

- Common feminine nouns ending in -e include:

  la clase (*the class*); la llave (*the key*); la gente (*the people*); la torre (*the tower*)

3 Exercises

1 Put the correct definite article (*el/la*) with the noun.

> *E.g.* libro → el libro

a vino	**d** colegio	**g** periódico	**j** niño
b cerveza	**e** chico	**h** revista	
c casa	**f** chica	**i** niña	

2 Put the correct definite article (*el/la*) with the noun.

a clase	**d** gente	**g** madre	**j** equipaje
b llave	**e** cine	**h** té	**k** torre
c aceite	**f** garaje	**i** café	

3 Give the feminine equivalents of the following.

a el hombre	**c** el padre	**e** el cantante
b el niño	**d** el chico	

4 Give the masculine equivalents of the following.

a la profesora	**c** la cantante	**e** la madre
b la señora	**d** la directora	

5 The following nouns are new to you. Put the correct definite article (*el/la*) according to the meaning.

a tía (*aunt*)	**e** hija (*daughter*)	**i** actor (*actor*)
b hijo (*son*)	**f** hermano (*brother*)	**j** abuela
c hermana (*sister*)	**g** enfermera (*nurse*)	(*grandmother*)
d tío (*uncle*)	**h** secretaria (*secretary*)	**k** marido (*husband*)
		l abuelo (*grandfather*)

6 Each noun here has a corresponding female/male form. What are they?

> *E.g.* el hijo (*son*) → la hija (*daughter*)

a el italiano (*Italian*)	**d** el ministro (*minister*)
b la rusa (*Russian*)	**e** el camarero (*waiter*)
c la secretaria (*secretary*)	

4 Nouns: more on genders

A Nouns which end in a consonant can belong to either gender, so you will need to learn these carefully.

- Some masculine nouns ending in a consonant include:
  el papel (*the paper*); el cartel (*the poster*); el arroz (*the rice*); el lápiz (*the pencil*)

- Some feminine words ending in a consonant include:
  la luz (*the light*); la piel (*the skin*); la habitación (*the room*); la capital (*the capital city*)

- All nouns ending in **-dad** or **-tad** are feminine.
  la ciudad (*the city, large town*); la universidad (*the university*)

B The word for *a/an (the indefinite article)* is **un** for masculine nouns and **una** for feminine nouns.
  un libro (*a book*); un cine (*a cinema*); una casa (*a house*); una universidad (*a university*)

C To make all nouns plural, add **-s** to words ending in a vowel and **-es** to words ending in a consonant. The word for *the* is **los** with masculine plural nouns and **las** with feminine plural nouns.
  los chicos (*the boys*); las chicas (*the girls*); los profesores (*the teachers*); las universidades (*the universities*)

- Nouns ending in **-z** change to **-ces** in the plural.
  los lápices (*the pencils*); los andaluces (*the Andalusians*)

- Nouns ending in **-ión**, like **habitación** (*room*), lose the accent when adding **-es**.
  las habitaciones (*the rooms*)

- Some plurals which are masculine can include the feminine.
  los hijos (*the sons and daughters, children*); los padres (*the parents*); los tíos (*the aunts and uncles*)

⚠ If there is likely to be any ambiguity, you can clarify what you mean by re-stating the nouns.
  los tíos y las tías (*the uncles and the aunts*)

4 Exercises

1 Give the correct definite article (*el/la*) with these nouns.

E.g. catedral → la catedral

a luz
b arroz
c ciudad
d piel
e cartel

f papel
g andaluz
h habitación
i lápiz
j catedral

2 Give the correct indefinite article (*un/una*) with the same nouns.

E.g. una catedral

3 Change the same nouns into the plural, adding *los* or *las* as appropriate.

E.g. las catedrales

4 Give the singular of the following nouns.

E.g. los chicos → el chico

a las casas
b los lápices
c las ciudades
d los carteles
e las universidades

f los papeles
g las luces
h las habitaciones
i los andaluces
j las pieles

5 Clarify the nouns to show that you are referring to both genders.

E.g. los tíos → los tíos y las tías

a los hijos
b los abuelos
c los niños
d los hermanos

e los sobrinos
f los nietos
g los padres

5 More on genders: exceptions (1)

This unit looks at nouns that are feminine by exception.

You already know some basic rules for genders of nouns. There are, however, some nouns which, from their endings, appear to be of one gender when in fact they are of the other.

A There are a very few nouns which end in -o, but which are, in fact, feminine. These are mostly words which have been shortened.

> la radio(grafía) (*radio*); la foto(grafía) (*photograph*); la moto(cicleta) (*motorbike*); la disco(teca) (*disco*)

These nouns take feminine articles.

> una radio (*a radio*); una foto (*a photo*)

⚠ **el radio** (*radius* or *radium*); American Spanish sometimes uses **el radio** for *a radio set* instead of **la radio**.

The following masculine-looking nouns are also feminine: **la modelo** (*(female) fashion model*); **la mano** (*hand*) (because it was feminine in Latin!).

Esta chica es una modelo muy hermosa.	*This girl is a very beautiful model.*
Dame la mano.	*Give me your hand.*

B Adjectives will also agree in the feminine.

Tengo una buena foto de Julio.	*I've got a good photograph of Julio.*
un coche de segunda mano	*a second-hand car*

⚠ **a la (mano) derecha/izquierda** (*on the right/left*)

A la (mano) derecha está la catedral.	On the right (-hand side) is the cathedral.

5 Exercises

1 Put the definite article with these nouns.

a mano   b radio   c foto   d moto   e disco

2 Now make the same nouns plural with the definite article (*las, los*).

3 Put the indefinitive article (*un, una*) with the same nouns.

4 Give the Spanish for the following.

a I have (**Tengo**) a good radio.

b The photo of the children is fantastic.

c Julio's motorbike is fast (**rápida**).

d María is a beautiful model.

e the house on the right

f the door (**la puerta**) on the left

g We are going (**Vamos**) to the disco.

h There are (**Hay**) many (**muchas**) discos here (**aquí**).

i I have a second-hand car.

j Give me your hands.

5 **Crucigrama.** *All the answers are feminine words ending in -o.*

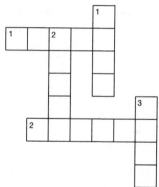

HORIZONTALES

1 ¿Hay un programa en la ...?

2 Juanita es una ... fantástica.

VERTICALES

1 Tengo una ... de Julio.

2 Vamos a la ...

3 Vamos en tu ...

6 More on genders: exceptions (2)

Many nouns which end in -a and which look feminine are masculine. This unit summarises these.

A An important group is formed of 'international' words of Greek origin, which end in **-ma**. Their meaning in English is generally obvious.

el dilema (*dilemma*); el problema (*problem*); el sistema (*system*); el esquema (*scheme*); el drama (*drama*); el programa (*program(me)*); el telegrama (*telegram*); el tema (*theme*)

B Other miscellaneous masculine words ending in **-a** include:

el cometa (*comet*); el tranvía (*tram*); el mapa (*map*)

… and nouns denoting a male person, such as:

el atleta (*athlete*); el guía (*guide*); el policía (*policeman*); el trompeta (*trumpet player*), el corneta (*bugler*)

⚠ You will come across some of these nouns with feminine articles, which gives them a different meaning.

la cometa (*kite*); la trompeta (*trumpet*); la corneta (*bugle*)

C Nouns ending in **-ista** are masculine unless specifically referring to a female.

el periodista (*journalist*); el turista (*tourist*); el dentista (*dentist*); el futbolista (*footballer*) and political words such as **socialista**.

D Some words can be either masculine or feminine, but with a different meaning.

la consonante (*consonant*), el consonante (*word rhyming with another*); la orden (*order, command*), el orden (*arrangement, tidiness*); la disco (*discoteque*), el disco (*record, disc*); la capital (*capital (city)*), el capital (*capital (money)*); la manzanilla (*camomile tea*); el manzanilla (*type of fortified wine*); la cólera (*rage*), el cólera (*cholera*)

⚠ A few nouns in recent years have evolved forms (not always officially recognized) to denote females, such as:

la jefa (*boss* (from **el jefe**)); la presidenta (*president* (from **el presidente**)); la estudianta (*student* (from **el estudiante**))

6 Exercises

1 Put the most appropriate article (*el, la, un, una*) with these nouns.

E.g. Quiero comprar _____ moto diferente. → Quiero comprar una moto diferente.

a ¿Tienes _____ foto de Luisa?
b Hay _____ programa en _____ radio.
c Tengo _____ moto verde.
d Vamos a _____ disco. Quiero bailar _____ chachachá.
e Quiero ver el museo. ¿Es usted _____ guía, señor?
f Juan López es _____ atleta internacional.
g No puedo ver _____ mapa – no tengo mis gafas.
h Julia es _____ modelo en _____ foto.
i Julio tiene _____ mano en escayola (*in plaster*).
j Vamos en _____ tranvía número uno.

2 Make these nouns plural.

E.g. el mapa → los mapas

a la modelo
b la disco
c el tranvía
d la mano
e la moto
f el cometa

3 Put in the article reflecting the most likely gender for the context.

a Mi hijo tiene _____ cometa.
b Julio hace _____ modelo de su casa.
c ¿Existe _____ cólera en aquel país?
d ¿Tienes telescopio? Quiero ver _____ cometa.
e ¿Qué círculo tiene _____ radio más grande?
f ¿Quién tiene _____ radio ahora?
g _____ trompeta toca _____ trompeta en la orquesta.
h Voy a Madrid porque es _____ capital.
i Voy al banco porque necesito _____ capital.
j Me gusta _____ modelo en el bikini blanco.

7 Nouns: still more on genders

This unit groups more nouns according to gender.

A Nouns which end in **-aje**, like **el garaje** (*the garage*), are masculine (see Unit 3). Also masculine are most nouns ending in a stressed syllable.

el valor (*valour*); el amor (*love*); el honor (*honour*); el champú (*shampoo*); el rubí (*ruby*); el bailarín (*dancer*)

- The days of the week and months of the year (see Unit 12) are masculine.

el lunes (*Monday*); el septiembre pasado (*last September*)

- Countries are masculine unless ending in unstressed -a.

Perú (*Peru*); Canadá (*Canada*); los Estados Unidos (*the USA*)

But **España** (*Spain*); **Francia** (*France*); **Inglaterra** (*England*) and many more are feminine as the final **-a** is not stressed.

B Compound nouns are masculine.

el lavaplatos (*dishwasher*); el paraguas (*umbrella*); el limpiacristales (*window cleaner*); el cumpleaños (*birthday*)

⚠ To make compound nouns plural, simply change **el** to **los**: **los paraguas** (*the umbrellas*).

C • Unit 4 told you that nouns ending in **-dad** or **-tad** are feminine: **la ciudad** (*city*). Nouns in **-tud** are likewise feminine: **la multitud** (*crowd*).

- Also feminine are nouns which end in **-umbre**.

la cumbre (*summit*); la muchedumbre (*crowd*).

- Nouns ending in **-is** and **-ie** are usually feminine:

la crisis (*crisis*); la serie (*series*)

- Nouns of more than one syllable ending in **-ión** are usually feminine.

la habitación (*room*); la reunión (*meeting*)

⚠ Nouns beginning with a stressed **a-** or **ha-** but which are feminine take **el** (not **la**) as their singular definite article and **un** as their singular indefinite article.

el agua (*water*), las aguas (*the waters*); el hambre (*hunger*); un arpa (*a harp*); un hacha (*an axe, hatchet*); el águila (*eagle*)

7 Exercises

1 Put in the correct definite article.

E.g. ciudad → la ciudad

a valor
b champú
c lunes
d rubí
e amor
f muchedumbre
g multidud
h crisis
i reunión
j serie

2 Put the correct article *el* or *la* with the following nouns.

a lavaplatos
b paraguas
c limpiacristales
d cumpleaños

3 Make the same nouns plural and give the correct article *los* or *las*.

4 Which countries are the odd ones out in gender?

a Portugal, Cuba, Perú
b Australia, Canadá, Uruguay
c Japón, Pakistán, China
d Chile, España, Panamá

5 Put the correct indefinite article, *un* or *una*, with the following nouns.

a hacha
b agua
c arpa
d águila

6 Put the correct definite article, *el* or *la*, with the same nouns.

7 Make the same nouns plural with the correct definite article.

8 The use of the definite article

This unit explains when you need to put in el, la, los or las in Spanish.

A In Units 3 and 4 we saw the definite articles according to gender (masculine or feminine) and number (singular or plural). Generally speaking, the inclusion or omission of the definite article is similar in English and Spanish.

	Masculine	Feminine
Singular	**el libro** (*the book*)	**la casa** (*the house*)
Plural	**los libros** (*the books*)	**las casas** (*the houses*)

Los tomates son buenos.	*The tomatoes are good.*
¿Tiene usted el número?	*Do you have the number?*
¿Tiene usted el pan y la fruta?	*Do you have the bread and the fruit?*
¿Tiene usted pan y fruta?	*Do you have bread and fruit?*
Hablo inglés.	*I speak English.*
¿Hay pan?	*Is there (any) bread?*

B Spanish, however, includes the article if making a general statement.

Los tomates son horribles.	*(All) tomatoes are horrible.*
No me gusta el vino.	*I don't like (any) wine.*
El inglés es difícil.	*English is difficult.*

C Spanish also includes the article with locations such as school, work, university, town, unlike English.

Estudia en la universidad.	*He's studying at university.*
Emilia está en la iglesia.	*Emilia is in church.*
Voy al trabajo.	*I'm going to work.*

D The article is used with titles when talking about someone.

¿Dónde está el señor López?	*Where is Mr López?*
La señorita García no está aquí.	*Miss García is not here.*

But **Buenos días, señor López** (*Good morning, Mr López*).

E Spanish uses the definite article with countries only if the country is limited in some way. Note, however, **la India** (*India*).

España es bonita.	*Spain is pretty.*
Vivía en la España de Franco.	*He was living in Franco's Spain.*

8 Exercises

1 **Put in the definite article if it is required.**

E.g. ¿Tiene usted _____ hijos? → ¿Tiene usted hijos?

a No me gustan _____ tomates.

b _____ pan francés es muy bueno.

c ¿Te gusta _____ vino?

d No bebo _____ vino.

e ¿Hay _____ pan?

f _____ español es difícil.

g _____ agua por favor.

h ¿Dónde vive _____ señor López?

i ¿Qué quieres, _____ vino o _____ café?

j _____ España es diferente.

k _____ España de los turistas es diferente.

2 **Translate the following into English.**

a España es bonita.

b El español es bonito.

c Teresa no habla español.

d Vivimos en la India.

e No me gusta el señor Gómez.

f Buenos días, señora García.

3 **Translate the following into Spanish.**

a I speak (**Hablo**) Spanish.

b Mr Ortega doesn't speak (**no habla**) English.

c The England of Mr Blair is very (**muy**) different.

d I don't like (**No me gusta**) coffee.

e I don't have (**No tengo**) wine.

f I don't have the wine.

g We live (**Vivimos**) in Spain.

h We live in tourist Spain.

i Where is (**está**) Miss García?

j Good morning, Miss García.

9 The indefinite article

> *The indefinite article (a, an) in Spanish agrees in gender (masculine or feminine) with its noun. This unit summarizes the main uses of the indefinite article.*

	Masculine	Feminine
Definite	el hombre (*the man*)	la casa (*the house*)
Indefinite	un hombre (*a man*)	una casa (*a house*)

A **Una** changes to **un** in front of a feminine noun or adjective beginning with a stressed **a-** or **ha-**, but not if the **a-** or **ha-** is unstressed.

> un arpa (*a harp*); un hacha (*an axe*); una ardilla (*a squirrel*)

B Spanish also has plural forms of the indefinite article, **unos** *(masculine)* and **unas** *(feminine)*: **unos tirantes** (*(a pair) of braces*).

The plural forms **unos** and **unas** can also mean *some*.

Hay unos hombres en la esquina.	*There are some men on the corner.*
Creo que hay unas galletas en la cocina.	*I think there are some biscuits in the kitchen.*

C The use of the indefinite article is generally similar to English.

> Una chica canta en un coro. *A girl is singing in a choir.*

There are some differences, however.

- The indefinite article is not used after **ser** (*to be*) or **hacerse** (*to become*) to denote professions, status, etc.

Soy estudiante.	*I'm a student.*
Mi padre es mecánico.	*My father is a mechanic.*

- It is not generally used after **tener** (*to have*) in the negative.

No tengo familia.	*I haven't got a family.*

- The indefinite article is usually omitted with **sin** (*without*) and **con** (*with*).

Lo abrí sin llave.	*I opened it without a key.*

- It is not used with **otro** (*other*), **cierto** (*certain*), or **tal** (*such a ...*).

Quiero otra habitación.	*I want another room.*

9 Exercises

1 Put the correct indefinite article instead of *el* or *la* with the following nouns.

E.g. la botella (*bottle*) → una botella

a la naranja (*orange*)
b el plátano (*banana*)
c la manzana (*apple*)
d el chico (*boy*)
e la niña (*girl*)

f la mesa (*table*)
g el coche (*car*)
h la luz (*light*)
j la ciudad (*city, town*)
j el libro (*book*)

2 Put *un* or *una* with the following nouns.

a habitación (*room*)
b hospital (*m.*) (*hospital*)
c hacha (*axe*)
d aldea (*village*)

e arpa (*harp*)
f autora (*author*)
g actriz (*actress*)
h ala (*wing*)

3 Put *unos* or *unas* with the following.

a casas
b hombres
c tijeras (*scissors*)
d tirantes

e legumbres (*vegetables*)
f euros
g chicos
h habitaciones

4 Give the Spanish for the following.

a another room
b another man
c another car
d a certain girl

e such an actress
f such students
g without a book
h without a key

5 Translate the following into Spanish.

a I am a student.
b We are (**somos**) mechanics.
c I have a book.
d I haven't a book.
e We have a house.
f We haven't a car.

10 Numbers

Spanish uses cardinal numbers when counting. These are the numbers from zero to 199.

0	cero	15	quince	30	treinta
1	uno/una	16	dieciséis	31	treinta y uno/una/un
2	dos	17	diecisiete	32	treinta y dos
3	tres	18	dieciocho	33	treinta y tres
4	cuatro	19	diecinueve		
5	cinco	20	veinte	40	cuarenta
6	seis	21	veintiuno/veintiuna	41	cuarenta y uno/una/un
7	siete	22	veintidós	42	cuarenta y dos
8	ocho	23	veintitrés		
9	nueve	24	veinticuatro	50	cincuenta
10	diez	25	veinticinco	60	sesenta
11	once	26	veintiséis	70	setenta
12	doce	27	veintisiete	80	ochenta
13	trece	28	veintiocho	90	noventa
14	catorce	29	veintinueve	99	noventa y nueve

A Uno becomes **una** in front of a feminine noun; **veintiuno** becomes **veintiuna**.

una casa (*one house*); veintiuna casas (*21 houses*)

B Uno becomes **un** in front of any masculine noun; **veintiuno** becomes **veintiún**. These changes also occur in front of a feminine noun beginning with a stressed **a-** or **ha-**.

un libro (*one book*); veintiún libros (*21 books*); veintiún hachas (*21 axes*)

⚠ Take special care when spelling **cuatro**, **catorce** and **quince**!

C All tens and units are linked with **y**. The numbers 16 to 19 and 21 to 29 may also be written as three separate words in older spelling: **diez y seis**; **veinte y uno**; **veinte y dos**, etc.

D 100 is **cien**. Cien becomes **ciento** in front of another lesser number.

Tengo cien dólares. *I have 100 dollars.*
ciento noventa y nueve *199*

E To say the numbers between 100 and 199, you simply join up the numbers with **ciento**.

Me faltan ciento cincuenta *I'm 151 euro short.*
y un euros.

10 Exercises

1 Write or say the following in full.

E.g. 23 días → veintitrés días

a 16 años
b 1 euro
c 4 casas

d 9 meses
e 10 chicas
f 28 días

g 21 hombres
h 1 águila
i 2 cervezas

2 Practise using numbers in a bar or restaurant.

E.g. 1 mesa para 2 → una mesa para dos

a 1 limonada, por favor.
b 3 cervezas por favor.
c 2 cafés, 1 con leche y 1 solo.
d ¿Hay una mesa para 4?
e 3 botellas de vino, 1 de blanco y 2 de tinto.

3 Use *más* (plus) and *menos* (minus) to do these sums.

E.g. 1 + 5 + 2 = ? → uno más cinco más dos son ocho.

a 3 + 4 + 2 = ?
b 10 − 3 + 4 = ?
c 9 + 9 + 8 = ?
d 21 − 17 − 2 = ?
e 11 + 13 + 5 = ?

**4 Put the numbers into words. Make sure you use the correct form
un, -ún or *una* with these expressions!**

a 21 euros
b 121 libros
c 131 casas
d 51 hombres
e 81 revistas

f 101 chicas
g 31 niños
h 161 cigarrillos
i 191 botellas
j 71 estudiantes

5 Ask for your room key.

E.g. 55 → La cincuenta y cinco, por favor.

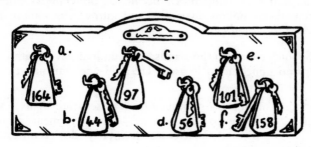

11 Numbers above 200

This unit looks at numbers from 200. The hundreds have masculine and feminine forms.

200	doscientos/doscientas	600	seiscientos/seiscientas
300	trescientos/trescientas	700	setecientos/setecientas
400	cuatrocientos/cuatrocientas	800	ochocientos/ochocientas
500	quinientos/quinientas	900	novecientos/novecientas

A Note the agreements in the following.

doscientas treinta y una casas	(*231 houses*)
cuatrocientos un pesos	(*401 pesos*)
quinientas cincuenta y una mujeres	(*551 women*)
seiscientos sesenta y un hombres	(*661 men*)

B Numbers above 999

1.000	mil
2.000	dos mil
3.000	tres mil, etc.
100.000	cien mil
999.000	novecientos noventa y nueve mil
1.000.000	un millón
2.000.000	dos millones, etc.

The same rules of agreement as above apply. Novecientas noventa y nueve mil novecientas noventa y una libras
999,991 pounds

⚠ Spanish separates thousands with a full point. The comma is used instead of a decimal point.
5,6 = cinco coma seis   (*five point six*)

C Round numbers involving **millón, millones**, etc. are followed by **de: un millón de habitantes** (*one million inhabitants*), but not otherwise: **un millón doscientas mil euros** (*one million two hundred thousand euro*).

⚠ Spanish counts in thousands, not hundreds, even with dates where no punctuation is used: 1999 (**el año**) **mil novecientos noventa y nueve.**

D Telephone numbers are either given as separate digits, as in English, or more usually divided into convenient groups. 232 24 56 89 (**el**) **doscientos treinta y dos veinticuatro cincuenta y seis ochenta y nueve**

11 Exercises

1 Write these years in full.

a 1066	f 1898
b 1215	g 1936
c 1492	h 1945
d 1588	i 2000
e 1789	j 2001

2 Give these telephone numbers in Spanish.

3 You are explaining these statistics for a model of car to a Spanish friend. State the figures in words.

a Motor: 1.984 centímetros cuadrados (*cc*)

b Potencia (*power*): 150 C (**caballos** (*horsepower*)) a 6.000 revoluciones

c Neumáticos (*tyres*): 195

d Dimensiones exteriores: 3,85/1,64/1,41 metros

e Velocidad (*speed*) máxima: 216 kilómetros por hora

f Aceleración 0–1 kilómetro: 30,4 segundos

g Consumo: 9 litros en 100 kilómetros

h Precio: 18.500 euros

12 Make a date: days and months

A summary of days, months, seasons and other time expressions.

A Spanish normally writes days and months with a small letter.

Los días de la semana (*Days of the week*)

lunes	*Monday*	viernes	*Friday*
martes	*Tuesday*	sábado	*Saturday*
miércoles	*Wednesday*	domingo	*Sunday*
jueves	*Thursday*		

Hoy es lunes. *Today is Monday.*

B The definite article (**el/los**) is used for *on*; **los** is used for repeated occasions.

el lunes (*on Monday*); los lunes (*on Mondays*)
Vamos al cine los domingos. *We go to the cinema on Sundays.*

C Time of day is expressed with **por la mañana** (*in the morning*); **por la tarde** (*in the afternoon/evening*); **por la noche** (*during the night*); **por la madrugada** (*in the early morning*).

Salimos el martes por *We are leaving on Tuesday*
la mañana. *morning.*

D **Los meses del año** (*Months of the year*)

enero	abril	julio	octubre
febrero	mayo	agosto	noviembre
marzo	junio	septiembre	diciembre

Voy de vacaciones en agosto. *I go on holiday in August.*

E To give the date, Spanish uses the order day, month, year.

Es el dos de mayo de mil *It's the second of May,*
novecientos noventa y nueve. *1999.*
martes trece *Tuesday 13th*
el uno de enero/el primero *1st January*
de enero
¿Cuál es la fecha?/ *What's the date?*
¿Qué fecha es?
¿A cuántos estamos hoy? *What is today's date?*
Estamos a diez de mayo. *It's the tenth of May.*

F In letters, the town of the sender is usually included as a heading.

Madrid, 28 de febrero de 2006 *Madrid, 28 February 2006*

G **Las cuatro estaciones** (*The four seasons*)

primavera	*spring*	otoño	*autumn*
verano	*summer*	invierno	*winter*

12 Exercises

1 Write the family birthdays in full.

E.g. Madre (1/X) → primero/uno de octubre

a Tío Pepe (22/V)
b Hermana Luisa (18/I)
c Gemelos (*twins*) (5/VIII)
d Hijo (6/III)
e Hija (8/IV)
f Raúl (30/IX)
g Luisa (15/II)
h Abuela (9/XII)

2 What are the following horoscope dates in Spanish?

a Aries: 21 March–21 April
b Tauro: 22 April–21 May
c Géminis: 22 May–21 June
d Cáncer: 22 June–22 July
e Leo: 23 July–22 August
f Virgo: 23 August–22 September
g Libra: 23 September–22 October
h Escorpio: 23 October–22 November
i Sagitario: 23 November–22 December
j Capricornio: 23 December–20 January
k Acuario: 21 January–19 February
l Piscis: 20 February–20 March

3 Which month is being referred to?

a A principios del año, tiene treinta y un días.
b El mes antes de junio con treinta y un días.
c El mes a mediados del año con treinta días.
d Este mes tiene un día más algunos años.
e En primavera; tiene treinta días.
f En otoño, con treinta días.
g A fines del año; tiene treinta y un días.
h Entre julio y septiembre, en verano.

4 Unjumble the months and seasons.

a vemaprira b ribal c bremidice d yoma e norevini
f liouj

5 Look at the following *refrán* (saying): *El clima* (climate) *de Madrid.*
Which are the *meses* being referred to?

'Nueve meses de invierno, tres meses de infierno.'

13 Time for more numbers

Telling the time in Spanish is very much like in English.

A ¿Qué hora es? (*What time is it?*)

Es la una.	*It's one o'clock.*
Son las dos.	*It's two o'clock.*
Son las tres, cuatro, cinco, etc.	*It's three o'clock, etc.*

⚠ La and las are used, as **hora** and **horas** are understood.

B • y media (*half past*)

Son las cinco y media. *It's half past five.*

• y cuarto/menos cuarto (*quarter past/quarter to*)

Son las seis menos cuarto. *It's a quarter to six.*
Es la una y cuarto. *It's a quarter past one.*

⚠ Take care to distinguish **cuatro** (*four*) and **cuarto** (*quarter*).

C Minutes past or to the hour are introduced with y or menos.

Son las cinco y diez. *It's ten past five.*
Son las cuatro menos veinte. *It's twenty to four.*

• With odd numbers of minutes, **minutos** is added for clarity, as in English.

Son las cinco y seis minutos. *It's six minutes past five.*

• y pico (just past); menos algo (*just before*); pasadas (*gone*)

Son las cinco y pico. *It's just after five.*
Son las doce menos algo. *It's coming up to twelve.*
Son las cuatro pasadas. *It's gone four.*

D To say *At what time?*, Spanish uses **a**.

¿A qué hora sales? *(At) what time are you going out?*

A las cinco en punto. *At five, sharp.*

With specific time by the clock, use **de la mañana** for *a.m.*, **de la tarde** or **de la noche** for *p.m.* and **de la madrugada** for the early morning.

¡Son las tres de la madrugada! *It's three a.m.!*

⚠ Mi reloj está adelantado/atrasado (*My watch is fast/slow*).

13 Exercises

1 Say what time these clocks show.

a 10.20 a.m.   **b** 2.05 p.m.   **c** 8.45 a.m.

d 11.30 a.m.   **e** just past 1.00 p.m.   **f** almost 9.00 p.m.

g 1.30 a.m.   **h** 12.45 a.m.   **i** 2.00 a.m.

2 Translate the following into Spanish.
   a The train leaves (**sale**) at ten a.m.
   b The film (**La película**) begins (**empieza**) at five on the dot.
   c Julio is coming (**viene**) at half past nine.
   d It's gone six!
   e My watch is slow.
   f I am going out (**Voy a salir**) just before ten.
   g Silence (**Silencio**) – it's five in the morning.
   h Is your watch fast?
   i It's a quarter to four.
   j It's just gone three.

14 Numbers: ordinals and timetables

Ordinal numbers like first, second and third are less commonly used in Spanish than in English. Nevertheless this unit deals with the important ones.

A Ordinal numbers are generally used only up to *tenth* in Spanish. After that the cardinal numbers are used.

primero	*first*	séptimo	*seventh*
segundo	*second*	octavo	*eighth*
tercero	*third*	noveno	*ninth*
cuarto	*fourth*	décimo	*tenth*
quinto	*fifth*		
sexto	*sixth*	último	*last*

⚠ Abbreviations such as 1°, 6ª mean **primero, sexta**, etc.

B **Primero** and **tercero** shorten to **primer** and **tercer** in front of a masculine singular noun.

el tercer hombre	*the third man*
la última página	*the last page*
Enrique octavo	*Henry VIII*
el siglo diecinueve	*the nineteenth century*
Luisa vive en el piso doce.	*Luisa lives on the twelfth floor.*

⚠ Note Spanish word order in expressions involving ordinals: **las tres primeras páginas** (*the first three pages*); **los cinco últimos días** (*the last five days*).

C For times with travel, transport, entertainment, Spanish uses the 24-hour clock, with minutes counted from one to 59.

El tren sale a las veinte treinta y cinco.	*The train leaves at 20.35 (8.35 p.m.).*
El concierto empieza a las veintidós (horas) y termina a las veintitrés quince.	*The concert starts at 22.00 (10 p.m.) and ends at 23.15 (11.15 p.m.).*

14 Exercises

1 Practise ordinals by reading the following out loud.

a Enrique VIII
b Carlos V
c Juan XXIII
d Alfonso XIII
e Juan Carlos I

f el piso 1°
g el piso 3°
h el siglo VII
i el piso XI
j el siglo XX

2 Use the train timetable to practise the 24-hour clock.

E.g. 1° Madrid–Aranjuez → El primer tren sale de Madrid a las siete cinco y llega a Aranjuez a las siete cincuenta y uno.

a 3° Madrid–Pinto
b 5° Villaverde Bajo–Toledo
c 1° Aranjuez–Toledo

d 2° (tarde) Madrid–Aranjuez
e 8° Valdemoro–Aranjuez
f último Madrid–Toledo

Madrid							→	Toledo
Madrid-At.	Villaverde Bajo	S. C. Industrial	Getafe I.	Pinto	Valdemoro	Aranjuez	C. Añover	Toledo
7.05	7.12	7.17	7.20	7.25	7.36	7.51	8.00	8.25
8.25	8.33	8.38	8.41	8.46	8.52	9.08	9.17	9.39
10.25	10.33	10.38	10.41	10.46	10.52	11.08	11.17	11.41
12.25	12.33	12.38	12.41	12.46	12.52	13.08	13.17	13.39
14.25	14.33	14.38	14.41	14.46	14.52	15.07	15.17	15.40
14.35	14.43	14.48	14.51	14.57	15.09	15.24	15.34	15.57
16.25	16.33	16.38	16.41	16.46	16.52	17.08		17.44
18.25	18.33	18.38	18.41	18.46	18.52	19.08	19.24	19.47
19.32	-	-	-	-	-	-		20.30
20.25	20.33	20.38	20.41	20.46	20.52	21.08	21.26	21.46
20.43	-	-	-	-	-	21.14	-	21.46

15 Words for time

A La hora (*time* (clock))

Use **la hora** when you are asking for time by the clock.

¿Qué hora es?	*What time is it?*
¿A qué hora empieza el partido de fútbol?	*(At) what time does the football match start?*

⚠ Spanish always requires **a** in such expressions.

B El tiempo (*time* (abstract sense))

No tengo tiempo para estudiar.	*I don't have time to study.*
Llevo aquí mucho tiempo esperándola.	*I have been waiting here for her for a long time.*
¿Cómo pasan el tiempo aquí?	*How do they pass/spend the time here?*
¿Qué pasatiempos tienes?	*What hobbies/pastimes do you have?*
Hace mucho tiempo había osos en la montañas.	*A long time ago there were bears in the mountains.*

C El tiempo can also refer to the weather. The context makes the meaning clear.

¿Qué tiempo hace?	*What's the weather like?*
Hace mal tiempo.	*The weather is bad.*

D La vez (*time*, (number of times))

La última vez que estuve aquí perdí mi dinero.	*The last time I was here I lost my money.*
Te lo digo por última vez.	*I'm telling you for the last time.*
Lo digo sólo una vez.	*I'll say it only once.*
Me llamaron dos veces.	*They rang me twice.*

Muchas veces (*often*); pocas veces (*seldom*); raras veces (*hardly ever, rarely*); a veces (*at times, sometimes*); algunas veces (*sometimes*)

Raras veces vamos a España. *We rarely go to Spain.*

⚠ The definite article is omitted with **vez** after **por**:

por primera vez (*for the first time*), por última vez (*for the last time*).

15 Exercises

1 Put in the correct word from the box.

a ¿Qué .... es?

b ¿Qué .... hace?

c ¿A qué ... sale el tren?

d Hace mal ... en diciembre.

e ¿Cuántas .... has visitado Madrid?

f Estoy aquí por primera ... .

g Comemos en un restaurante muchas .... .

h No tenemos .... para descansar.

tiempo	hora	veces	tiempo	tiempo	hora	vez	veces

2 Give the Spanish for the following.

a the first time

b for the first time

c twice

d What is the time?

e We don't have time.

f sometimes

g at times

h seldom

3 Give the English for the following.

a He ido a España muchas veces.

b No tengo la hora.

c No tengo tiempo.

d Escribo por última vez.

e Estamos aquí por segunda vez.

f Le visitamos raras veces.

4 Fill in the crossword. One of the clues does not fit!

a ¿Qué _____ es?

b Vamos a la playa muchas _____ .

c Te lo digo por última _____ .

d No tenemos _____ .

16 Adjectives

Adjectives are words that describe nouns, for example, green tree, tall man, the house is big.

A Adjectives in Spanish agree with the noun to which they refer in gender (masculine or feminine) and number (singular or plural).

Adjectives which end in **-o** change to **-a** (feminine singular), **-os** (masculine plural) and **-as** (feminine plural).

	Singular	Plural
Masculine	un libro pequeño (*a small book*)	libros pequeños (*small books*)
Feminine	una casa pequeña (*a small house*)	casas pequeñas (*small houses*)

B Adjectives agree even when separated from the noun.
La casa es pequeña.   *The house is small.*
Los libros son pequeños.   *The books are small.*

C Not all adjectives have separate feminine forms.

- Adjectives ending in **-e** have no separate feminine form.
  María está triste.   *María is sad.*

- Most adjectives ending in a consonant have no separate feminine form.
  una falda azul   *a blue skirt*

- Adjectives ending in **-or** and most in **-ón** do, however, have feminine forms. Those in **-ón** drop the accent.
  Su esposa es mandona.   *His wife is bossy.*

  ⚠ **Marrón** (*brown*) has no feminine form.

  las botas marrones   *the brown boots*

- Adjectives of nationality, like **español** (*Spanish*), **inglés** (*English*), **francés** (*French*) and **alemán** (*German*) do have feminine forms. Any final accent is dropped before such endings.
  las mujeres inglesas   *the English women*
  Esta revista es alemana.   *This magazine is German.*

D Most Spanish adjectives come after the noun.
Aquí hay parques magníficos.   *There are magnificent parks here.*

16 Exercises

1 Give the feminine singular form of these adjectives.

E.g. negro (*black*) → negra; azul (*blue*) → azul.

a rojo (*red*)   f verde (*green*)
b blanco (*white*)   g gris (*grey*)
c amarillo (*yellow*)   h marrón (*brown*)
d purpúreo (*purple*)   i celeste (*sky blue*)
e rosado (*pink*)

2 Give the masculine singular of these feminine forms.

E.g. francesa (*French*) → francés

a española   f irlandesa (*Irish*)
b italiana   g alemana
c inglesa   h japonesa (*Japanese*)
d rusa (*Russian*)   i americana
e griega (*Greek*)   j australiana

3 Give the feminine plural of these adjectives.

E.g. blanco (*white*) → blancas; triste (*sad*) → tristes

a negro   f celeste
b pequeño   g pobre (*poor*)
c rico (*rich*)   h fácil (*easy*)
d bonito (*pretty*)   i difícil
e hermoso (*beautiful*)   j diferente (*different*)

4 Make these expressions plural.

E.g. la chica francesa → las chicas francesas

a el chico italiano   f la esposa mandona
b la casa azul   g la falda gris
c la revista inglesa   h la bota marrón
d el actor americano   i el hombre diferente
e la chica trabajadora   j la chica triste

5 Give the Spanish for the following.

a a pretty girl   f The magazine is Spanish
b the pretty girls   g Ana is hardworking.
c The house is white.   h Luisa and María are
d The houses are white.   hardworking.
e The women are English.   i Kylie is Australian.
     j The girls are Spanish.

17 More on adjectives

This unit continues a summary of the use of adjectives.

In Unit 16 we saw that adjectives in Spanish usually come after the noun.

    la casa blanca   *the white house*

A Some adjectives regularly go in front of the noun, as in English.

- Adjectives showing quantity usually go in front. These include **mucho** (*much, many*); **poco** (*little, few*); **varios** (*several*); **algunos** (*some*); **bastante/suficiente** (*enough*); **ambos** (*both*) and numbers.

muchos libros	*many books*	bastante vino	*enough wine*
poco dinero	*little money*	varias casas	*several houses*
dos chicas	*two girls*		

- Adjectives can go in front of the noun if they state a natural characteristic.
    la blanca nieve   *the white snow*

- Subjective judgements similarly put the adjective first.
    Es una buena película.   *It's a good film.*

- If the adjective comes after an expression with **qué**, Spanish adds **más** (*more*) or **tan** (*such*).
    ¡Qué chica más bonita!
    ¡Qué chica tan bonita!   *What a pretty girl!*

B A few adjectives shorten when they come in front. This usually only happens in the masculine singular.
    un libro bueno → un buen libro   (*a good book*)
    un vino malo → un mal vino   (*a bad wine*)
    el capítulo primero → el primer capítulo (*the first chapter*)
    el hombre tercero → el tercer hombre (*the third man*)

Alguno (*some*) and **uno** (*one*) also shorten.

    ¿Hay algún bar por aquí?   *Is there a bar round here?*
    Hay un bar en la plaza.   *There's a bar in the square.*

C Some adjectives change meaning according to their position.
    un pobre hombre *a poor (wretched) man*; un hombre pobre *a poor (penniless) man*; un nuevo coche *a new (different) car*; un coche nuevo *a (brand-)new car*; un gran general (*a great general*); un general grande (*a tall general*)

⚠ **Grande** becomes **gran** in front of any singular noun.
    Gran Bretaña   *Great Britain*

17 Exercises

1 **Give the Spanish for the following.**

  a many books
  b few houses
  c a lot of wine
  d some girls
  e the white snow
  f both men
  g enough money
  h enough euro
  i several boys
  j little money

2 **Translate the following into Spanish.**

  a We live (**Vivimos**) in a small house.
  b There is (**Hay**) a good film on television.
  c Some general lives here.
  d He is a great man.
  e He is a tall man.
  f I live in Great Britain.
  g The poor boy has no friends (**no tiene amigos**) .
  h The poor man has no money (**dinero**).
  i The third book is not good.
  j The first chapter is bad.

18 Combinations of adjectives and nouns

Sometimes you will need to talk about a combination of items which may be of different number and gender.

A • Adjectives covering more than one noun of the same gender agree with that gender in the plural.

Tengo muchos amigos y compañeros.
I have many friends and companions.

Come patatas y sardinas fritas.
He is eating fried potatoes and sardines.

• With nouns of different genders, use masculine plural adjectives.

Lleva botas y calcetines negros.
He is wearing black boots and socks.

Hay muchos chicos y chicas.
There are many boys and girls.

B Sometimes you may need more than one adjective, for example, *I live in a little white house.* You have a couple of possibilities.

• You can make a noun sandwich. This is common when one adjective customarily comes in front of the noun.

Vivo en una pequeña casa blanca.
I live in a little white house.

• The adjectives may be linked with **y** (*and*).

Es una chica inteligente y trabajadora.
She is an intelligent and hard-working girl.

⚠ Remember to change **y** to **e** in front of **i-** or **hi-**.

Es un estudiante trabajador e inteligente.
He is a hard-working and intelligent student.

C Compound adjectives like *dark-red* are invariable.

una falda rojo oscuro
a dark-red skirt

A noun may be used as an invariable adjective.

un coche (de color) naranja
an orange car

camisas café
coffee-coloured shirts

unos coches modelo
model cars

18 Exercises

1 Make the adjective agree as necessary.

E.g. una casa (blanco y negro) → una casa blanca y negra
una casa y un jardín (grande) → una casa y un jardín grandes

a casa (pequeño/blanco)
b (mucho) niños y niñas
c faldas y blusas (amarillo)
d chicas y profesoras (bonito)
e chicas y chicos (trabajador)
f periódicos y revistas (alemán)
g revistas y películas (español)
h un general (gran/importante)
i un general (grande/importante)
j un libro (buen/inglés)

2 Add the adjective required.

E.g. una blusa (*light-blue*) → una blusa azul claro

a unas botas (*dark-green*)
b una camisa (*orange*)
c una falda (*light-yellow*)
d unos calcetines (*dark-grey*)
e unos vaqueros (*light-blue*)
f una blusa (*coffee-coloured*)
g la casa (*show*)
h los coches (*model*)

3 Translate the following into Spanish.

a I want to see (**Quiero ver**) the show house.
b She is wearing (**Lleva**) a dark-green skirt.
c We live in a little blue house.
d There is a small orange car in the garage.
e Do you have some Spanish books and magazines?

4 Fill the gaps with appropriate adjectives taken from the box.

Vivo en un a _____ pueblo b _____ con c _____ casas
d _____. Las casas tienen jardines e _____ y f _____ con rosas
g _____ y violetas h _____. En mi jardín hay unas rosas
especiales – son i _____ y son muy j _____. Los habitantes
visitan mi jardín porque son muy k _____ y quieren ver esta
rosa l _____.

---

amarillas   azul claro   azules   bonito   bonitos   curiosos
diferente   grandes   muchas   pequeño   raras   viejas

19 The formation of adverbs

Adverbs are used to describe actions and in English often end in -ly like deeply, loudly, slowly. In a similar way, Spanish adds -mente to the corresponding adjective.

alegre → alegremente (*happily*) triste → tristemente (*sadly*)

A The adjective and **-mente** were originally considered as separate words, so any accent on the basic adjective is retained when it becomes an adverb.

fácil → fácilmente (*easily*)

B Adjectives which have a separate feminine form add **-mente** to this.

lento/ lenta → lentamente (*slowly*)
serio/seria → seriamente (*seriously*)
rápido/rápida → rápidamente (*quickly*)

When Spanish has a string of adverbs, only the final one takes **-mente**, though feminine singular adjectives are used in anticipation.

Juan sirve rápida, seria y amablemente. | *Juan serves quickly, seriously and kindly.*

C A few adverbs are special forms.

bueno (*good*); bien (*well*) malo (*bad*); mal (*badly*)

D Some adverbs are identical to the adjective.

mejor (*better*); peor (*worse*); mucho (*a lot*); poco (*a little/little*); tarde (*late*); temprano (*early*); más (*more*); menos (*less*); demasiado (*too (much)*); bastante (*enough*)

Usted habla demasiado. | *You talk too much.*

E • **Más, menos, demasiado** and **bastante** can be used as intensifiers with other adverbs.
Hable menos rápidamente. | *Speak less quickly.*
Juan canta bastante bien. | *Juan sings quite well.*

• Muy (*very*) can also be used to modify adverbs.
Luisa habla muy precisamente. | *Luisa speaks very precisely.*

• The adjective **tanto** (*so much*) becomes **tan** (*so*).
España es tan bonita. | *Spain is so pretty.*

• When **alto/fuerte** and **bajo** are used figuratively with the meaning *loudly* and *softly*, the unchanged adjective form is kept.
Hable alto. | *Speak loudly.*

19 Exercises

1 Form adverbs from the following adjectives.

E.g. alegre → alegremente.

a diferente
b difícil
c fácil
d formal
e natural
f elegante
g mayor
h principal

i inteligente
j cruel
k evidente
l responsable
m raro
n rápido
o claro
p estupendo

q lento
r nervioso
s calmado
t tranquilo
u serio
v franco
w divino
x furioso

2 You are describing how someone reacted to a recent incident. Complete the sentences with the appropriate adverbs.

E.g. Juan estaba furioso – gritó _____ . → Juan estaba furioso – gritó furiosamente.

a Luisa es una persona sincera – explicó todo _____ .
b Julio es un buen conductor – condujo _____ .
c El profesor es muy inteligente – describió la situación _____ .
d Normalmente la policía es puntual – llegó _____ .
e Rodrigo tiene un carácter malo – actuó _____ .
f El incidente fue muy rápido – todo ocurrió _____ .
g El inspector es un hombre serio – habló _____ .
h Soy una persona sincera – lo digo _____ .
i Tú eres un conductor cuidadoso – viaja _____ .

3 Make up sentences using two adverbs.

E.g. Pedro habla (buen) (rápido). → Pedro habla bien y rápidamente.

a Julio canta (claro) (triste).
b Enrique trabaja (malo) (lento).
c Rodrigo actúa (serio) (profesional).
d Emilio conduce (rápido) (peligroso).
e El niño habla (poco) (bajo).
f Trabajamos (intenso) (responsable).
g Escribo (lento) (inteligente).
h Tú escribes (mucho) (bueno).
i Francisco viste (bueno) (elegante).

20 Comparisons

In English, we use words like more or less to compare quantities.
This unit deals with comparisons in Spanish.

A To say *more than* or *less than*, use **más que** and **menos que**.
Tengo más dinero que Julio. *I have more money than Julio.*
Tenemos menos tiempo que tú. *We've less time than you.*
Julio trabaja más que Ignacio. *Julio works harder than Ignacio.*

B However if *more than* or *less than* refers only to quantity, use **más de** and **menos de**.

Bebe más de dos litros   *He drinks more than two litres*
de vino.   *of wine.*
Trabajamos menos de dos   *We work less than two hours*
horas al día.   *per day.*

C If the comparison is with an abstract, use **más/menos de lo que**.
Cuesta más de lo que piensa. *It costs more than he thinks.*
Me duele menos de lo que   *It hurts less than I expected.*
esperaba.

Note also the use of **del que, de la que, de los que, de las que** agreeing with specific nouns.

Tiene más dinero del que dice. *He/She has more money*
                                than he/she says.

Tiene más cerveza de la   *He/She has more beer than*
que dice.   *he/she says.*

Tiene más libros de los   *He/She has more books than*
que dice.   *he/she says.*

Tiene más revistas de las   *He/She has more magazines*
que dice.   *than he/she says.*

D To say that two comparisons are the same, use **tanto como** and make the **tanto** agree with the object referred to.

Tengo tanta cerveza como   *I have as much beer*
Julio.   *as Julio.*
Tengo tantas revistas como   *I have as many magazines*
Julio.   *as Julio.*

With an adjective or adverb, **tanto** becomes **tan**.

Soy tan inteligente como   *I am as intelligent as Ignacio.*
Ignacio.
Leo tan rápidamente   *I read as quickly as you.*
como tú.

20 Exercises

1 **Make comparisons.**

> *E.g.* Julio tiene libros/Juana → Julio tiene más libros que Juana.

a Julia tiene vestidos/Luisa
b Ignacio bebe vino/Francisco
c Madrid tiene habitantes/Granada
d Yo hablo español/inglés
e Los españoles comen carne/pescado

2 **Say you don't have as much as someone else using *tanto como*.**

> *E.g.* tengo amigas/Luisa → No tengo tantas amigas como Luisa.

a como carne/Luisa
b escribo cartas/mi madre
c compro pescado/tú
d recibo dinero/mi jefe
e soy inteligente/el profesor

3 **Fill the blanks with *que, de, de lo que, del que, de la que, de los que, de las que*, as necessary.**

a Un coche cuesta más _____ una moto.
b Un coche cuesta menos _____ dice mi padre.
c Mi coche usa menos gasolina _____ piensas.
d Mi coche usa menos aceite _____ gasolina.
e En Madrid hay más parques _____ dice este libro.
f Tú necesitas menos camisas _____ tienes.
g El billete cuesta más dinero _____ tengo.
h Voy al cine más frecuentemente _____ tú.
i Julia tiene más _____ veinte pares de zapatos.

21 Comparison of adjectives and adverbs

This unit looks at the comparative forms of adjectives and adverbs like prettier, more quickly, as clearly.

A Más / menos with adjectives

- Superiority is indicated by **más** + adjective + **que**.

  La ciudad es más bonita   *The town is prettier than*
  que la playa.   *the beach.*

- Adverbs are compared in the same way.

  Juan escribe más rápidamente   *Juan writes more quickly than*
  que Luisa.   *Luisa.*

- Inferiority is likewise shown using **menos**.

  La playa es menos bonita   *The beach is less pretty than*
  que la ciudad.   *the town.*
  Luisa escribe menos claramente   *Luisa writes less clearly*
  que Juan.   *than Juan.*

- Similarity is shown with **tan** + adjective/adverb + **como**.

  Luisa escribe tan claramente   *Luisa writes as clearly as*
  como Catalina.   *Catalina.*

B Just as English has some irregular forms like *better*, so does Spanish.

> mejor (*better*); peor (*worse*); mayor (*older, more important*);
> menor (*younger, less important*); superior (*upper*); inferior
> (*lower*).

⚠ These adjectives have no separate feminine form.

  El libro es mejor que   *The book is better than*
  la película.   *the film.*

C To say *even (worse)* etc., use **aun**.

  La película es aun peor que   *The film is even worse than*
  la novela.   *the novel.*

D Mejor and peor can be used as adverbs.

  Tú hablas español mejor   *You speak Spanish better*
  que yo.   *than I do.*

The forms **más bueno** and **más malo** usually refer to moral qualities; **más grande** and **menos grande** refer to physical size, whereas **mayor** and **menor** refer to age.

  Madrid es más grande   *Madrid is bigger than Seville.*
  que Sevilla.

21 Exercises

1 Join the sentences to make one sentence comparing the three descriptions.

E.g. Luisa es inteligente. Julio. Yo → Luisa es más inteligente que Julio pero menos inteligente que yo.

a Barcelona es grande. Sevilla. Madrid.
b Carlos es valiente. Federico. Juan.
c Luisa conduce rápidamente. Mi hermana. Julia.
d Paco canta bien. Miguel. Julio.
e La torre es alta. La iglesia. La catedral.
f El general es importante. El ministro. El presidente.
g El teatro es caro. El cine. La ópera.
h El actor es famoso. La actriz. El director.
i El pescado es bueno. La carne. La fruta.
j Mi novia es guapa. Mi hermana. Tu esposa.

2 This time, practise using *tan(to) como* using the same prompts.

E.g. Luisa es tan inteligente como Julio pero no es tan inteligente como yo.

3 Make your own comparisons.

E.g. Un caballo es más grande que un perro pero no es tan grande como un elefante.

Here are some suggested words you can use.

Nouns

hotel, pensión, palacio (*palace*), casa (*house*), piso (*flat*), mar (*sea*), río (*river*), lago (*lake*), estanque (*pond*), vino, cerveza (*beer*), limonada, vinagre (*vinegar*), hermana (*sister*), prima (*female cousin*), sobrina (*niece*), calle (*street*), autopista (*motorway*), carretera (*road*), moto (*motorbike*), coche (*car*), tren (*train*), tigre (*tiger*), león (*lion*), gato (*cat*)

Adjectives

bonito (*kind, nice*), guapo (*good-looking*), dulce (*sweet*), seco (*dry*), amargo (*bitter*), alto (*tall*), ancho (*wide*), estrecho (*narrow*), largo (*long*), rápido (*fast*), lento (*slow*), feroz (*ferocious*), fuerte (*strong*), peligroso (*dangerous*) – and any others you can think of. Good luck!

22 Superlatives

We see superlatives around us every day, especially in adverts: the whitest wash of all, the best lemonade in the world, the most expensive ingredients and so on.

A The good news is that superlatives in Spanish are very similar to the comparative forms, except that you add the definite article (**el, la, los, las**) or a possessive ajective (**mi, tu**, etc.).

COMPARATIVE

Quiero ver un deporte más peligroso.	*I want to watch a more dangerous sport.*

SUPERLATIVE

Quiero ver el deporte más peligroso del mundo.	*I want to watch the most dangerous sport in the world.*

⚠ **Éste es mi mejor amigo** (*This is my best friend*).

B After a superlative, use **de** to translate *in*.

Luis es el estudiante más inteligente de la clase.	*Luis is the most intelligent student in the class.*

C Another way is to form an 'absolute superlative' by adding **-ísimo** to the basic adjective. This often has the force in English of *ever so ...* or *extremely*.

Luisa es guapísima.	*Luisa is ever so good-looking.*
Este pueblo es feísimo.	*This little town is extremely ugly.*

You will have to watch your spelling rules.

rico → riquísimo	largo → larguísimo
feliz (happy) → felicísimo	elegante → elegantísimo
difícil → dificilísimo	

⚠ **-ísimo** always needs an accent.

D Adverbs usually form their superlatives with **muy** (*very*) or **extremadamente** (*extremely*).

Hablan muy rápidamente.	*They speak very quickly.*

E **Muchísimo** (*very much*); **poquísimo** (*very little*)

Los chicos estudian muchísimo para el examen.	*The boys are working very hard for the exam.*
Aquí la gente trabaja poquísimo.	*Here, people work very little.*

22 Exercises

1 Invent some advertising slogans.

E.g. vino; vendido; el país → el vino más vendido del país
a periódico; leído; el mundo
b película; vista; el año
c chocolate; rico; Europa
d coche; popular; el continente
e piel; suave; todas
f banco; cooperativo; América
g música; vibrante; capital
h playas; limpias; costa
i precios; económicos; ciudad
j selección; variada; región

2 You've had enough! Complain about your treatment. Use *más* or *menos* as necessary.

E.g. habitación sucia hotel → Tengo la habitación más sucia del hotel.

a coche viejo compañía   f dolor terrible todo
b asiento malo teatro   g dentista simpático pueblo
c secretaria trabajadora oficina h día aburrido fábrica
d colega hablador departamento i vacaciones largas colegio
e esposa fea mundo   j plato asqueroso restaurante

3 Practise absolute superlatives using *-ísimo*. Pick adjectives from the box.

E.g. ¿Qué tal el chocolate? → Es sabrosísimo. (*How's the chocolate? It's really tasty.*)
¿Qué tal...
a el vino? b el coche? c la casa? d el traje?
e la playa? f las patatas? g los caramelos?
h los ejercicios? i las chicas? j las discos?

---

elegante cómodo sabroso dulce bueno fácil
guapo vivo rico rápido

---

23 Demonstrative adjectives and pronouns

Demonstratives are words that show or point out something, like this, that, those *and* these.

A Demonstrative adjectives agree in gender and number with the nouns to which they refer, and they normally go in front of the noun.

There are three demonstrative adjectives in Spanish. In addition to **este** (*this*), Spanish distinguishes between **ese** (*that near you*) and **aquel** (*that over there*).

- **este** (*this*)

	Masculine	Feminine
Singular	este libro (***this book***)	esta casa (***this house***)
Plural	estos libros (***these books***)	estas casas (***these houses***)

- **ese** (*that (near you)*)

	Masculine	Feminine
Singular	ese libro (***that book***)	esa casa (***that house***)
Plural	esos libros (***those books***)	esas casas (***those houses***)

- **aquel** (*that (over there – remote)*)

Singular	aquel libro (***that book***)	aquella casa (***that house***)
Plural	aquellos libros (***those books***)	aquellas casas (***those houses***)

B When the demonstratives stand on their own, an accent is placed on the stressed syllable to show that they are pronouns.

- **éste, ésta, éstos, éstas** (*this one, these ones*)
  Mi casa es ésta – éstas son   *My house is this (one) – these*
  mis hermanas.   *are my sisters.*

- **ése, ésa, ésos, ésas** (*that one, those ones*)
  ¿Qué revista es ésa?   *What magazine is that (one)?*

- **aquél, aquélla, aquéllos, aquéllas** (*that one, those ones*)
  ¿Qué montañas son aquéllas? *What mountains are those?*

⚠ **Esto, eso, aquello**

If something has not yet been identified, so consequently has not been given a gender, use these neuter pronouns.
  ¿Qué es eso? ¡Es horrible!   *What's that? It's horrible!*

C **Esto, eso** and **aquello** never take an accent and are never used as adjectives.

23 Exercises

1 Put in the correct form of *este*, *esta*, *estos*, *estas*.

E.g. patatas → estas patatas

a coche   b botas   c chica   d chicos   e casas   f hombre
g película   h estudiantes.

2 Repeat the exercise, this time with *ese*.

3 Finally, repeat the exercise with *aquel*.

4 Practise using demonstrative pronouns.

E.g. ¿Qué chica es (ése)? → ¿Qué chica es ésa?

a ¿Qué fruta es (éste)?
b ¿Qué es (ése)?
c ¿Qué botas son (aquél)?
d ¿Qué pueblo es (éste)?
e ¿Qué ciudad es (aquél)?

5 Which do you prefer? Use the demonstrative pronouns.

E.g. ¿Qué botas prefieres? éste/aquél → ¿Éstas o aquéllas?

a ¿Qué casa prefieres? ése/éste
b ¿Qué libro prefieres? aquél/éste
c ¿Qué camisas prefieres? éste/ése
d ¿Qué vaqueros prefieres? éste/aquél
e ¿Qué revistas y periódicos prefieres? éste/ése

6 Put in the demonstrative adjective or pronoun as necessary.

E.g. (este) casa es grande → Esta casa es grande.
      (este) es la casa de mi amigo → Ésta es la casa de mi amigo.

a (aquel) chicos son inteligentes.
b ¿Qué estudiantes son (aquel)?
c ¿Qué es (aquel)? ¿Es carne?
d (este) chica es muy bonita.
e (esta) es mi hermana.
f (aquel) montañas son bonitas.
g ¿Qué montañas son (aquel)?
h ¿Qué es (este)?
i ¿Qué chica es (ese)?
j ¿De quién es (aquel) falda?

24 Possessive adjectives

Possessive adjectives indicate ownership and correspond to my, your, his, etc. in English.

A Possessive adjectives come in front of the noun. Like other adjectives in Spanish, they agree in gender and number with the noun to which they refer.

(yo)	mi/mis	(nosotros)	nuestro/a/os/as
(tú)	tu/tus	(vosotros)	vuestro/a/os/as
(él, ella, usted)	su/sus	(ellos, ellas, ustedes)	su/sus

- *my*: mi libro (*my book*); mis libros (*my books*); mi casa (*my house*); mis casas (*my houses*)

- *your (familiar singular)*: tu libro (*your book*); tus libros (*your books*); tu casa (*your house*); tus casas (*your houses*)

- *his/her/your (polite)*: su libro (*his, her, your book*); sus libros (*his, her, your books*); su casa (*his, her, your house*); sus casas (*his, her, your houses*)

- *our*: nuestro libro (*our book*); nuestros libros (*our books*); nuestra casa (*our house*); nuestras casas (*our houses*)

- *your (familiar plural)*: vuestro libro (*your book*); vuestros libros (*your books*); vuestra casa (*your house*); vuestras casas (*your houses*)

B To avoid ambiguity, since **su** can mean *his, her, their, your* (singular polite) and *your* (plural polite), you can specify who the **su** refers to by adding **de él, de ella, de ellos, de ellas, de usted** or **de ustedes**.

su coche de usted *your car*

You can also say simply **la casa de usted**, etc.

⚠ The possessive adjectives agree with the thing possessed not the person who owns it. Hence **su casa** means *his, her, their, your house* and **sus casas** means *his, her, their, your houses*.

24 Exercises

1 Make these expressions plural.

E.g. mi amigo → mis amigas

a nuestra hermana
b tu coche
c su habitación
d vuestra universidad
e mi clase

f su bicicleta
g nuestro amigo
h su casa
i mi revista
j tu periódico

2 Add *de él, de ella, de usted, de ellos, de ellas* or *de ustedes* for clarity.

E.g. His house → su casa de él

a their (*feminine*) house
b their (*masculine*) houses
c her sister
d her sisters
e your (*singular*) newspaper

f your (*plural*) newspaper
g his father
h her father
i their (*feminine*) parents
j his parents

3 Correct the possessive adjectives.

E.g. ¿Es el libro de Julio? (*our*) → No, es nuestro libro.

a ¿Es el coche de Juan? (*my*)
b ¿Es el vino de Juanita? (*your (familiar)*)
c ¿Es la revista de Julio? (*her*)
d ¿Son las botas de Pedro? (*our*)
e ¿Son los periódicos de Ana? (*their (feminine)*)

4 Translate the following into Spanish.

a Your newspaper is interesting, sir.
b Our house is small and white.
c Do you have my boots?
d Their car is green.
e Her jeans are blue.
f Juanito, do you want your shirt?
g Our money is in the bank.
h My parents live in his house.
i Their house is in Madrid.
j Children, your socks (**calcetines**) are here.

25 Possessive pronouns

> *Possessive pronouns are words like* mine *and* yours *which refer to a noun or nouns already identified.*

Su coche es blanco pero el mío es azul.	*His car is white but mine is blue.*

A Possessive pronouns agree in gender and number with the noun they represent.

	Singular		Plural	
	Masculine	Feminine	Masculine	Feminine
mine	**el mío**	**la mía**	**los míos**	**las mías**
yours (fam.)	**el tuyo**	**la tuya**	**los tuyos**	**las tuyas**
his, hers yours (pol.)	**el suyo**	**la suya**	**los suyos**	**las suyas**
ours	**el nuestro**	**la nuestra**	**los nuestros**	**las nuestras**
yours (fam.)	**el vuestro**	**la vuestra**	**los vuestros**	**las vuestras**
theirs, yours (pol.)	**el suyo**	**la suya**	**los suyos**	**las suyas**

Éste es mi vino, ¿dónde está el tuyo?	*This is my wine, where is yours?*
Nuestros padres trabajan mucho pero los suyos trabajan poco.	*Our parents work hard but his work little.*

B **El suyo** may be clarified with **de él, de usted**, etc.

Mi revista es ésta – ¿Cuál es la (suya) de usted?	*This is my magazine – which is yours?*

C With names, use **el de, la de, los de, las de** + the name.

mi coche y el de Julio	*my car and Julio's*
nuestras botas y las de Ana y Pedro	*our boots and Ana and Pedro's*

D After **ser** (*to be*), possessive pronouns usually drop the definite article.

Este libro es mío – aquél es tuyo.	*This book is mine – that one is yours.*
Esta habitación es nuestra.	*This room is ours.*

E The long forms of the possessives like **mío**, etc., may occasionally be used as adjectives but must come after the noun.

¡Dios mío!	*My God!*

Note also expressions like **un amigo mío** (*a friend of mine*).

⚠ **Muy señor mío** (*Dear Sir* (in formal letters)).

25 Exercises

1 Play a game of one-upmanship.

> *E.g.* Tu casa es grande. → Tu casa es grande, pero la mía es más grande.

a Tu coche es rápido.
b Tu familia es inteligente.
c Tus padres son trabajadores.
d Tus hermanas son estúpidas.
e Tu trabajo es difícil.
f Tu habitación es bonita.
g Tu amiga es hermosa.
h Tus botas son elegantes.
i Tu colegio es famoso.
j Tus tías son ricas.

2 Practise possessive pronouns.

> *E.g.* (los libros) → Tengo los míos pero los tuyos están en casa.

a las botas
b la botella de vino
c el diccionario
d los calcetines negros
e los vaqueros

3 Practise using *el de ...*, *la de ...*, etc.

> *E.g.* trabajo (*hers*) → mi trabajo y el de ella

a casa (*your* (polite))
b coche (*Julio*)
c padres (*theirs*)
d dinero (*hers*)
e vaqueros (*his*)

4 Practise possessives after *ser* (to be).

> *E.g.* Este libro es (yo). → Este libro es mío.

a Esta casa es (tú).
b Estos vaqueros son (nosotros).
c Estas faldas son (vosotras).
d Este dinero es (usted).
e Esta camisa es (yo).
f Este coche es (Julio).
g Este vino es (ella).
h Estos amigos son (él).

26 Subject pronouns

Subject pronouns (I, you, he, etc.) are not used as frequently in Spanish as in English, as the verb ending itself usually makes clear who the subject is. They may, however, be included for clarity or emphasis.

Tú trabajas mucho pero yo prefiero dormir.	*You work hard but I prefer to sleep.*

A The personal pronouns are first, second or third person.

	Singular	Plural
1st person	yo (*I*)	nosotros/nosotras (*we*)
2nd person	tú (*you* (familiar))	vosotros/vosotras (*you* (familiar))
3rd person	él (*he*) ella (*she*) usted (*you* (formal))	ellos (*they* (masculine)) ellas (*they* (feminine)) ustedes (*you* (formal))

B • **Yo** is written with a small letter except as the first word of a sentence.

Yo soy profesor. El profesor, soy yo.	*I'm a teacher. The teacher – that's me.*

- **Nosotros, vosotros** and **ellos** distinguish gender: **nosotras somos alumnas** (*we* (girls) *are pupils*). As all Spanish nouns are masculine or feminine, **él, ella, ellos** and **ellas** refer also to things, not just people.

- Spanish has four forms for *you* to distinguish degrees of familiarity and number. **Tú** and **vosotros** are singular and plural and express familiarity – family, friends, close colleagues. They are used with second-person verb endings, singular and plural as appropriate. **Usted** and **ustedes** are used to express formality or politeness. They are always used with third-person verb endings (like extremely formal English *How is your majesty? How are your excellencies?*)

¿Cómo están ustedes, señoras y señores?	*How are you, ladies and gentlemen?*

- **Usted** and **ustedes** are often written **Vd.** and **Vds.** (**Ud.** and **Uds.** are also used, particularly in America). **Vosotros** can sound old fashioned or has religious, poetic overtones. In America (and in some parts of southern Spain) **ustedes** is used for the plural *you* in all cases.

26 Exercises

1 Add personal subject pronouns for emphasis.

> *E.g.* _____ bebo → yo bebo

a _____ trabajo.
b _____ trabajamos.
c ¿_____ trabajáis, chicos?
d ¿Dónde están _____ , señores?
e _____ es española pero _____ es inglés.
f ¿Cómo está _____ , señora?

2 Add the necessary subject pronouns.

a ¿Quién es? Soy _____ .
b ¿Quiénes son? Somos _____ .
c ¿Sois _____ , Isabel y Juan?
d ¿Sois _____ , Luisa y María?
e ¿Son _____ , señores?
f ¿Es _____ , señor López?

3 Use subject pronouns to combine the pairs of sentences and show the contrast.

> *E.g.* Trabajo por la mañana. Trabajas por la tarde. → Yo trabajo por la mañana, pero tú trabajas por la tarde.

a Vas a Madrid. Voy a Barcelona.
b Coméis carne. Comemos pescado.
c Somos profesoras. Sois alumnas.
d Viven (= las chicas) en el campo. Viven (= los chicos) en la ciudad.
e Prefiero vino. Prefiere (= *you*) cerveza.
f Escuchan (= *you*) música clásica. Escucho música pop.

27 Disjunctive personal pronouns

Disjunctive pronouns are used after prepositions.

Disjunctive (or prepositional) personal pronouns are used in both English and Spanish in such expressions as *for him*, *without us*, *from them*. All disjunctive means is that the pronoun is separated (dis-joined) from the verb.

A The good news is that most disjunctive pronouns in Spanish are the same as the subject pronouns.

Tengo un regalo para él y para ella.	*I have a present for him and for her.*
Una botella de vino para nosotros y champán para ustedes.	*A bottle of wine for us and champagne for you.*

B The bad news is that **yo** changes to **mí** and **tú** changes to **ti** after a preposition. Note that **mí** has an accent, but **ti** does not.

¿Es la carta para mí o para ti? *Is the letter for me or for you?*

⚠ After some prepositions, the ordinary subject pronouns are used instead of **mí** and **ti**. These include **según yo** (*according to me*), **entre tú y yo** (*between you and me*), **salvo, excepto, menos** (*except*).

Todos excepto yo. *Everyone except me.*

C To summarize, disjunctive pronouns are as follows.

	Singular	Plural
1st person	(para) mí	(para) nosotros/nosotras
2nd person	(para) ti	(para) vosotros/vosotras
3rd person	(para) él	(para) ellos
	(para) ella	(para) ellas
	(para) usted	(para) ustedes

Conmigo (*with me*), **contigo** (*with you*), **consigo** (*with oneself*)

The preposition **con** (*with*) combines with **mí** and **ti** to create two special forms, **conmigo** and **contigo**.

¿Quieres ir conmigo?	*Do you want to go with me?*
Siempre quiero estar contigo.	*I always want to be with you.*

Consigo (*with oneself*) is used with any third person to refer back to the same subject.

Juan lleva mucho dinero consigo.	*Juan takes a lot of money with him.*
Ustedes traen la comida consigo.	*You bring the food with you.*

27 Exercises

1 Complete the sentence with the appropriate pronoun.

> *E.g.* Hoy es mi cumpleaños – ¿tienes un regalo para _____ ?
> → ¿tienes un regalo para mí?

a Hoy es tu cumpleaños – tengo un regalo para _____ .

b Hoy es el cumpleaños de Juan – tengo un regalo para _____ .

c Hoy es su cumpleaños, don José – tengo un regalo para _____ .

d Hoy es su aniversario, señores – tengo un regalo para _____ .

e Hoy es nuestro aniversario – ¿tenéis un regalo para _____ ?

f Claro, mamá y papá – tenemos un regalo para _____ .

g Niñas, tengo limonada para _____ .

h Mi hermana y yo estamos enfermas – ¿tiene usted medicina para _____ ?

2 Add correct form; *yo*, *mí* or *migo*.

a para _____	**d** delante de _____
b con _____	**e** salvo _____
c sin _____	**f** entre tú y _____

3 Talk about Juan and Luisa. Use *consigo, con él, con ella, con ellos* as necessary.

a Luisa va al cine _____ .

b Luisa tiene mucha comida _____ .

c Juan ha perdido su dinero en la lotería – está muy enojado (*angry*) _____ .

d Luisa ha perdido el dinero de Juan – está muy enojado _____ .

e Luisa ya no quiere salir _____ .

f Esta tarde voy a salir _____ .

28 Direct object pronouns

> *Direct object pronouns are words like it, them, me, us, him which replace nouns.*

A In English, we put object pronouns after the verb: *I eat it*; *they know us*, etc. Spanish normally places the object pronoun in front of the verb: **lo como** (*I eat it*); **nos conocen** (*they know us*).

B Spanish object pronouns reflect the gender and number of the noun being replaced.

	Singular	Plural
1st person	me	nos
2nd person	te	os
3rd person	lo / la	los (*masculine*) / las (*feminine*)

¿Dónde está el chocolate?	*Where is the chocolate?*
No lo veo.	*I don't see it.*
(**lo = el chocolate**)	
No veo la cerveza	*I don't see the beer,*
¿la has bebido?	*have you drunk it?*
(**la = la cerveza**)	

C **lo, la, los** and **las** refer to both people and things. In educated usage in Spain, many people use **le** rather than **lo** to refer to a masculine, singular person.

Le conozco./Lo conozco.	*I know him.*

⚠ Usted and ustedes, the polite words for *you*, are third-person pronouns, so the corresponding direct object forms are also **lo, la, los** and **las**.

La conozco, María.	*I know you, María.*
¿Los señores de López?	*Mr and Mrs López –*
¡No los vi!	*I didn't see you!*

D To make the expression negative, **no** comes in front of the object pronoun but after any subject.

Yo no te conozco.	*I don't know you.*
No te he visto nunca.	*I've never seen you.*

E When two verbs are used together, for example, *I am going to buy it*, the object pronoun goes either in front of the first verb or is added to the infinitive to make one word, but NEVER goes between the verbs.

Lo voy a comprar./	*I'm going to buy it.*
Voy a comprarlo.	
Queremos verlos./	*We want to see them.*
Los queremos ver.	

1 Use object pronouns instead of the nouns.

> *E.g.* ¿Quieres el libro? → Lo tengo.

a ¿Quieres la cerveza?
b ¿Quieres los cigarrillos?
c ¿Quieres las patatas?
d ¿Quieres pan?
e ¿Quieres mucho dinero?
f ¿Quieres agua?

2 Choose the appropriate object pronoun, *te, os, lo, la, los, las*.

> *E.g.* Señora → La oigo.

a Juanita, hijita
b Alumnos
c Señor
d Julio, ¡amigo!
e Hijas
f Señores
g Señoritas
h Mamá y papá

3 Practise the order of object pronouns.

> *E.g.* (el café) (beber) he bebido → No lo he bebido, voy a beberlo.

a (la cerveza) (beber) he bebido
b (la casa) (limpiar) he limpiado
c (yo) (ducharse) he duchado
d (el coche) (conducir) he conducido
e (los niños) (ver) he visto
f (las botellas) (lavar) he lavado

29 Indirect object pronouns

> *Indirect objects are words like* (to) him, (to) me, *that show the recipient of a verb.*

A In English, the indirect pronouns are sometimes introduced with *to*: *I show the book to him* (*I show him the book*). Spanish does not require a preposition: **le muestro el libro; me da el libro.**

B As with the direct object pronouns (see Unit 28), Spanish usually places the indirect object in front of the verb.

	Singular	Plural
1st person	me (*(to) me*)	nos (*(to) us*)
2nd person	te (*(to) you*)	os (*(to) you*)
3rd person	le (*(to) him, her, you*)	les (*(to) them, you*)

You can see that the first and second persons are the same as the direct object pronouns. In the third person **le** and **les** are used for either gender.

| Le doy el libro. | *I give him/her/you* (polite) *the book.* |
| Les doy el libro. | *I give them/you* (plural) *the book* |

C If there is any ambiguity, you can clarify who the **le/les** refers to by adding **a** with a disjunctive pronoun (see Unit 27): **a él, a ella, a usted, a ellos, a ellas, a ustedes,** but you still keep the **le/les** as well!

| Le doy el libro a usted. | *I give the book to you.* |
| No les hablo a ustedes. | *I'm not talking to you.* |

D When two verbs come together, the same word order as with direct object pronouns applies.

| Quiero decirle la verdad./ | *I want to tell him/her/* |
| Le quiero decir la verdad. | *you the truth.* |

E When two object pronouns come together, any first person takes precedence over a second or third person.

| Me lo presenta. | *He is presenting it to me.* |

F With two third-person object pronouns, the indirect comes in front of the direct. The first **le/les** changes to **se.**

| Se lo entrego. | *I'm handing it to him/her/ you/them.* |

⚠ With two object pronouns tacked on the end of an infinitive, an accent is always needed to maintain the stress.

| No voy a decírselo. | *I'm not going to say it to him,* etc. |

29 Exercises

1 Supply the appropriate indirect object pronoun.

   E.g. (*Us*) da el vino. → Nos da el vino.

a (*You*) doy la limonada, hijo.

b (*Us*) entrega la limonada.

c (*Me*) da la limonada.

d (*Him*) digo la verdad.

e (*Them*) entregamos el vino.

f (*Her*) damos el libro.

g (*You*) doy un descuento, señor.

h (*You*) entrego el paquete, señor y señora.

**2 Emphasize or clarify the person referred to in exercise 1 (*him,
them, her, you,* etc.) by adding *a* with the appropriate disjunctive
pronoun.**

   E.g. Nos da el vino a nosotros.

3 Put the supplied object pronouns in the correct order.

a dice (lo, me)

b quiero hablar (le)

c No puedo decir (te, lo)

d entregamos (te, las)

e doy (te, lo)

f presenta (nos, lo)

**4 Use the alternative position, putting the object pronouns after
the infinitive. Remember an accent is needed with two pronouns.**

   E.g. Le quiero decir la verdad → Quiero decirle la verdad.

a No lo puedo decir.

b Se lo quiero decir.

c No les quiero dar un descuento.

d No se lo quiero dar.

e No se lo queremos entregar.

f ¿Por qué no me quieres dar el vino?

g ¿Por qué no me lo quieres dar?

h Se lo voy a pagar.

i No te lo puedo confesar.

j ¿No me lo vas a preguntar?

30 Indefinite words: *someone*, *something*, etc.

English has a number of words or expressions beginning with some- or any-, for example someone, anybody, something, to refer to specific but undefined situations.

A **algo** (*something/anything*)

¿Quiere usted algo más?	*Do you want anything else?*
Hay algo en el armario.	*There's something in the cupboard.*

⚠ **Algo** can also be used with an adjective to mean *somewhat* or *rather*.

Esto es algo difícil.	*This is rather difficult.*

B **alguien** (*someone*)

Hay alguien en la casa.	*There's someone in the house.*
¿Conoces a alguien aquí?	*Do you know anyone here?*

⚠ **Alguien** takes a personal **a** (see Unit 94).

C **alguno** (*some*)

Like **uno**, **alguno** agrees with the noun.

Luisa conoce algunas ciudades de América.	*Luisa knows some cities in America.*
Alguna gente prefiere dormir.	*Some people prefer to sleep.*
Juan trabaja en algún colegio en Madrid.	*Juan is working in some school in Madrid.*

⚠ **Alguno** becomes **algún** in front of a masculine singular noun.

D **alguna parte** (*somewhere*)

Vive en alguna parte del sur.	*He lives somewhere in the south.*
Hay servicios por alguna parte aquí.	*There are toilets somewhere round here.*

E **cualquiera** (*any one*)

¿Qué libro? – Cualquiera.	*Which book? – Any (one).*
Cualquiera puede hacerlo.	*Anyone can do it.*

⚠ **Cualquiera** becomes **cualquier** in front of any singular noun and **cualesquier** in front of any plural noun.

El tren sale en cualquier momento.	*The train is leaving at any moment.*
Se venden en cualesquier tiendas.	*They are sold in any shops.*

30 Exercises

1 Make *alguno* agree with its noun.

> *E.g.* Necesito alg___ libros → Necesito **algunos** libros.

a ¿Tiene usted alg___ naranjas?
b Felipe estudia en alg___ universidad.
c ¿Necesitas alg___ dinero?
d Alg___ españoles prefieren café con leche.
e Este hombre es alg___ mecánico o carpintero.
f Creo que todavía hay alg___ lobos en España.
g ¿Has invitado a alg___ amigas a comer?

2 Fill the blanks with the appropriate indefinite word from the box.

a Para mí la ópera es _____ interesante.
b Hay _____ en mi habitación – ¿eres tú, Julio?
c _____ gente piensa que el vino es malo.
d Necesito _____ más – un kilo de patatas.
e La conocí en _____ .
f Creo que hay un hotel por _____ en el centro.
g ¿_____ ha telefoneado? Sí, tu amigo Juan.
h Creo que hay _____ servicios en la plaza.
i Si viene _____ inglés, voy a practicar mi lengua.
j Creo que hay _____ sobre España en este libro.

algo	algo	algo	alguien	alguien	algún
alguna	alguna parte	alguna parte	algunos		

3 Put *cualquiera* into the correct form.

a Necesito _____ medicina.
b Puedes leerlo en _____ periódico.
c Estamos contentos con _____ habitación.
d ¿Qué periódico quieres? _____ .
e ¿Qué mariscos prefieres? _____ .
f No es difícil, _____ puede hacerlo.
g Felipe lo hizo por _____ razón.
h Me gustaría pasar las vacaciones en _____ playa.

31 Negative words: *no one, never, nothing*

You can't always agree to everything, so you need to learn how to say no!

A The simplest way is to put **no** in front of the verb.

Hablo español pero no hablo   *I speak Spanish but I don't*
  portugués.   *speakPortuguese.*

B **No** comes after any subject pronoun but before any reflexive or object pronoun.

Yo no te escucho.   *I'm not listening to you.*
Usted no se levanta tarde.   *You don't get up late.*

C **Nunca** (*never*) is used in the same way.

Tú nunca me ayudas.   *You never help me.*
No vuelvo allí nunca jamás. *I'm never ever going back there.*

D Unlike English, Spanish allows (indeed requires) two or more negative words in the same expression.

Nadie nunca hace nada.   *No one ever does anything.*

If a negative word comes after the verb, Spanish requires **no** or another negative word in front.

Nadie trabaja aquí./   *No one works here.*
No trabaja aquí nadie.

⚠ Do not add **no** if a negative word is already present before the verb.

Nadie aquí habla español. *No one here speaks Spanish.*

E **Nadie** used as the object of a verb requires personal **a**.

No conozco a nadie aquí.   *I don't know anyone here.*

F **Ninguno** is the corresponding negative form of **alguno** (*some*).

No hay ningunas entradas   *There are no tickets for the*
  para el concierto.   *concert.*

⚠ **Ninguno** becomes **ningún** in front of a masculine singular noun.

No he visto ningún hotel.   *I haven't seen any hotel.*

Note that **alguno** used after a negative verb and placed after its noun has an emphatic but negative meaning.

No hay remedio alguno.   *There's no alternative at all.*

31 Exercises

1 **Make the following sentences negative, using *no*.**
a Yo estudio mucho.
b Luisa tiene entradas.
c Nosotros nos levantamos tarde.
d Usted lo ha visto.
e Ellos se han levantado.
f Esta paella le gusta.

2 **Answer these questions in the negative.**

E.g. Tú siempre bebes vino. → Yo nunca bebo vino.
a Yo siempre como patatas.
b Juan llega tarde con frecuencia.
c Alguien me ha ayudado en la casa.
d Algún español vive aquí.
e Mucho es interesante aquí.
f Alguna chica trabaja mucho.

3 **Re-write your answers from exercise 2 putting *no* in front of the verb.**

E.g. Yo no bebo vino nunca.

4 **Put the appropriate negative words in the gaps to describe one of life's unfortunates.**
Pedro a _____ tiene dinero. b _____ tiene dinero. No tiene c _____ amigos y d _____ le quiere. e _____ trabaja porque f _____ ha encontrado g _____ trabajo en h _____ pueblo. En fin, el pobre hombre no tiene i _____ .

5 **Translate the following into Spanish.**
a I never eat potatoes.
b Julio speaks Spanish but doesn't speak Portuguese.
c There are no tickets left for the cinema.
d Luisa never helps me.
e Juan never gets up late.
f Luisa doesn't know anyone here.
g You never help anyone.
h No one ever drinks anything in this town.
i I don't like anything here.
j I'm not coming back ever again.

32 Negatives: *neither, nor, no longer*

> *In Unit 31 we saw that Spanish allows more than one negative word in one expression. Here are some more you may need.*

A **ni … ni …** (*neither … nor …*)

Yo no tengo ni casa ni dinero. *I have neither house nor money.*

Ni Juan ni Pedro me   *Neither Juan nor Pedro ever*
   ayuda nunca.   *helps me.*

B **tampoco** (*neither*)

Tú no comes pescado –   *You don't eat fish – me*
   yo tampoco.   *neither.*

Julio no me ayuda tampoco. *Julio doesn't help me either.*

C **ni siquiera** (*not even*)

No tengo ni siquiera un euro. *I don't have even a euro.*

D Negative words such as **nada**, **nadie** and **nunca** are needed after **sin** (*without*), **antes de/que** (*before*), **más/menos que** (*more/less than*) where English uses *anything, anyone, ever,* etc.

Julio salió sin decir nada. *Julio went out without saying*
                              anything.

Luisa terminó el examen   *Luisa finished the exam*
   antes que nadie.   *before anyone.*

Te quiero más que nunca.   *I love you more than ever.*

E Pessimistic expressions like **es imposible** (*it's impossible*) are also followed by negatives.

Es imposible hacer nada   *It's impossible to do anything*
   aquí.   *here.*

F **ya no** (*no longer*)

Ya no fumo.   *I no longer smoke.*

G **todavía no/no … todavía** (*not yet, still not*)

Luisa todavía no se ha levantado./
Luisa no se ha levantado   *Luisa has not got up yet.*
   todavía.

Todavía can be replaced with **aún**.

Aún no sabía qué hacer.   *I still didn't know what to do.*

⚠ The expressions **en la vida** and **en absoluto**, which look positive, are emphatic negatives!

En la vida he comido carne. *I have never eaten meat in*
                              my life.

¿Quieres probar los mariscos? *Do you want to try the*
   En absoluto.   *shellfish? Absolutely not.*

32 Exercises

1 **Put in the appropriate negative word.**

E.g. Pedro no come pescado _____ . → Pedro no come pescado tampoco.

a No como patatas y no como fruta _____ .

b No bebo _____ vino _____ cerveza.

c María no habla inglés _____ .

d No tengo _____ una peseta.

e Esta carne no es buena, _____ es barata.

f Es imposible comer _____ en este restaurante terrible.

g Julio come más que _____ .

h Luisa antes bebía mucho pero _____ bebe vino.

2 **Insert *ya* or *todavía* as appropriate in these expressions.**

a No he decidido _____ qué hacer.

b _____ no fumo porque es malo para la salud.

c Cuando vivía en España hablaba bien, pero _____ no recuerdo los verbos.

d ¿_____ no has terminado tu trabajo?

e ¿Qué quieres estudiar? _____ no sé.

f Luisa _____ no sabe que Julio _____ no come pescado.

g María _____ no sabe qué hora es porque _____ no ha terminado de beber.

h Si tú _____ no me quieres, me voy.

3 **Supply a suitable response from the box.**

a ¿Qué quieres hacer?

b ¿Cuándo piensas ir a una corrida (*bullfight*)?

c ¿Quieres ir a la corrida?

d ¿No quieres ir al restaurante?

e ¿Qué zapatos prefieres?

f ¿Quién canta?

g ¿Qué has dicho?

h ¿Has comido algo tan malo?

i ¿Has decidido?

j No has comido la carne, ¿no vas a comer el pescado?

nunca	nada	nadie	en la vida	en absoluto
tampoco	todavía no	ya no	ningunos	nada

33 Relative pronouns: *que, quien, el cual*

Spanish uses **que** (*which*) and **quien** (*who*) in a similar way. **Que** and **quien** do not have accents when used as relative pronouns.

A **que** (*which, who*)
- **Que** can refer to persons or things.

La casa que está en el campo es muy bonita.	*The house which is in the country is very pretty.*
El libro que lees no es muy interesante.	*The book (which) you are reading isn't very interesting.*
La mujer que ves en la foto es española.	*The woman (who/whom) you see in the photo is Spanish.*

⚠ English sometimes leaves out the relative pronouns when they refer to the object of the verb. Spanish, however, always includes them.

- **Que** may be used after **a**, **de** and **con** when referring to a thing, but not to a person.

Ésta es la casa de que te hablaba.	*This is the house I was talking to you about.*

⚠ In everyday English, we can put words like *to, about* and *with* at the end of the sentence: *with which I was writing* → *I was writing with*. This must never be done in Spanish.

B **el cual, la cual** (*which*)

With other prepositions, **que** is replaced with **el cual, la cual, los cuales** or **las cuales**.

la casa delante de la cual hay un jardín magnífico	*the house in front of which there is a wonderful garden*
los chicos para los cuales compramos los regalos	*the children for whom we bought the presents*
los chicos, a quienes dabas clasas, ahora viven en otra ciudad.	*The children (whom) you used to teach now live in another town.*

C **quien, quienes** (*who, whom*)
- If the relative pronoun refers to a person, and is the object of the verb, **que** can be replaced by **a quien** (**a quienes** if plural).

La mujer a quien conociste en Madrid ha muerto.	*The woman (whom) you met in Madrid has died.*
Los chicos, a quienes dabas clasas, ahora viven en otra ciudad.	*The children (whom) you used to teach now live in another town.*

33 Exercises

1 Join the two sentences into one using *que*.

E.g. El hombre lleva gafas. El hombre trabaja en el jardín. → El hombre que trabaja en el jardín lleva gafas.

a La chica es la hermana de Luisa. La chica canta bien.
b El vino no me gusta. El vino se hace aquí.
c La fruta es mala. La fruta se vende en el mercado.
d El libro fue interesante. Me recomendaste el libro.
e El hotel era muy caro. Nos quedamos en el hotel.
f El mecánico trabaja bien. El mecánico repara mi coche.

2 Use *quien, quienes, a quien, a quienes* as appropriate to link these sentences.

E.g. La señora López trabaja aquí desde septiembre. Es directora del colegio. → La señora López, quien es directora del colegio, trabaja aquí desde septiembre.

a Estos actores reciben mucho dinero. Son los protagonistas principales.
b Las actrices son populares. Viste a las actrices anoche.
c El inglés es profesor de idiomas. Lo conocimos en Londres.
d Los cantantes han grabado un disco nuevo. Hablábamos de los cantantes.
e Julio se ha marchado a América. Luisa salía con Julio.
f El niño lo ha perdido todo. Diste el dinero al niño.

3 Fill the gaps with the appropriate form of *el cual, la cual, los cuales, las cuales*.

E.g. La casa en _____ vivo es muy vieja. → La casa en la cual vivo es muy vieja.

a El mar debajo de _____ hay petróleo es muy profundo.
b La plaza cerca de _____ vives es muy grande.
c Aquí ves la iglesia enfrente de _____ está el bar.
d Los coches con _____ trabaja el mecánico son viejos.
e Abrió el armario en _____ guardaba la comida.
f Estas son las llaves sin _____ salieron.

34 Question words

We use question words like how? what? when? where? who? to request information.

Spanish question words are all written with an accent on the stressed syllable and are preceded by an upside-down question mark (¿).

A **¿Qué?** (*What? Which?*)

| ¿Qué es esto? | *What's this?* |

B **¿Cuál?/¿Cuáles?** (*Which?* (identified more closely))

| ¿Cuál es la ciudad más grande de la región? | *Which is the biggest town in the region?* |
| ¿Cuáles son los platos típicos? | *Which are the typical dishes?* |

⚠ **¿Cuál?** and **¿Cuáles?** are not used next to a noun in correct Spanish. Use **¿Qué?** instead.

| ¿Qué platos son los típicos? | *Which dishes are typical?* |

C **Qué** may be used after a preposition.

| ¿En qué habitación están ustedes? | *What room are you in?* |
| ¿De qué película hablas? | *What film are you talking about?* |

⚠ Unlike everyday English, the preposition must never go at the end of the sentence in Spanish.

D **¿Quién?/¿Quiénes?** (*Who?*)

| ¿Quién es esa chica? | *Who is that girl?* |
| ¿Quiénes son esas chicas? | *Who are those girls?* |

E **¿A quién?/¿A quiénes?** (*Who(m)* as a direct object)

| ¿A quién viste allí? | *Who(m) did you see there?* |
| ¿A quiénes quieren? | *Who(m) do they love?* |

F **¿De quién?/¿De quiénes?** (*Whose?*)

| ¿De quién es este coche? | *Whose car is this?* |
| ¿De quiénes son aquellos coches? | *Whose cars are those?* |

⚠ Note the different word order in Spanish.

34 Exercises

1 Ask questions using **¿Qué? ¿Quién?** or **¿Quiénes?**

> *E.g.* ¿_____ es paella? → ¿Qué es paella?

a ¿_____ son mariscos?   e ¿_____ es la capital de España?
b ¿_____ es el presidente?   f ¿_____ libro prefieres?
c ¿_____ significa esto?   g ¿_____ es tu mejor amigo?
d ¿_____ son los estudiantes?   h ¿_____ son los cantantes?

2 Ask questions with **¿Quién?, ¿A quién?, ¿Con quién?, ¿De quién?** as necessary.

> *E.g.* ¿_____ viste en el pueblo? → ¿A quién viste en el pueblo?

a ¿_____ habla?   f ¿_____ sale Julio?
b ¿_____ conoces?   g ¿_____ es la mujer de Juan?
c ¿_____ es Julio?   h ¿_____ escribes la carta?
d ¿_____ es usted?   i ¿_____ es la casa?
e ¿_____ vieron los niños? j ¿_____ hablan los chicos?

3 Use **¿Qué?** or **¿Cuál?/¿Cuáles?** to form questions.

> *E.g.* ¿_____ de los libros has leído? → ¿Cuáles de los libros has leído?

a ¿_____ de las películas has visto?
b ¿_____ película has visto?
c ¿_____ de los dos libros prefieres?
d ¿_____ es la chica que te gusta?
e ¿_____ de los platos son típicos?
f ¿_____ plato es español?
g ¿_____ es la capital de Inglaterra?
h ¿_____ es el hermano mayor?

35 Questions: *where? when? how? why?*

This unit looks at some more important question words and summarizes those you have met.

A **¿Dónde?** (*Where?*)
    ¿Dónde vive usted?   *Where do you live?*

⚠ **¿Adónde?** (old English *whither?*), should correctly be used with movement, though this is frequently not observed.
    ¿Adónde vas?   *Where are you going?*

B **¿Cuándo?** (*When?*)
    ¿Cuándo piensas casarte?   *When do you intend to get married?*

C **¿Cómo?** (*How?*)
    ¿Cómo se va a la plaza?   *How does one get to the square?*
    ¿Cómo está Juan?   *How is Juan?*

With **ser**, **¿cómo?** asks *what is* (something/someone) *like?*
    ¿Cómo es Juan?   *What is Juan like?*

¿Cómo? is used to request repetition or show surprise.
    Hoy no hay clase.   *There's no lesson today.*
    ¿Cómo?   *What?*

D **¿Cuánto?** (*How much?*) agrees with the noun referred to.
    ¿Cuánta paella quiere?   *How much paella do you want?*
    ¿Cuántos cigarrillos tienes?   *How many cigarettes do you have?*

    ¿Cuánto es?/¿Cuánto vale?   *How much is it?*
    ¿Cuánto son? ¿Cuánto valen?   *How much are they?*

E **¿Por qué?** (*Why? For what reason?*), **¿Para qué?** (*Why? For what purpose?*)
    ¿Por qué no puedes ir al cine?   *Why can't you go to the cinema?*
    ¿Para qué haces eso?   *Why are you doing that?*

⚠ Don't forget **¿Por qué?** (two words, accent needed) (*Why?*) but **porque** (one word, no accent) (*because*).

F In reported (or indirect) speech, such as *She asked me what I was doing*, the question word retains the accent: **Me preguntó qué hacía.**
    Me dijeron cuántos cigarrillos   *They told me how many*
      tenían.   *cigarettes they had.*
    No sabía dónde vivías.   *I didn't know where you lived.*

35 Exercises

1 Imagine you are a reporter interviewing a famous person. Put in the appropriate question words.

a ¿_____ vive usted?
b ¿En _____ ciudad, exactamente?
c ¿_____ hermanos o hermanas tiene?
d ¿_____ es su director preferido?
e ¿_____ de sus filmes prefiere?
f ¿_____ no trabaja usted ahora en España?
g ¿_____ casas tiene en América?
h ¿_____ pasa usted su tiempo libre?
i ¿_____ planes tiene para el futuro?
j ¿_____ va usted mañana?

2 You have a bad telephone line and you need the caller to repeat everything. Which question words do you use?

E.g. Quiero hablar con Luisa. → ¿Quién?

a Soy yo, Paco.
b Voy al pueblo.
c Voy a ir en coche.
d Paso por tu casa esta mañana.
e Tengo que comprar dos libros.
f Quiero una novela y un libro de texto.
g Los necesito porque tengo exámenes.
h También voy a comprar algo para los niños.
i Voy a comprarlo en el mercado.
j Es más barato.

3 Complete the sentences.

a ¿_____ son las ciudades importantes?
b ¿_____ es paella?
c ¿_____ está Barcelona?
d ¿_____ son los Reyes de España?
e ¿_____ valen las entradas?
f ¿_____ es Granada?
g ¿_____ habitantes tiene?
h ¿_____ día es hoy?
i ¿_____ es el presidente?
j ¿_____ fue el problema?

36 Common conjunctions: *and, or*

A conjunction is a word that links elements in a phrase or sentence. Two common English conjunctions are and and or.

A Y = *and*

Julio y Julia hablan español.	*Julio and Julia speak Spanish.*
Julio come pescado y patatas.	*Julio eats fish and potatoes.*
Julio come pescado y Julia come fruta.	*Julio eats fish and Julia eats fruit.*

When **y** comes before a word beginning with **i-** or **hi-**, it is changed to **e**.

Julia e Isabel comen mucho.	*Julia and Isabel eat a lot.*
Madre e hija salen juntas.	*Mother and daughter go out together.*

B O = *or*

¿Es usted inglés o español?	*Are you English or Spanish?*
Necesito un bolígrafo o un lápiz.	*I need a biro or a pencil.*

When **o** comes before a word beginning with **o-** or **ho-**, it is changed to **u**.

Hay diez u once personas en el restaurante.	*There are ten or eleven people in the restaurant*
Busco un restaurante u hotel.	*I'm looking for a restaurant or hotel.*

⚠ Between figures, **o** is usually written **ó** for clarity.

100 ó 200 pesos	*100 or 200 pesos*
22 ó 23	*22 or 23*
en 4 ó 5 días	*in 4 or 5 days*

C Ni = *n(or)*

After a negative verb, Spanish uses **ni**.

No tengo dinero ni casa.	*I haven't money or home.*
No bailo ni canto.	*I don't dance or sing.*

You can also say:

No tengo ni amigos ni colegas.	*I have neither friends nor colleagues.*
Ni canto ni bailo.	*I neither sing (n)or dance.*

36 Exercises

1 Join the two expresions with *y*.

E.g. Tengo dos hijas → Tengo un hijo y dos hijas.
a Tengo una casa. Tengo un jardín.
b Luisa habla inglés. Luisa habla español.
c Tenemos un coche. Tenemos dos bicicletas.
d Ana sale con Pedro. Ana sale con Julio.
e Muchos chicos estudian en el colegio. Muchas chicas estudian en el colegio.

2 Join the expressions with *o*.

E.g. Voy al cine. Voy al teatro. → Voy al cine o al teatro.
a Prefiero pescado. Prefiero carne.
b Usted es alemán. Usted es inglés.
c Bebo cerveza. Bebo vino.
d Pasamos las vacaciones en la playa. Pasamos las vacaciones en la montaña.
e Julio quiere ser profesor. Julio quiere ser mecánico.

3 Link the expressions with *y* or *e* as necessary.

a Juan _____ Ignacio
b Ignacio _____ Juan
c vino _____ aceite
d padres _____ hijos
e restaurantes _____ hoteles
f libertad _____ aire libre
g calefacción central _____ aire acondicionado
h rocas _____ islas
i el libro es romántico _____ interesante
j la película es larga _____ muy interesante

4 Use *o* or *u* as necessary.

a Antonio _____ Octavio _____ horchata?
b Octavio _____ Antonio horror
c siete _____ ocho
d ¿Es septiembre _____ octubre?
e julio _____ agosto
f ¿Quiere usted limonada
g un libro de amor _____
h odio _____ adoro
i ¿Es usted turista _____ hotelero?
j Habla _____ escribe.

37 Conjunctions: *but, however, nevertheless*

Spanish has different ways of expressing the conjunction but.
This unit looks at them and equivalent expressions.

A **Pero** = *but*

This is used in most cases.

Como mucho pero bebo poco.	*I eat a lot but drink little.*
Dame el dinero, pero si te mueves yo tiro.	*Give me the cash, but if you move, I'll shoot.*
Julia trabja hoy pero está muy enferma.	*Julia is working today but she's very ill.*
No trabajo hoy pero tengo que ir a la oficina.	*I'm not working today but I have to go to the office.*

B **Sino** = *but*

When a negative notion is replaced by the positive or corrected equivalent, use **sino** (not **pero**) to translate *but*.

Ésta no es Luisa sino Julia.	*This isn't Luisa but Julia.*
¡No estamos de vacaciones sino de juerga!	*We're not on holiday but on a binge!*
Julia no entra sino sale.	*Julia's not coming in but going out.*

With verb equivalents, **sino que** is often used.

No saludo sino que me ahogo. *I'm not waving but drowning.*

⚠ Sino is not used when both elements are negative.

No saludo pero no me ahogo tampoco.	*I'm not waving but I'm not drowning either.*

C **Sin embargo** = *however*

Estoy en casa; sin embargo no puedo verte.	*I'm at home, however I can't see you.*

D **No obstante** = *nevertheless*

Pedro es rico; no obstante nunca paga la cuenta.	*Pedro is rich; nevertheless he never pays the bill.*

37 Exercises

1 Combine the two sentences using *pero*.

> *E.g.* Estoy en casa. No descanso. → Estoy en casa pero no descanso.

a Pedro vive en Madrid. Pedro no es madrileño.
b Alberto vive en Lisboa. Alberto no habla portugués.
c Mi padre es mecánico. Mi padre no tiene coche.
d Vivimos en la costa. No nos gusta la playa.

2 Combine the two sentences using *sino*.

> *E.g.* No es Luisa. Es María. → No es Luisa sino María.

a No como patatas. Como legumbres.
b No es española. Es americana.
c No estoy casado. Estoy soltero.
d No hablo italiano. Hablo inglés.

3 Fill the blanks with *pero* or *sino*.

a Quiero comprar un coche _____ no tengo bastante dinero.
b No quiero comprar un coche _____ una moto.
c No quiero comprar un coche _____ no quiero usar los trenes.
d Voy a salir con Adolfo _____ es un hombre algo feo.
e No voy a salir con Adolfo _____ con Julio.
f No quiero a María _____ ella me quiere mucho.
g María no es española _____ argentina.
h No vive en Madrid _____ Buenos Aires.
i No vive en Madrid _____ su hermana vive allí.
j No es su hermana _____ su hermano que vive allí.

4 Translate the following into Spanish.

a Julio and Julia eat oranges (**naranjas**) or grapes (**uvas**).
b Héctor and Ignacio don't eat fish (**pescado**) or fruit (**fruta**) but they eat a lot.
c Is his wife María or Octavia?
d Neither María or Octavia but Luisa.
e She doesn't speak French and Italian but Spanish and English.

38 Regular verbs: the present tense

Spanish verbs fall into three basic groups according to their infinitive. This unit covers the regular forms.

A The infinitive is the part of the verb you look up in the dictionary. It corresponds to the English *to speak, to eat, to live,* etc. In English, *to* is the usual sign of the infinitive, and is a separate word. In Spanish, the infinitive is just one word, and the group is shown by the final two letters: **-ar, -er** or **-ir**.

hablar (*to speak*); comer (*to eat*); vivir (*to live*)

B In English there are usually only two personal forms in the present tense, for example, *eat, eats.* We need to add *I, you, he,* etc. to show the subject.

Spanish, on the other hand, shows the subject by the ending of the verb. There are six forms for each group; three singular and three plural.

		Hablar	Comer	Vivir
Singular	1	hablo (*I speak*)	como (*I eat*)	vivo (*I live*)
	2	hablas (*you speak*)	comes (*you eat*)	vives (*you live*)
	3	habla (*he/she/it speaks, you speak*)	come (*he/she/it eats, you eat*)	vive (*he/she/it lives, you live*)
Plural	1	hablamos (*we speak*)	comemos (*we eat*)	vivimos (*we live*)
	2	habláis (*you speak*)	coméis (*you eat*)	vivís (*you live*)
	3	hablan (*they/you speak*)	comen (*they/you eat*)	viven (*they/you live*)

C *I* and *we* are known as 'first person', the first people you think about when the ship goes down! You (singular and plural) are second persons – the next people on your mind! *He, she* and *it* (singular) and *they* (plural) are third persons – those who are left!

D Spanish distinguishes between *you* in the singular (**tú**) and plural (**vosotros**). The second person forms are 'familiar', used when talking to family, friends and people of your age or status.

There are also third-person forms for *you* (**usted** and **ustedes**) which are 'polite' or 'formal' forms – they take third-person verb endings as if to avoid direct address! They are used with strangers, in a formal situation or if you are not sure about status. If in doubt, use these when speaking to someone you don't know.

1 **Give the required forms of the following basic verbs.**

E.g. I (hablar) → hablo

a *we* (hablar)
b *we* (comer)
c *we* (vivir)
d *you* (*familiar singular*) (comer)
e *he* (vivir)
f *they* (comer)
g *you* (*polite singular*) (hablar)
h *I* (comer)
i *you* (*familiar plural*) (vivir)
j *you* (*polite plural*) (hablar).

2 **Practise the full present tense of the following verbs.**

a beber (*to drink*)   d escribir (*to write*)
b fumar (*to smoke*)   e charlar (*to chat*)
c leer (*to read*)

3 **Fill the gaps with the verb form from the box.**

a Pedro _____ vino.   e _____ con mis amigos.
b _____ en Madrid.   f _____ un libro.
c _____ cartas.   g _____ la catedral.
d _____ cigarrillos.   h _____ patatas.

bebe	charlo	come	escribes	fuman
	lee	visitamos	vivimos	

4 **Translate the following into Spanish.**

a We eat paella.
b They smoke cigarettes.
c I visit the cathedral.
d Juan reads a book.
e We chat with friends.
f They drink wine.
g He lives in Madrid.
h You (*polite*) drink wine.

39 Funny first persons

Many first-person singular forms of the present tense have peculiarities. This unit summaries some of them.

A First persons in **-go**.

A number of verbs from the **-er** and **-ir** groups insert a **g** before the final **-o** of the first person. This **g** disappears in the other forms of the present tense, which behave normally! An example is **salir** (*to go out, leave*).

SALIR   salgo, sales, sale, salimos, salís, salen.

Salgo de la casa.   *I go out of the house.*

B Other common verbs with **-g-** in the first person singular include **caer** (*to fall*) → **caigo, caes, cae**, etc; **poner** (*to put*) → **pongo, pones, pone; traer** (*to bring*) → **traigo, traes, trae; hacer** (*to do, make*) → **hago, haces, hace; tener** (*to have*) → tengo, tienes, tiene.

Tengo un coche.   *I have a car.*

C **Venir** (*to come*) behaves like **tener**, but with **-ir** endings: **vengo, vienes, viene, venimos, venís, vienen**.

D The first person singular of the present tense of most verbs ends in **-o**. However, verbs of one syllable, end in **-oy**.

ser (*to be*) → soy (*I am*)   dar (*to give*) → doy (*I give*)

E **Ir** (*to go*) is irregular. Its endings are similar to **dar. Estar** (*to be*) has similar endings.

IR   voy, vas, va, vamos, vais, van.
DAR   doy, das, da, damos, dais, dan.
ESTAR   estoy, estás, está, estamos, estáis, están.

F **Saber** (*to know*) and **ver** (*to see*) have irregular first person singulars.

SABER   sé, sabes, sabe, sabemos, sabéis, saben.
VER   veo, ves, ve, vemos, veis, ven.

G Verbs in **-ecer, -ocer** and **-ucir** have **-zco** in their first persons, for example **conocer** (*to know, be acquainted*), **ofrecer** (*to offer*) and **conducir** (*to drive*).

CONOCER
    conozco, conoces, conoce, conocemos, conocéis, conocen.
OFRECER
    ofrezco, ofreces, ofrece, ofrecemos, ofrecéis, ofrecen.
CONDUCIR
    conduzco, conduces, conduce, conducimos, conducís, conducen.

Similarly **parecer** (*to seem*); **aparecer** (*to appear*); **obedecer** (*to obey*); **traducir** (*to translate*); **producir** (*to produce*); **introducir** (*to introduce*); **reducir** (*to reduce*).

39 Exercises

1 Give the first person singular and plural (*I* and *we* forms) of the following verbs.

a salir
b poner
c hacer
d traer
e caer

2 Give the first persons singular and plural of the following verbs.

E.g. hablar → hablo; hablamos

a dar
b ir
c saber
d conducir
e conocer
f ver

3 Give the Spanish for the following.

a I translate
b I produce
c I seem
d I appear

e I offer
f I introduce
g I reduce
h I obey

4 Give the third person plural (*they* form) of the same verbs.

5 Translate the following into Spanish.

a We produce the money.
b I know (**conocer**) Madrid.
c He translates the book.
d I go to Madrid.
e I know (**saber**) Spanish
f I am Spanish.
g I give the wine.
h He sees the film (**la película**).
i He seems sad (**triste**).
j I appear on the television (**en la televisión**).

40 Present tense: spelling changes

This unit covers the main spelling changes you have to look out for when giving different forms of the present.

A Changes affecting the first person singular.

- Verbs ending in -ger like **coger** (*to pick*); **escoger** (*to choose*). The **g** changes to **j** in the first person singular.
  cojo (*I pick*); escojo (*I choose*)

- Verbs ending in -cer like **vencer** (*to overcome*); **cocer** (*to boil*), **torcer** (*to twist*). The **c** changes to **z**.
  venzo (*I overcome*); **cuezo** (*I boil*); **tuerzo** (*I twist*)

- Verbs in **-guir** like **seguir** (*to follow, continue*); **distinguir** (*to distinguish*) drop the **u** before **o**.
  sigo (*I follow*); distingo (*I distinguish*)

B Changes affecting other forms of the present.

- Verbs like **continuar** (*to continue*); **enviar** (*to send*); **prohibir** (*to forbid*); **reír** (*to laugh*) take an accent on the **u** or **i** when this weak vowel is stressed.

CONTINUAR	ENVIAR	PROHIBIR	REÍR
continúo	envío	prohíbo	río
continúas	envías	prohíbes	ríes
continúa	envía	prohíbe	ríe
continuamos	enviamos	prohibimos	reímos
continuáis	enviáis	prohibís	reís
continúan	envían	prohíben	ríen

Try reciting the verbs out loud to remember the stress.

- Verbs like **oír** (*to hear*); **huir** (*to flee*) insert **y** in certain forms.

OÍR   oigo, oyes, oye, oímos, oís, oyen.
HUIR huyo, huyes, huye, huimos, huis, huyen.

C Radical-changing verbs starting with o- or e- like **oler** (*to smell*) and **errar** (*to wander*) put **h** before -**ue** and change **ie** to **ye**.

OLER   huelo, hueles, huele, olemos, oléis, huelen.
ERRAR yerro, yerras, yerra, erramos, erráis, yerran.

40 Exercises

1 Give the *yo* (*I*) and *tú* (*you*) forms of the present tense.

E.g. oír → oigo; oyes

a oír
b ofrecer
c seguir
d coger
e conocer
f huir
g reír
h escoger
i prohibir
j continuar

2 Give the *yo* (*I*) and *nosotros* (*we*) forms of the present tense.

E.g. enviar → envío; enviamos

a errar
b reír
c enviar
d continuar
e oler

3 Put the correct form of the missing verb in the gap.

a Julio siempre _____ en el cine. (**reír**)
b Yo no _____ flores en el parque. (**coger**)
c Juan _____ un regalo para su madre. (**escoger**)
d Yo no _____ Londres. (**conocer**)
e Los ladrones _____ por la calle. (**huir**)
f El niño no _____ a su madre. (**oír**)
g Tú siempre _____ una carta a tu familia. (**enviar**)
h Este vino _____ mal. (**oler**)
i Luisa y Felipe _____ hablando. (**continuar**)
j El policía nos _____ aparcar. (**prohibir**)

4 Translate the following into Spanish.

a We hear the music.
b I choose a present (**un regalo**).
c The child runs off.
d He sends a letter.
e The potatoes smell good.
f We follow the car.
g Julio and Luisa laugh in the cinema.
h Are you laughing, children?
i The girls pick flowers.
j I offer the wine.

41 To be or not to be: *ser* and *estar*

A These are the present tenses:

	SER	ESTAR	
yo	soy	estoy	*I am*
tú	eres	estás	*you are*
él, ella, usted	es	está	*he/she/it is, you are*
nosotros	somos	estamos	*we are*
vosotros	sois	estáis	*you are*
ellos, ellas, ustedes	son	están	*they/you are*

You will see that **ser** is irregular. **Estar** behaves like **dar,** but is stressed on the endings throughout – notice the need for accents on most of its forms.

B Fortunately there are some basic rules which cover most uses of these verbs.

- Use **ser** when a noun or pronoun follows as complement.
  Soy profesor. *I'm a teacher.*
  Mi madre es enfermera. *My mother is a nurse.*
  Somos estudiantes de inglés. *We are students of English.*
  ¿Eres tú, María? *Is that you, María?*

- The noun may be implied and not actually stated.
  Somos (ciudadanos) ingleses. *We're English.*
  Es el (día) dos de mayo. *It's the second of May.*
  Son las tres (horas) de la tarde. *It's 3 p.m.*
  No soy (mujer) española. *I am not Spanish.*

- **Estar** is used to show position or location.
  Madrid está en España. *Madrid is in Spain*
  Juan está en la universidad. *Juan is at university.*
  Estoy aquí en casa. *I am here at home.*
  ¿Dónde están los servicios? *Where are the toilets?*

41 Exercises

1 Put in the correct form of the present tense of *ser*.

E.g. Nosotros _____ mecánicos. → Nosotros somos mecánicos.

a Tú _____ estudiante.

b Juan _____ mecánico.

c Julio y Pedro _____ amigos.

d Yo _____ turista.

e Madrid _____ la capital de España.

f Vosotros _____ ingleses.

g Hoy _____ lunes.

2 Put in the correct form of the present tense of *estar*.

E.g. Londres _____ en Inglaterra. → Londres está en Inglaterra.

a Los estudiantes _____ en la clase.

b ¿Dónde _____ Julio?

c Juan y Pedro _____ en la ciudad.

d ¿Dónde _____ los servicios?

e El hotel _____ en la plaza Mayor.

f Nosotros _____ en casa.

g ¿_____ María? No, no _____ aquí.

h ¿Vosotros _____ en Madrid?

i Yo _____ en el café.

j Ustedes no _____ en el centro de la ciudad.

3 Put in the correct form of *ser* or *estar* as necessary.

E.g. Emilio y tú _____ estudiantes. → Emilio y tú sois estudiantes.

a Buenos Aires _____ la capital de Argentina.

b Buenos Aires _____ en Argentina.

c María _____ española.

d María _____ en España.

e Los hombres _____ mecánicos.

f Los mecánicos _____ en el garaje.

g ¿Tú _____ en casa?

42 *Ser* and *estar* with adjectives

> *Either* ser *or* estar *can be used with adjectives, but they have different implications.*

A **Ser** is used to show inherent characteristics (the nature of things).

Manolo es inteligente.	*Manolo is intelligent.*
Juanita es bonita y delgada.	*Juanita is pretty and slim.*
El hielo es frío.	*Ice is cold.*
América es grande.	*America is big.*
Viajar en avión es rápido.	*Travelling by plane is fast.*
Me gusta este libro – es divertido.	*I like this book – it's funny.*

B **Estar** is used to show accidental qualities (e.g. what has happened to something or someone).

Julio está triste porque está constipado.	*Julio is sad because he's got a cold.*
Mi café está frío.	*My coffee is cold.*
Esta taza está vacía.	*This cup is empty.*
¡Estás muy alegre esta mañana!	*You seem very cheerful this morning!*
¡Qué constipado estoy!	*How cold-ridden I am!*
¡Qué bonita estás con ese vestido!	*How pretty you look in that dress!*

C With a past participle, **ser** shows an action in process (the passive) whereas **estar** describes the state resulting from that action.

La puerta es abierta por el profesor.	*The door is being opened by the teacher.*
Ahora la puerta está abierta.	*Now the door is open.*

D **Estar** is also used to form continuous tenses with the gerund (see Unit 43):

Estoy escribiendo una carta.	*I'm writing a letter.*
¡Mira!, estás fumando en la cocina.	*Look, you're smoking in the kitchen.*
Ahora están abriendo las puertas.	*Now they're opening the doors.*

42 Exercises

1 Put in the correct form of *ser* with the adjective to show inherent characteristics.

E.g. Tú _____ inteligente. → Tú eres inteligente.

a Ramiro _____ inteligente. **d** Ustedes _____ simpáticos.

b Tú y yo _____ tímidos. **d** Tú _____ bonita, Juana.

c Juan y Pedro _____ estúpidos. **f** Yo _____ alto y gordo.

2 Put in the correct form of *estar* with the adjective to show accidental qualities.

E.g. Tú _____ mala hoy, Ana. → Tú estás mala hoy, Ana.

a Julio _____ triste hoy.

b Juanita y Luisa _____ constipadas.

c Yo _____ contento porque hace sol.

d Tú y yo _____ alegres porque no hay clase.

e ¡Qué bonita _____ con ese vestido negro, Susana!

f La profesora _____ furiosa porque no trabajamos bien.

3 Complete this letter to a new penfriend by filling the gaps with the correct forms of *ser/estar*.

Yo me llamo Julio y **a** _____ estudiante y **b** _____ estudiando la historia, que **c** _____ muy difícil pero interesante. Hoy **d** _____ lunes y voy a la universidad pero no **e** _____ bien. Por desgracia **f** _____ muy constipado. Mis amigos también **g** _____ malos y **h** _____ en casa. La universidad **i** _____ en las afueras de la ciudad y **j** _____ muy grande con muchos estudiantes. Ya **k** _____ las nueve y media y hoy **l** _____ la clase del doctor López que **m** _____ un hombre muy antipático y **n** _____ furioso si un estudiante **o** _____ ausente o mal preparado.

43 The gerund: continuous and progressive tenses

This unit examines ways of emphasising actions in progress.

A The gerund in Spanish corresponds to the verb ending in *-ing* in English. It is used when two or more actions take place at the same time.

Iban por la calle, cantando
y riendo.

They were going along the street, singing and laughing.

B The gerund is formed by replacing the infinitive endings **-ar**, **-er** and **-ir** as follows.

cantar (*to sing*) → cantando (*singing*)
comer (*to eat*) → comiendo (*eating*)
escribir (*to write*) → escribiendo (*writing*)

C Verbs like **leer** (*to read*) and **creer** (*to believe*) change the **i** to **y** (**leyendo, creyendo**).

Continuaron leyendo.

They went on reading.

D A small cluster of **-ir** verbs which are radical changing have irregular gerunds. These include the following:

morir (*to die*) → muriendo; dormir (*to sleep*) → durmiendo; pedir (*to ask, request*) → pidiendo; repetir (*to repeat*) → repitiendo; seguir (*to follow, continue*) → siguiendo; reír (*to laugh*) → riendo; decir (*to say*) → diciendo.

The gerund is used after **estar** (*to be*) (see Unit 41) to form 'progressive' tenses, which emphasise an action actually taking place.

Niños, vuestra madre está
hablando.

Children, your mother is speaking.

Mira, el tren está saliendo.

Look, the train is leaving.

E **Estar** can be used in any appropriate tense.

Los pájaros estaban cantando
y volando por el cielo.

The birds were singing and flying across the sky.

⚠ Use the infinitive and not the gerund in expressions such as the following:

Me gusta leer.

I like reading.

Ver es creer.

Seeing is believing.

F The gerund is used after two verbs, **continuar** and **seguir**, to mean *to continue, to go on …ing*.

Julio continuó hablando.

Julio kept on talking.

43 Exercises

1 Give the gerunds of the following verbs.

a hablar   f leer
b fumar   g escribir
c buscar   h vivir
d ver   i pedir
e beber   j dormir

2 Change the ordinary present into the continuous present.

E.g. hablamos → estamos hablando.

a estudiamos   f salís
b reímos   g escribes
c muere   h espera
d roban   i seguimos
e aprendo   j repiten

3 Choose a gerund from the box to fill the gaps in this story.

El otro día me levanté **a** _____ porque el sol estaba **b** _____ en el cielo. Los pájaros estaban **c** _____ y **d** _____ círculos en el cielo. Bajé las escaleras, **e** _____ una a otra y entré en la cocina donde mi madre estaba **f** _____ el desayuno y mi padre estaba **g** _____ el periódico. Mis hermanos estaban **h** _____ porque estaban **i** _____ la televisión, **j** _____ la conversación; el perro estaba **k** _____ con un hueso. Después de diez minutos salí **l** _____ porque tuve que coger el autobús que se estaba **m** _____ a la parada.

acercando	brillando	cantando	corriendo	haciendo
jugando	leyendo	preparando	repitiendo	riendo
	saltando	viendo	volando	

44 Radical-changing verbs

In some verbs, the root vowel changes when the stress falls on it. Such verbs are usually known as radical-changing, root-changing or stem-changing verbs.

Radical-changing verbs can come from any of the three groups (-ar, -er or -ir). The change doesn't affect the first and second persons plural (**nosotros** and **vosotros**) because the stress doesn't fall on the root vowel.

A Root o → ue

CONTAR (*to count, relate*)	PODER (*to be able/can*)	DORMIR (*to sleep*)
cuento	puedo	duermo
cuentas	puedes	duermes
cuenta	puede	duerme
contamos	podemos	dormimos
contáis	podéis	dormís
cuentan	pueden	duermen

B Root e → ie

PENSAR (*to think*)	QUERER (*to want*)	SENTIR (*to feel*)
pienso	quiero	siento
piensas	quieres	sientes
piensa	quiere	siente
pensamos	queremos	sentimos
pensáis	queréis	sentís
piensan	quieren	sienten

C Some common verbs like **tener** (*to have*) and **venir** (*to come*) do not have a radical change in the first person if they have already inserted -**g**-; the rest of the verb, however, follows the above pattern.

TENER   tengo, tienes, tiene, tenemos, tenéis, tienen.
VENIR   vengo, vienes, viene, venimos, venís, vienen.

D There are also a few verbs in the -**ir** group that change the root **e** to **i**.

PEDIR (*to request*)   pido, pides, pide, pedimos, pedís, piden.

Some common verbs like this are: **seguir** (*to follow, continue*); **repetir** (*to repeat*); **servir** (*to serve*); **reír** (*to laugh*); **sonreír** (*to smile*).

44 Exercises

1 Fill in the missing forms of the radical-changing verbs.

a DECIR (*to say*) digo, dices, dice, decimos, decís, _____ .

b FREGAR (*to scrub*) friego, _____ , friega, fregamos, fregáis, friegan.

c PERDER (*to lose*) _____ , pierdes, pierde, perdemos, perdéis, pierden.

d VOLVER (*to return*) _____ , _____ , _____ , volvemos, volvéis, _____ .

e REÍR (*to laugh*) río, _____ , _____ , reímos, reís, _____ .

2 Put the verb in the correct form to tell the story.

Todos los días, cuando yo me (**a** vestir), Julia me (**b** servir) el café que (**c** hervir) en la cocina. Yo (**d** pensar) que Julia y los hijos (**e** tener) mucho más que hacer en la casa pero Julia me (**f** sonreír) mientras (**g** seguir) trabajando. A las diez, los vecinos (**h** venir) y siempre (**i** repetir) las noticias del día. (**j** Decir) que (**k** querer) una taza de café también y nos (**l** contar) todos sus chistes. Julia y yo (**m** reír) mucho y los vecinos (**n** reír) también. Sus chistes nos (**o** divertir) siempre. Pero, después de media hora yo no (**p** poder) más – (**q** perder) mucho tiempo. Yo (**r** sonreír), y (**s** pedir) perdón y (**t** volver) a mi trabajo. Por la tarde me (**u** sentir) un poco cansado, y (**v** dormir) la siesta – Julia (**w** dormir) también porque (**x** tener) sueño.

45 Reflexive verbs: personal actions

Reflexive verbs are very common in Spanish and frequently translate the idea of a person or thing becoming or getting something.

A Reflexive verbs are used with a reflexive pronoun agreeing with (or 'reflecting') the subject. The reflexive pronoun is attached to the end of the infinitive: **lavarse** (*to get washed*). When the verbs have a personal ending, the reflexive pronoun goes in front of the verb.

LAVARSE (*to get washed*)	PONERSE (*to put on*)	VESTIRSE (*to get dressed*)
me lavo	me pongo	me visto
te lavas	te pones	te vistes
se lava	se pone	se viste
nos lavamos	nos ponemos	nos vestimos
os laváis	os ponéis	os vestís
se lavan	se ponen	se visten

⚠ Remember that **usted** and **ustedes** are treated as third persons so they take the reflexive pronoun **se**.

B Compare these verbs used reflexively and non reflexively.

Lavo los platos.	*I wash the dishes.*
Me lavo en el cuarto de baño.	*I get washed in the bathroom.*
Acostamos al bebé.	*We put the baby to bed.*
Nos acostamos.	*We go to bed.*

Other verbs like this include **levantarse** (*to get up*); **bañarse** (*to have a bath/ go bathing*); **ducharse** (*to have a shower*); **maquillarse** (*to put on make-up*); **desnudarse** (*to get undressed*); **quitarse** (*to take off (clothing)*); **dormirse** (*to fall asleep*); **divertirse** (*to have a good time*).

Me pongo el pijama.	*I put on my pyjamas.*
Se visten rápidamente.	*They get dressed quickly.*
Los niños se divierten mucho en el circo.	*The children have a good time/ enjoy themselves at the circus.*

C Note the word order if subject pronouns are used for emphasis, or the verb is negative.

Yo me lavo pero tú no te lavas. *I get washed but you don't.*

45 Exercises

1 Put in the reflexive pronoun to match the verb endings.

E.g. levantas → te levantas

a lavas   d bañan   g viste
b levantamos   e baño   h levantas
c ducháis   f ponemos   i bañamos

2 Give the infinitives.

E.g. te lavas → lavarse

a nos levantamos   d te vistes   g se acuesta
b se ducha   e me maquillo   h nos ponemos
c nos bañamos   f os laváis   i se divierten

3 Give the Spanish for the following.

a I get washed.   f We lift up the bottle.
b I wash the car.   g She goes to bed.
c We bathe in the sea (**el mar**).   h She puts the baby to bed.
d I bath the baby.   i They get up.
e We get up.   j I put on my pyjamas
                        (**el pijama**).

4 Say what you do at the following times.

46 More on reflexive verbs

Spanish also has several reflexive verbs which indicate or emphasise types of movement or change of position.

A Several verbs suggest movement away when they are reflexive. An example is **ir** (*to go*) and **irse** (*to go away*).

IRSE   me voy, te vas, se va, nos vamos, os vais, se van.

¡Me voy!	*I'm off!*
Los niños se van por la calle.	*The children go off down the street.*

Like **irse** are **marcharse** (*to go away*); **escaparse** (*to escape*).

Si no pagas, me marcho.   *If you don't pay, I'm leaving.*

B A reflexive verb is sometimes used for emphasis: **caer** (*to fall*); **caerse** (*to fall down, over*).

¡Cuidado! ¡Vas a caerte!   *Careful – you'll fall over!*

C Other verbs involving movement are reflexive, especially if an object is not stated: **detenerse, pararse** (*to stop*); **moverse** (*to move*); **perderse** (*to get lost*); **pasearse** (*to go for a stroll, walk*).

El autobús se para por enfrente.	*The bus stops opposite.*
Estoy cansado – no puedo moverme.	*I'm tired – I can't move.*

D There are two ways to combine reflexive verbs with other verbs; you can use either word order.

Voy a divertirme./Me voy a divertir.	*I'm going to have a good time.*

⚠ Never put the reflexive pronoun between the two verbs.

46 Exercises

1 Give the correct forms of the following reflexive verbs.

E.g. (yo) irse → me voy

a (tú) irse

b (yo) marcharse

c (usted) pasearse

d (ellos) pararse

e (él) caerse

f (nosotros) irse

g (ellos) escaparse

h (tú) marcharse

i (nosotros) perderse

j (ellas) pasearse

2 Give the correct form of the verb in brackets.

E.g. El tren (pararse) en la estación. → El tren se para en la estación.

a El coche (pararse) en el garaje.

b La policía (parar) los coches.

c Yo siempre (perder) dinero.

d Yo siempre (perderse) en Madrid.

e El niño (caerse) mucho en la playa.

f Las hojas (caer) en octubre.

g La policía (detener) a los ladrones.

h Luisa (detenerse) para ver el tráfico.

i ¿Quiere usted (mover) su coche? No puedo salir.

j Julio no va a (moverse) porque está cansado.

3 Form a future phrase with *ir a* and the reflexive verb given. Give both possible word orders. Remember to change the reflexive pronoun according to the subject!

E.g. irse (yo) → voy a irme; me voy a ir

a bañarse (tú)

b perderse (usted)

c ponerse (nosotros)

d divertirse (ellos)

e lavarse (vosotros)

f vestirse (ellos)

g escaparse (él)

h caerse (tú)

47 General statements

A Like English, Spanish usually refers to a specific subject.

Juan bebe vino.   *Juan drinks wine.*
Los españoles hablan español. *Spaniards speak Spanish.*

Sometimes, however, you want to make a general statement.

En España beben mucho   *In Spain they drink a lot*
  vino.   *of wine.*

In this sentence, *they* means 'people in general'. Spanish, like English, can simply use the third person plural (the *they* form) of the verb.

Dicen que va a llover.   *They say it's going to rain.*

Spanish also uses the reflexive **se** with a singular verb.

Se dice que va a llover.   *It is said it's going to rain.*
Aquí se habla español.   *They speak Spanish here./*
                                     Spanish is spoken here.

This construction is very common when the verb does not take a direct object, and corresponds to the English *one*.

Aquí se vive bien.   *One/You/People live well here.*
Se estudia mucho.   *One/You/People study hard.*

B **Se puede** is a useful expression to ask if something is permitted.

¿Se puede aparcar aquí?   *Can one park here?*
¿Se puede pagar con tarjeta *Can you pay by credit card?*
  de crédito?

C With a reflexive verb which already has a **se**, **uno** is used as the subject.

En el campo uno se levanta   *In the countryside people get*
  temprano.   *up early/one gets up early.*
Uno se divierte mucho en   *You have/One has a good time*
  la fiesta.   *at the party.*

You can also use **la gente** (*people*), again with a singular verb.

En España la gente   *In Spain, people are kind.*
  es simpática.

47 Exercises

1 Use the third person plural to complete these sentences.

E.g. En Inglaterra (comer muchas patatas). → En Inglaterra comen muchas patatas.

a En España (beber mucho vino).
b En este pueblo (tener una fiesta típica).
c En la costa (tomar el sol).
d En la playa (nadar en el mar).
e En Barcelona (visitar la catedral).
f En Málaga (comer bien).
g Aquí (no trabajar mucho).
h En aquel país (ganar mucho dinero).

2 Make general statements, using *se*.

E.g. Aquí (comer bien). → Aquí se come bien.
En esta tienda (vender) recuerdos. → En esta tienda se venden recuerdos.

a Aquí (hablar portugués).
b En este pueblo (beber mucho).
c (estudiar mucho) en este colegio.
d (salir) por las escaleras.
e En España (fumar mucho).
f En este restaurante (comer bien).
g En aquella fábrica (trabajar mucho).
h En este país (vivir bien).

3 Use *uno* to make general statements with reflexive verbs.

E.g. Aquí (divertirse mucho). → Aquí uno se divierte mucho.

a Durante las vacaciones (levantarse tarde).
b Los fines de semana (acostarse a las dos).
c Después de beber mucho (sentirse mal).
d Los domingos (no despertarse hasta mediodía).
e Durante las vacaciones (no acordarse del trabajo).
f Después de nadar (dormirse) en la playa.

4 Use *se puede* to ask if something is allowed.

E.g. Quiero aparcar. → ¿Se puede aparcar aquí?

a Quiero pagar con dinero inglés.
b Quiero telefonear.
c Quiero comprar sellos.
d Quiero sacar fotos.
e Quiero cambiar dinero.
f Quiero usar una tarjeta de crédito.
g Quiero nadar.
h Quiero visitar la catedral.

48 Liking and disliking: *gustar*

> To express the idea of liking, Spanish uses the verb
> gustar – *literally* to be pleasing.

A **Gustar** is used 'back-to-front', with the indirect object pronoun to show who is doing the liking (or disliking); it is used in the third person singular (**gusta**) if one thing is liked, or in the third person plural (**gustan**) if more than one thing is liked. In other words, the thing(s) being liked are the *subject* of the verb.

(no) me gusta	(no) me gustan
te gusta	te gustan
le gusta	le gustan
nos gusta	nos gustan
os gusta	os gustan
les gusta	les gustan

| Les gusta el vino. | *They like the wine* (lit. *to them is pleasing the wine.*) |
| Les gustan las patatas. | *They like the potatoes* (lit. *to them are pleasing the potatoes*). |

B The definite article is used to show general likes or dislikes.
Me gusta el queso. *I like cheese.*

C If what you like or dislike is a verb, or verbs, the singular **gusta** is used.
Me gusta bailar y cantar. *I like singing and dancing.*

D If a name or a particular person or persons are referred to, they are introduced with **a**.
A Juan le gusta el cine. *John likes cinema.*
A Julia no le gustan las naranjas. *Julia doesn't like oranges.*
A las chicas les gusta esta tienda. *Girls like this shop.*

E The personal indirect object pronouns can be intensified for clarity or emphasis by adding the disjunctive pronouns (see Unit 27) with **a**.
A mí me gusta bailar, pero a ti no te gusta. *I like dancing, but you don't.*

⚠ You can only use one personal pronoun in front of **gustar**.

F Since **gustar** means *to be pleasing*, any other personal verb ending needs care.
Me gustas. *I fancy you* (lit. *you are pleasing to me*).

48 Exercises

1 Say whether the person likes or dislikes something.

> *E.g.* Juan   ☺ cantar → A Juan le gusta cantar.

a María   ☹ el vino blanco.
b Julio y Julia   ☺ el teatro.
c yo   ☹ trabajar.
d Julia   ☺ salir con Julio.
e tú   ☺ ¿la paella?
f tu y yo   ☹ las novelas románticas.
g el padre   ☺ su casa.
h los españoles   ☹ la comida inglesa.
i Julio   ☺ beber y fumar.
j los ingleses   ☺ ir a España.

2 Say you used to like something but not any more.

> *E.g.* el vino → Me gustaba el vino antes, pero ya no.

a las tortillas
b estudiar
c nadar y tomar el sol
d beber los vinos dulces
e los vinos secos.

3 Say that two people went somewhere or did something and that one person liked it but the other didn't.

> *E.g.* Julio (Julia) bebió el vino. → Julio bebió el vino y le gustó; Julia bebió el vino pero no le gustó nada.

a Julio (Julia) fue al cine.
b Yo (mi marido) probé el vino.
c Julio y Julia (Juan y Juana) visitaron el museo.
d Julia (Julio) vio las películas.
e Julia y yo (tú y María) comimos en el restaurante.

49 More verbs with indirect objects

Besides gustar, Spanish has a number of expressions using verbs with indirect object pronouns.

A **Doler** (*to be aching, be hurting*)

Me duele la cabeza.	*I have a headache (lit. to me is aching the head).*
Me duelen los pies.	*I have sore feet (lit. to me are aching the feet).*

Me (*to me*) is an indirect pronoun. It indicates the person being affected. The indirect object pronoun is kept even when a specific person is mentioned.

A Julio le duelen las piernas. *Julio's legs are aching.*

If, however, you want to say that someone is hurting you, say:

Me haces daño.	*You're hurting me.*
El dentista siempre me hace daño.	*The dentist always hurts me.*

B There are other more pleasant verbs that follow the same pattern: **encantar** (*to delight*); **chiflar** (*to captivate, drive crazy*); **apetecer** (*to appeal to*).

Me encanta el vino.	*I love the wine.*
A Julia le encantan las gambas.	*Julia loves prawns.*
No me apetece salir esta noche.	*I don't feel like going out tonight.*

C Other common expressions of this type include:

- (**me**, etc.) **hace falta** (*I need*)

Me hace falta descansar.	*I need to rest.*
Le hacen falta unos buenos amigos.	*He could do with some good friends.*

- **me falta** (*I'm short of* (lit. *to me is lacking*))
- **me importa** (*it matters to me*)

Francamente, cariño, no me importa un pepino.	*Frankly, my dear, I don't give a damn.* (lit. *it doesn't matter a cucumber to me!*)

- **me queda** (*I have ... left*)

Me quedan sólo diez libras. *I've only ten pounds left.*

- **me conviene** (*it suits me*)
- **me sienta** (*it suits/looks good on me*)

Te sienta bien ese vestido. *That dress suits you.*

- **a mí me toca** (*it's my turn*)

49 Exercises

1 **Match these questions to the answers.**

a ¿Por qué no vienes al bar?   1 Me duele la espalda.
b ¿Qué le pasa, señor?   2 Me chifla el fútbol.
c ¿Cuánto dinero tienes, Juan?   3 Me quedan cinco dólares.
d ¿Por qué te pones este jersey?   4 No me apetece una cerveza.
e ¿Por qué ves la televisión?   5 Me sienta bien el rojo.

2 **Complete the sentences with an expression from the box.**

a ¡Ay! Me _____ el diente.
b ¿Dónde hay una farmacia? Me _____ comprar aspirinas.
c No te _____ aspirinas. Te _____ dos en este paquete.
d Voy al partido esta noche porque me _____ el Real Madrid.
e Me _____ la ópera.
f Si no quieres ir al cine, voy solo. No me _____ .
g A ti te _____ lavar los platos.
h Julio quiere comprar el periódico pero le _____ un euro.
i Sí, mañana me _____ .
j Te _____ bien la falda. Es muy elegante.

chifla   conviene   duele   encanta   falta   hace falta
hacen falta   importa   quedan   sienta   toca

3 **Translate the following into Spanish.**

a Luisa has toothache.
b She needs to go to the dentist.
c You're hurting me, doctor.
d Julio thinks cars are really great.
e Julia doesn't give a damn.
f It's Juan's turn to sing.
g You've one euro left.
h Blue doesn't suit you very well.
i I love potaotes.
j Does tomorrow suit you?

50 Impersonal expressions

Impersonal expressions are statements like it is difficult to
sleep; *it is forbidden to smoke.*

Impersonal expressions such as **es posible** (*it's possible*) are used
with three main constructions.

A If the expression refers to a general situation, i.e. no particular
person is included, you may follow with the verb in the
infinitive.

Es difícil estudiar.	*It's difficult to study.*
No es posible ir en autobús.	*You/One can't go by bus.*
Hace falta ir a pie.	*You/One must go on foot.*
Es mejor usar el ascensor.	*It's better to use the lift.*
Está prohibido aparcar.	*It's forbidden to park.*

B To relate the expression to a particular person, use an indirect
object.

Me es difícil trabajar.	*I find it hard to work.*
Te es imposible llegar a tiempo.	*You can't get there on time.*
Nos hace falta esperar aquí.	*We have to wait here.*

C When mention is made of a specific case, a subjunctive verb is
found, especially when the speaker is expressing a personal
opinion or making a value judgement.

Hay mucha niebla y es imposible que venga.	*It's very foggy and it's impossible for him to get here.*
Lo más importante es que usted trabaje mucho.	*The most important thing is that you work hard.*
Es curioso que David no hable bien el español.	*It's strange that David does not speak Spanish well.*

⚠ The subjunctive verb may have to be in a past tense.

Sería importante que Julio viniera a tiempo.	*It would be important for Julio to come on time.*
Habría sido inútil que los bomberos entrasen en el edificio.	*It would have been useless for the firemen to go into the building.*

50 Exercises

1 **Answer each question with an appropriate infinitive expression.**

> *E.g.* ¿Dónde cojo el autobús? (imposible) → Es imposible coger un autobús.

a ¿Dónde alquilo un coche? (difícil)

b ¿Se puede aparcar aquí? (está prohibido)

c Estoy muy cansado. ¿Qué recomienda usted – ir en taxi o a pie? (es más rápido)

d La reparación es urgente. ¿Debo ir al taller? (más vale)

e ¿Se recomienda comer temprano? (preferible)

2 **Complete the expressions using an indirect object.**

> *E.g.* (Yo) Es imposible dormir → Me es imposible dormir.

a (Julia) Hace falta salir.

b (Nosotros) Es posible quedar aquí.

c (Julia y Julio) Es fácil hablar.

d (Tú) Hace falta dormir.

e (El profesor) Se prohíbe entrar.

3 **Link the phrases as appropriate.**

> *E.g.* posible/Juan/venir → Es posible que Juan venga.

a preferible/Julio/no cantar

b inútil/nosotros/rehusar

c probable/mi padre/visitar Madrid

d preciso/los estudiantes/estudiar mucho

e injusto/tú/pagar siempre

51 Talking about the past: the preterite tense

We use the preterite or simple past tense to indicate completed actions carried out in the past.

A These are the regular forms of the preterite.

HABLAR (to speak)	COMER (to eat)	ESCRIBIR (to write)
hablé	comí	escribí
hablaste	comiste	escribiste
habló	comió	escribió
hablamos	comimos	escribimos
hablasteis	comisteis	escribisteis
hablaron	comieron	escribieron

B Note the following
- -er and -ir verbs share the same set of endings.
- The **nosotros** (we) form is the same as in the present tense for -ar and -ir verbs, but different for -er verbs.
- Stressed -ó or -ió is the third person singular form in the preterite (not to be confused with the first-person -o ending in the present tense).

  Ayer visité a mi amigo en Londres.
  Yesterday I visited my friend in London.

  Julio cogió el bocadillo y se lo comió en seguida.
  Julio picked up the sandwich and ate it straight away.

  Viví seis años en París.
  I lived for six years in Paris.

- Sometimes the spelling will have to change.
  EMPEZAR (to begin)   empecé, empezaste, etc.
  LLEGAR (to arrive)   llegué, llegaste, etc.
- Accent marks are not needed for verbs of one syllable such as **ver** (to see), **dar** (to give).
  VER   vi, viste, vio, vimos, visteis, vieron.
- Dar has -er/-ir endings in the preterite, like **ver**.
  DAR   di, diste, dio, dimos, disteis, dieron.

  Ayer vi la televisión.
  Yesterday I watched television.

  Mi amigo me dio un regalo.
  My friend gave me a present.

C ayer (*yesterday*); anoche (*last night*); anteayer (*the day before yesterday*), el año/lunes pasado (*last year/Monday*) etc.; hace cinco años (*five years ago*) etc.

51 Exercises

1 Give the preterite for the following verbs.

E.g. tú (hablar) → tú hablaste

a él (saltar = *to jump*)
b nosotros (abrir = *to open*)
c ustedes (correr = *to run*)
d yo (cerrar = *to close*)
e vosotros (escuchar = *to listen*)
f nosotros (sentarse = *to sit down*)
g ellos (volver = *to return*)
h tú (sentir = *to feel*)
i ellos (contestar = *to reply*)
j yo (repetir = *to repeat*)

2 Form questions using the preterite which would invite the following responses.

E.g. Pasamos las vacaciones en Chile → ¿Dónde pasaron ustedes las vacaciones?

a Me levanté a las ocho.
b Vivimos muchos años allí.
c El libro costó seis euros.
d Bebí cerveza.
e No me gustó nada la película.
f Comí en un restaurante.
g Viajamos en coche.
h Pasamos un día terrible.
i Decidí comprar los zapatos negros.
j El tren salió a las diez en punto.

3 Fill the gaps with the appropriate verb from the box to make a logical sequence.

Anoche me **a** _____ temprano. Me **b** _____ en seguida pero, después de una hora, **c** _____ un ruido terrible y me **d** _____ . Me **e** _____ en la cama y **f** _____ . ¿Qué es?, **g** _____ pero nadie **h** _____ . De repente **i** _____ pasos detrás de la puerta. ¿Quién es?, **j** _____ a gritar, y **k** _____ a temblar de miedo. Luego algo, o alguien, **l** _____ a la puerta. **m** _____ de la cama y **n** _____ a la puerta. La **o** _____ pero no **p** _____ nada al principio. ¿Quién es?, **q** _____ en voz baja. Luego, en el pasillo algo se **r** _____ . Una figura oscura se me **s** _____ . No la **t** _____ , pero **u** _____ a una persona vieja, delgada y melancólica. **v** _____ la puerta y **w** _____ llamar a la policía.

abrí acercó acosté cerré contestó corrí decidí
descubrí desperté dormí empecé escuché grité llamó
movió oí reconcí repetí salté senté sentí vi volví

52 The preterite: radical changing verbs in *-ir*

A very few verbs have stem changes in the preterite. You will have already met some of these in the present tense.

A The good news is that no verbs in **-ar** or **-er** have radical changes in the preterite. However, a cluster of verbs from the **-ir** group do change their stem in the third-person forms of the preterite.

B The first type changes **e** to **i**.

PEDIR (*to ask for, request*) pedí, pediste, pidió, pedimos, pedisteis, pidieron

Other verbs like **pedir** are **seguir** (*to follow, continue*); **sentir** (*to feel*); **repetir** (*to repeat*); **servir** (*to serve*); **hervir** (*to boil*); **divertirse** (*to have a good time*); **arrepentirse** (*to repent, regret*).

Juan me pidió dinero.	*Juan asked me for money.*
Los camareros sirvieron la comida.	*The waiters served the meal.*
Julio se divirtió mucho.	*Julio had a very good time.*

C The second type changes **o** to **u**.

DORMIR (*to sleep*) dormí, dormiste, durmió, dormimos, dormisteis, durmieron

MORIR (*to die*) changes in the same way.

Anoche durmieron bien.	*Last night they slept well.*
El general Franco murió en 1975.	*General Franco died in 1975.*

⚠ Only the third persons change.

D The irregular verbs **ir** (*to go*) and **ser** (*to be*) share the same forms in the preterite: **fui, fuiste, fue, fuimos, fuisteis, fueron.**

Ayer fui a Londres a visitar a mi amigo.	*Yesterday I went to London to visit my friend.*
Julio fue al cine con sus amigos.	*Julio went to the cinema with his friends.*
Pedro y Juan fueron buenos amigos.	*Pedro and Juan were good friends.*
Los ladrones fueron cogidos por la policía.	*The robbers were caught by the police.*
La reunión fue abierta por el presidente.	*The meeting was opened by the president.*

⚠ Don't confuse **fui** (*I went, I was*) and **fue** (*he went, he was*). Ir and ser is the only preterite that ends in **-e** in the third person!

52 Exercises

1 Give the preterite of the following verbs.

> _E.g._ yo, ella (dormir) → dormí, durmió

a yo, tú (dormir)   f ellos, ella (morir)
b él, nosotros (pedir)   g tú, ella (repetir)
c él, vosotros (sentir)   h yo, usted (divertirse)
d usted, ustedes (dormir)   i él, nosotros (servir)
e yo, ellos (sentir)   j yo, ellos (seguir)

2 Fill in the gaps using _pedir, servir, repetir_ and _seguir_ to tell the story.

Ayer, en un bar yo **a** _____ una cerveza. El camarero me
b _____ vino.

— No, cerveza, **c** _____ .
— Usted me **d** _____ vino, señor.
— No, cerveza, **e** _____ .
— ¿Cerveza? **f** _____ el camarero.
— Sí, cerveza, yo **g** _____ .
— No, usted me **h** _____ vino, **i** _____ repitiendo el camarero.

Pero por fin el camarero me **j** _____ la cerveza que **k** _____ .

3 Give the correct forms of the preterite of _ser_ and _ir_.

> _E.g._ (nosotros) al cine → Fuimos al cine.

a (yo) a Madrid.
b (Luisa) a la ciudad.
c (vosotros) a casa.
d (los niños) al colegio.
e (usted) a un restaurante.
f (yo) a visitarlo.
g (el médico) al hospital.
h (tú y yo) al bar.
i (ustedes) a comer.
j (Julio) a dormir.
k (mi tío) mecánico.
l (yo) visto por mis amigos.
m (Alfonso) rey de España.
n (nosotros) sorprendidos por el tráfico.
o (el ladrón) cogido por la policía.

53 The *pretérito grave*

> *A group of verbs forms the preterite in a slightly different way,
> known as the* pretérito grave.

A The **pretérito grave** endings are: -e, -iste, -o, -imos, -isteis, -ieron.

ESTAR (*to be*)	PONER (*to put*)	VENIR (*to come*)
estuve	puse	vine
estuviste	pusiste	viniste
estuvo	puso	vino
estuvimos	pusimos	vinimos
estuvisteis	pusisteis	vinisteis
estuvieron	pusieron	vinieron

Me puse el mejor traje.   *I put on my best suit.*

B Unlike the so-called regular preterites, **pretérito grave** verbs are
not stressed on the end. Never put an accent mark on them. To
add to the fun, the stem of the verb usually changes in a
somewhat unpredictable way.

All verbs of this sort, whether -ar, -er or -ir, share the same set
of endings.

C Other common verbs in this cluster are:
poder (*to be able*)   pude, pudiste, ...
andar (*to walk, function (machinery)*)   anduve, anduviste, ...
saber (*to know*)   supe, supiste, ...
querer (*to want, love*)   quise, quisiste, ...
tener (*to have*)   tuve, tuviste, ...
hacer (*to do, make*)   hice, hiciste, ...

Julio no pudo abrir   *Julio was not able to open*
  la puerta.   *the door.*
Las chicas hicieron una   *The girls made a pie.*
  empanada.

D Remember the spelling rules concerning c/z (Unit 1) with **hacer**
(*to do, make*): the c changes to a z in the third person singular
(**hizo**).

Hizo sus deberes anoche.   *He did his homework
                            last night.*

E Verbs ending in -ucir like **conducir** (*to drive*) all change the ending
to -uje: conducir → conduje; producir (*to produce*) → produje

F One more thing to remember: after a -j- you write -eron instead of
-ieron. DECIR (*to say*)   dije, dijiste, dijo, dijimos, dijisteis, dijeron

Por fin dijeron la verdad.   *At last they told the truth.*

53 Exercises

1 Tell your friend you did it yesterday.

E.g. ¿Quieres traducir la carta? → Traduje la carta ayer.

a ¿Quieres hacer una tortilla?
b ¿Vas a estar en el jardín esta tarde?
c ¿Por qué no quieres decir la verdad?
d ¿Piensas conducir el coche hoy?
e Ten la bondad de poner la mesa.

2 Share the blame.

E.g. No lo dije yo. → Lo dijimos todos.

a No lo hice yo.
b No lo traduje yo.
c No estuve allí yo.
d No conduje yo.
e No puse la mesa yo.
f No pude comer todo el chocolate yo.

3 Translate the verbs to say what Julio and Julia got up to yesterday.

Ayer, Julia (**a** *wanted*) salir con Julio. Julia (**b** *said*) 'Hay una película buena en el cine que (**c** *produced*) un director famoso'. Julio no le (**d** *made*) caso (*pay attention*). Julia (**e** *put*) un billete de banco en la mesa. 'Ahora podemos ir', (**f** *he said*). '¿A qué hora termina la película?' (**g** *said*) los niños. '(**h** *I said*) que (**i** *I put*) las horas de las sesiones en tu bolso', (**j** *said*) uno de los niños. Entonces Julia (**k** *knew*) lo que (**l** *did*) los niños, y por fin Julia (**m** *was able*) encontrar el horario. Julia y Julio (**n** *drove*) a la ciudad y pronto (**o** *came*) al cine. Todos (**p** *had*) buena suerte porque la película, el viaje y los buenos actores (**q** *put*) un buen fin al día.

54 The imperfect tense

The imperfect tense is used to describe actions in the past which were repeated, in process or not necessarily completed.

A There is usually no specific reference to the action's start or end, hence the name 'imperfect'. Examples in English are: *I used to go*, *I was going*, *I would go*. It is used with expressions like **todos los días** (*every day*), **con frecuencia** (*frequently*), **muchas veces/a menudo** (*often*). Spanish has only two sets of endings. The stress stays on the same syllable throughout.

B Only two verbs (**ser** (*to be*) and **ir** (*to go*)) have strange imperfects. **Ver** (*to see*) reflects its old infinitive form, **veer**, by inserting an extra **e** before the endings.

> Veían la televisión en vez de estudiar.   *They would watch television instead of studying.*

HABLAR	COMER	VIVIR	SER	IR	VER
hablaba	comía	vivía	era	iba	veía
hablabas	comías	vivías	eras	ibas	veías
hablaba	comía	vivía	era	iba	veía
hablábamos	comíamos	vivíamos	éramos	íbamos	veíamos
hablabais	comíais	vivíais	erais	ibais	veíais
hablaban	comían	vivían	eran	iban	veían

⚠ Note the need for an accent on **hablábamos**, and the **-í-** throughout the **-er** and **-ir** verbs.

As the first and third persons singular are identical, a subject pronoun may be required for clarity.

> Antes (yo) nunca comía carne.   *I never used to eat meat.*
>
> Todos los días hablábamos italiano.   *We would speak Italian every day.*
>
> Vivían entonces en Nerja.   *They were living in Nerja at that time.*
>
> Te llamaba – ¿dónde estabas?   *I was calling you – where were you?*

C Spanish can also emphasise habit or custom by using **soler** (*to be in the habit of*) with an infinitive.

> Solíamos ir de vacaciones a España.   *We normally went to Spain for our holidays.*

54 Exercises

1 **Reply using the imperfect.**

E.g. ¿Qué hacías? (una paella) → Hacía una paella
a ¿Con quién hablabas? (Pedro)
b ¿Adónde ibais vosotros? (a la ciudad)
c ¿Qué bebías? (vino tinto)
d ¿Qué cantaba Julio? (una canción romántica)
e ¿Quiénes eran estas señoras? (las profesoras de mi hija)
f ¿Cómo pensaban ir ustedes? (en coche)
g ¿A qué jugaban los chicos? (al fútbol)
h ¿Qué veía Luisa? (una telenovela)
i ¿Dónde solías comprar la fruta? (en el mercado)
j ¿Qué solían fumar? (tabaco negro)

2 **Say what you no longer do.**

E.g. fumar (yo) → Fumaba antes, pero ya no.
a Cantar (yo)   f escribir (Julio e Isabel)
b ser estudiantes (nosotros)   g estudiar (tú y yo)
c nadar (Luisa)   h ver los partidos (ustedes)
d practicar deportes (tú)   i ayudar (vosotros)
e ir de paseo (yo)   j leer mucho (yo)

3 **Complete this story, inserting the appropriate verb forms for the imperfect.**

Cuando nosotros (**a** ser) niños, (**b** vivir) en un pueblo pequeño. Nuestros abuelos (**c** vivir) en el mismo pueblo. Mi padre (**d** ser) mecánico en la ciudad y mi madre (**e** trabajar) por la mañana también. Cuando ella (**f** volver) a casa, (**g** comer) todos juntos y después mis hermanos y yo (**h** jugar) en el parque. Todos los días mi padre (**i** ir) a su trabajo muy temprano y cuando (**j** entrar) en la casa (**k** estar) muy cansado. Mi padre (**l** beber) algo, (**m** ver) la televisión y (**n** dormir) un poco. Nosotros (**o** pasar) las tardes en casa y a las diez todos nos (**p** acostar) y (**q** esperar) otro día.

55 The preterite and imperfect compared

Choosing whether to use imperfect or preterite when talking about the past is normally fairly straightforward.

A The preterite is used for a specific, completed action.

El año pasado Julio ganó   *Last year Julio won the*
la lotería.   *lottery.*

B The imperfect is used for repeated or general actions.

Cuando era niño estudiaba   *When I was a child I would*
mucho.   *study a lot.*

C Usually an English verb such as *used to (study)*, *was (studying)*, *would (study)* is a clear indication for the imperfect, whereas *went*, *visited*, *won* suggest a preterite. Care is sometimes needed, however.

Cuando éramos niños fuimos   *When we were children we*
a Madrid.   *went to Madrid.*

(**fuimos** = preterite, one occasion implied)

Cuando éramos niños íbamos   *When we were children we*
a Madrid todos los veranos.   *went to Madrid every*
   summer.

(**íbamos** = imperfect, as the action was repeated)

D The preterite is used with actions that imply a beginning or end when a time duration is stated – even if that time period is a long one.

Vivimos allí cuarenta años.   *We lived there for 40 years.*

⚠ The imperfect is used for setting the scene or explaining the situation. The preterite is used for a specific event.

Mientras tomábamos café   *While we were having coffee*
en la terraza, empezó   *on the terrace, it started*
a llover.   *to rain.*

E With certain verbs, a change of tense from imperfect to preterite can have a different emphasis or meaning.

Sabía el precio.	*I knew the price.*
Supe el precio.	*I found out the price.*
Conocía a Julio en Madrid.	*I knew Julio in Madrid.*
Conocí a Julio en Madrid.	*I met Julio in Madrid.*
No querían venir.	*They did not want to come.*
No quisieron venir.	*They refused to come.*

F Only the imperfect is used to tell the time in the past.

¿Qué hora era?   *What time was it?*
Eran las cinco y media.   *It was half past five.*

55 Exercises

1 **Contrast imperfect and preterite.**

E.g. Mientras Julio (estar) en la ciudad, un ladrón le (robar) el dinero. → **Mientras Julio estaba en la ciudad, un ladrón le robó el dinero.**

a Cuando tú (estar) en el jardín, el teléfono (sonar).

b Mientras mi madre (preparar) la comida, yo (ir) al bar.

c Cuando (pasar) nuestras vacaciones en España, alguien (robar) el coche.

d Mientras usted (estar) fuera, la compañía (tratar) de entregar un paquete.

e Mientras Luisa (hacer) las compras, un accidente (ocurrir) en la plaza.

f Cuando nosotros (ser) niños, un día (ir) al parque de atracciones.

g Mientras los vecinos (ver) la televisión, el gato (coger) el pez.

h ¿Qué hora (ser) cuando tú (llegar)?

2 **What was the weather like when ...?**

E.g. Ignacio/salir - hacer sol → **Hacía sol cuando Ignacio salió.**

a Luisa/comprar la fruta/hacer frío

b Mi madre/ir a la ciudad/el sol brilla

c Nosotros/entrar/llover

d Mi padre/ir a trabajar/nevar

e Yo/salir a nadar/hacer viento

f Los estudiantes/comenzar a estudiar/hacer sol

3 **Complete the story with the preterite or imperfect of the verbs as necessary.**

El otro día (**a** hacer) sol, así nosotros (**b** decidir) salir al campo. (**c** Hacer) un poco frío y nos (**d** poner) el abrigo y los guantes. Luisa no (**e** querer) venir pero por fin la (**f** persuadir) su novio, que también (**g** venir) con nosotros. Nosotros no (**h** coger) paraguas porque no (**i** llover) cuando (**j** salir). (**k** Ser) las once en punto. Después de media hora (**l** llegar) a un bosque y (**m** entrar). (**n** Ser) muy tranquilo porque nadie (**o** estar) allí. De repente Juan (**p** oír) algo raro. (**q** Ser) el ruido de una tormenta. Inmediatamente (**r** empezar) a llover y (**s** tener) que volver corriendo a casa. Cuando (**t** llegar), (**u** estar) completamente calados (*drenched*) por la lluvia. Pero, ¡qué sorpresa! La puerta (**v** estar) abierta. Alguien se (**w** mover) en la casa. ¿Quién (**x** poder) ser? ...

56 The future tense

A The future tense is formed by adding personal endings
(originally from **haber** (*to have*)) to the infinitive. The good
news is that all verbs (**-ar, -er, -ir**) share the same set of endings.

HABLAR	COMER	VIVIR
hablaré	comeré	viviré
hablarás	comerás	vivirás
hablará	comerá	vivirá
hablaremos	comeremos	viviremos
hablaréis	comeréis	viviréis
hablarán	comerán	vivirán

⚠ All the endings are stressed, so remember the need for accent
marks on all the endings except for **nosotros**.

B The future tense corresponds to the English verb with *shall* or
will (or simply *'ll*) and explains what will happen at some future
time.

Mañana hablaremos más. *Tomorrow we shall
speak again.*

¿Comerás paella en España? *Will you eat paella in Spain?*
La próxima vez escribirá *Next time he'll write a letter.*
una carta.

C Although the endings are always the same, a few verbs change
their forms before adding the endings. This is usually to make
the words easier to say.

QUERER (*to want, love*) querré, querrás, …
PODER (*to be able*) podré, podrás, …
SABER (*to know*) sabré, sabrás, …
DECIR (*to say*) diré, dirás, …
HACER (*to do, make*) haré, harás, …

D Another group inserts **-d-** before the ending.

PONER (*to put*) pondré, pondrás, pondrá, …
SALIR (*to go out, leave*) saldré, saldrás, …
TENER (*to have*) tendré, tendrás, …
VENIR (*to come*) vendré, vendrás, …
VALER (*to be worth*) valdré, valdrás, …

Después de las vacaciones *After the holidays we shall
tendremos que trabajar. have to work.*
Un día esta casa valdrá *One day this house will be
mucho dinero. worth a lot of money.*

56 Exercises

1 Say that the person will do something tomorrow, using the future tense.

> *E.g.* No bebo el vino hoy. → Beberé el vino mañana.

a No pago la cuenta hoy (*pay the bill*).
b Luisa no contesta a la carta (*answer the letter*).
c Julio y Pedro no reparan el coche (*repair the car*).
d No vemos la película (*see the film*).
e Tú no vuelves a casa (*go back home*).
f Usted no escribe la carta (*write the letter*).
g Emilio no va a la ciudad (*go to town*).
h No dormimos aquí (*sleep here*).
i No me levanto temprano (*get up early*).
j Vosotros no os bañáis en el mar (*bathe in the sea*).

2 Repeat the exercise, but watch out – these verbs undergo changes in the future!

a No tengo el dinero (*have the money*).
b Los niños dicen la verdad (*tell the truth*).
c Tú no haces una paella (*make a paella*).
d Ustedes no salen (*go out*).
e No me pongo el traje (*put on my suit*).
f No vale la pena (*be worthwhile*).
g Julio no viene conmigo (*come with me*).
h El mecánico no puede reparar el coche (*can't fix the car*).
i Yo no sé la dirección (*know the address*).
j Ella no compone la música (*compose the music*).

3 Say what you'll do if Julio doesn't arrive on time.

> *E.g.* ir al teatro → Iremos al teatro.

a comer a solas (*eat alone*)
b acostarse (*go to bed*)
c estar tristes (*be sad*)
d salir al bar (*go out to the bar*)
e visitar a los vecinos (*visit the neighbours*)
f ver la televisión (*watch television*)
g hacer mucho ruido (*make lots of noise*)
h poner la mesa (*lay the table*)
i saber la verdad (*know the truth*)
j decir algo a su familia (*say something to his family*)

57 More on the future

*Spanish has a variety of ways to talk about the future.
This unit summarises the main expressions.*

A To express actions in the future, Spanish can use the future tense
(see Unit 56).

Nos visitará todos los años.	*He will visit us every year.*
Un día iremos a América.	*One day we'll go to America.*

B Particularly in conversation, the ordinary present tense is used
when it is clear that the immediate future is intended.

Lo hago ahora mismo.	*I'll do it right now.*
Te llamo mañana.	*I'll call you tomorrow.*

The present is also common with information or instructions.

¿Sirvo el café?	*Shall I serve the coffee?*
¿Doblamos aquí?	*Shall we turn here?*
Dame el dinero o tiro.	*Give me the money or
I'll shoot.*

C As in English, **ir a** (*to be going to*) with the infinitive is very
common.

Esta tarde vamos a
descansar.	*We're going to rest this
afternoon.*
Si no te doy el dinero,
¿qué vas a hacer?	*If I don't give you the money,
what will you do?*

D You can use the verb **pensar** with the infinitive to mean *to
intend*.

Después de los estudios
pensamos casarnos.	*After our studies we intend to
get married.*
Juanito, ¿no piensas lavar
los platos?	*Juanito, aren't you going to
wash the dishes?*

E You can also use the verb **querer** (*to want*) with the infinitive.

Luisa quiere trabajar mañana.	*Luisa wants to work tomorrow.*
No queremos hacerlo.	*We won't do it.*

57 Exercises

1 Express the future by using the present.

E.g. hacerlo (*do it*) → ¿Lo hago ahora?

a escribir la carta (*write the letter*)
b servir el café (*serve the coffee*)
c doblar a la izquierda (*turn left*)
d lavar los platos (*do the dishes*)
e cortar el césped (*mow the lawn*)
f reparar el coche (*mend the car*)
g llenar el depósito (*fill the tank*)
h enchufar la aspiradora (*plug in the vacuum cleaner*)
i llamarles (*call them*)
j salir (*go out*)

2 Contrast the future tense with *ir a* + infinitive.

E.g. hablaremos → vamos a hablar

a Comeremos mucho.
b Juan beberá una cerveza.
c Luisa irá a la universidad.
d Tú visitarás América.
e Tendrás problemas.
f Ustedes escribirán muchas cartas.

3 Use *pensar* + the infinitive to reply to the questions.

E.g. ¿Irás a la universidad? → Sí, pienso ir a la universidad.

a ¿Lavarás los platos?
b ¿Saldrás con Julio?
c ¿Juan comerá toda la paella?
d ¿Usted pagará la cuenta?
e ¿Servirás la comida?
f ¿Ustedes hablarán con el director?

4 Practise with *querer* (*to want*) by replying to the questions in exercise 3.

E.g. Sí, quiero ir a la universidad.

58 The conditional tense

> *The conditional tense is used to say what would happen in certain circumstances.*

A This tense corresponds to the English *should* or *would* when talking about some theoretical possibility.

En ese caso hablaría con el médico.
In that case I should speak to the doctor.

B The conditional tense is also used to report 'the future-in-the-past'.

Juan dijo que compraría un coche.
Juan said that he would buy a car.

C The conditional tense is formed by adding endings (originally from the imperfect of **haber**) to the infinitive, in the same way that the future tense (see Unit 56) added endings derived from the present tense of **haber**. As with the future, all verbs share the same sets of endings.

HABLAR	COMER	VIVIR
hablaría	comería	viviría
hablarías	comerías	vivirías
hablaría	comería	viviría
hablaríamos	comeríamos	viviríamos
hablaríais	comeríais	viviríais
hablarían	comerían	vivirían

The endings are stressed on the same letter throughout, and all endings need **í**.

A mí no me gustaría comer calamares.
I wouldn't like to eat squid.

D The same infinitives which change to form the future change in the same way to form their conditional.

QUERER (*to want*)	querría, ...	PONER (*to put*)	pondría, ...
PODER (*to be able*)	podría, ...	SALIR (*to go out, leave*)	saldría, ...
SABER (*to know*)	sabría, ...	TENER (*to have*)	tendría, ...
DECIR (*to say*)	diría, ...	VENIR (*to come*)	vendría, ...
HACER (*to do, make*)	haría, ...	VALER (*to be worth*)	valdría, ...

Sin tu ayuda no tendríamos nada.
Without your help we would have nothing.

58 Exercises

1 Julio does something but his twin Pedro uses the conditional to say that he wouldn't.

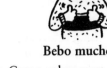

Bebo mucho.   No bebería mucho.

a Como calamares.   f Trabajo mucho.
b Voy a pie.   g Digo la verdad.
c Veo la televisión.   h Escribo una carta.
d Salgo con Luisa.   i Puedo llegar a tiempo.
e Hablo con el médico.   j Sé la dirección.

2 Fill the blanks with the conditional of the appropriate verb.

E.g. Si tuviera tiempo yo _____ el coche (reparar). → Si tuviera tiempo yo repararía el coche.

a Si tuviera tiempo yo _____ una paella.
b Si tuvieras tiempo tú _____ los platos.
c Si tuviera tiempo Juan _____ en el mar.
d Si tuvieran tiempo ustedes _____ visitar la ciudad.
e Si tuviéramos tiempo _____ las cartas.
f Si tuviera tiempo Juanito _____ al fútbol.
g Si tuvierais tiempo vosotros _____ un vaso de limonada.
h Si tuviera tiempo usted _____ conmigo.
i Si tuviera tiempo yo te _____ la verdad.
j Si tuvieras tiempo tú _____ en el jardín.

> decir   escribir   hacer   jugar   lavar   nadar
> poder   tomar   trabajar   venir

59 The present perfect tense

*The present perfect tense is one of many tenses that use **have** to express completed or perfected actions.*

A The present perfect (sometimes called just the perfect) is used, as in English, to talk about recent time.

| Hemos hablado con tu profesor. | *We have spoken to your teacher.* |

B Spanish forms such tenses in the same way, using a form of the verb **haber** (*to have*) next to a past participle (e.g. *spoken*).

Note that **haber** not **tener** is used. This is its irregular present tense.

HABER (*to have*)   he, has, ha, hemos, habéis, han

C The past participle is, fortunately, more regular.

HABLAR	COMER	VIVIR
hablado	comido	vivido

Once again, **-er** and **-ir** verbs follow the same pattern.
Verbs like **leer** (*to read*), **creer** (*to believe*) need an accent: **leído**, **creído**.

D As in English, the past participle does not change.

| Has comido mucho. | *You have eaten a lot.* |

E To make the verb negative, put **no** in front of **haber**. Do not split up **haber**, the past participle and any object or reflexive pronouns.

| Tú no te has levantado todavía. | *You haven't got up yet.* |

F Some past participles (not from **-ar** verbs) are irregular.

- decir (*to say*) → dicho; hacer (*to do, make*) → hecho; escribir (*to write*) → escrito; poner (*to put*) → puesto; ver (*to see*) → visto; romper (*to break*) → roto; morir (*to die*) → muerto; freír (*to fry*) → frito

- Verbs ending in **-brir** have past participles ending in **-bierto**.
  abrir (*to open*) → abierto; cubrir (*to cover*) → cubierto

- Verbs ending in **-olver** have past participles ending in **-uelto**.
  volver (*to return*) → vuelto; resolver (*to resolve*) → resuelto

- Compounds such as **describir, imponer, devolver** are similarly irregular.
  describir (*to describe*) → descrito; imponer (*to impose*) → impuesto; devolver (*to give back*) → devuelto

59 Exercises

1 Say you have already done what you are asked to do, using the present perfect tense.

E.g. ¿Quieres abrir la ventana? → He abierto la ventana.

a ¿Quieres terminar la carta? f ¿Quieres ir al mercado?
b ¿Quieres hablar con el médico? g ¿Quieres limpiar las ventanas?
c ¿Quieres salir con Julio? h ¿Quieres leer el periódico?
d ¿Quieres buscar el dinero? i ¿Quieres llamar a la policía?
e ¿Quieres beber el café? j ¿Quieres servir el té?

2 Give the correct form of the present perfect.

E.g. We have spoken (hablar) → Hemos hablado.

a They have eaten (**comer**).
b Have you (**tú**) finished (**terminar**)?
c They have believed (**creer**).
d He has seen (**ver**).
e We have put (**poner**).
f He has died (**morir**).
g You (**vosotros**) have broken (**romper**).
h I have described (**describir**).

3 Practise using object and reflexive pronouns combined with the present perfect.

E.g. ¿Por qué lo leen ustedes ahora? → Porque no lo hemos leído todavía.

a ¿Por qué lo beben ahora? f ¿Por qué se duchan ahora?
b ¿Por qué la escuchan ahora? g ¿Por qué se duermen ahora?
c ¿Por qué los pintan ahora? h ¿Por qué se levantan ahora?
d ¿Por qué lo comen ahora? i ¿Por qué los fuman ahora?
e ¿Por qué las leen ahora? j ¿Por qué les hablan ahora?

4 Practise forming the present perfect with irregular past participles.

E.g. ¿Cuándo piensan escribir la carta? → Ya han escrito la carta.

a ¿Cuándo piensan decir la verdad?
b ¿Cuándo piensan devolver el dinero?
c ¿Cuándo piensan abrir la puerta?
d ¿Cuándo piensan freír el pescado?
e ¿Cuándo piensan poner la mesa?
f ¿Cuándo piensan volver a casa?
g ¿Cuándo piensan hacer la paella?
h ¿Cuándo piensan describir sus planes?
i ¿Cuándo piensan resolver el problema?
j ¿Cuándo piensan morir?

60 The future perfect tense

This compound tense with haber *anticipates completed actions in the future.*

A The future perfect describes an action or event that will have taken place at some time in the future; the tense is similarly formed in Spanish and English.

Lo habrán terminado pronto. *They will have finished it soon.*

B The future perfect is formed by the future tense of **haber** (*to have*) and the past participle.

HABER   habré, habrás, habrá, habremos, habréis, habrán

Habré hablado con el médico.	*I shall have spoken to the doctor.*
Habremos comido todo.	*We will have eaten everything.*
Habrán salido.	*They will have gone out.*

⚠ Remember the irregular past participles (see Unit 59).

Lo habrás escrito.	*You will have written it.*
Habrán hecho la paella.	*They will have made the paella.*

C The future perfect can also suggest probability, as in English.

Habrá muerto.   *He will have died.*

D Some useful expressions which may be used with the future perfect include:

pronto (*soon*); **para finales de la semana** (*by the end of the week*); **para las tres** (*by three o' clock*); **para entonces** (*by then*); **antes de** + infinitive (*before*).

Lo habré leído antes de salir.	*I shall have read it before I go out.*

Remember the word order as with other compound tenses: subject + **no** + object/reflexive pronoun + **haber** + past participle.

Tú no te habrás acostado.	*You won't have gone to bed.*
Ellos no se habrán casado.	*They won't have got married.*

60 Exercises

1 Give the future perfect of the following verbs.

> *E.g.* yo (tomar *to take*) → yo habré tomado

a yo (beber = *drink*)
b él (llegar = *arrive*)
c nosotros (comer = *eat*)
d usted (leer = *read*)
e ellos (contestar = *reply*)
f ustedes se (casarse = *get married*)
g tú (llamar = *call*)
h vosotros (dormir = *sleep*)
i yo (dar = *give*)
j nosotros (ir = *go*)

2 Repeat the exercise, but watch out – the following verbs have irregular past participles.

a tú (ver = *see*)
b nosotros (freír = *fry*)
c yo (poner = *put*)
d ella (volver = *return*)
e ustedes (decir = *say*)
f tú (hacer = *make*)
g nosotros (escribir = *write*)
h ellos (romper = *break*)
i yo (devolver = *give back*)
j usted (morir = *die*)

3 Use the future perfect to suggest the likely event.

> *E.g.* morir → Julio habrá muerto.

a volver
b salir
c decidir
d casarse
e acostarse
f levantarse
g resolver el problema
h freír las patatas
i decir la verdad

4 Build sentences with the future perfect using the suggestions below.

> *E.g.* Luisa/llegar/a Madrid → Luisa habrá llegado a Madrid.

a Pedro/terminar/su libro
b Yo/pintar/la casa
c Julia y Emilio/casarse
d Tú y Julio/freír/el pescado
e El pobre hombre/morir
f Tú y yo/recibir/el dinero
g Usted/hacer/una paella
h Tú/escribir/la carta
i Ellos/irse/del pueblo
j Ustedes/ver/la película

61 The past perfect tense

The past perfect is another 'compound tense' formed with haber (to have) and a past participle.

A The past perfect (or 'pluperfect') tense corresponds to the English *had* with the past participle, for example, *I had spoken, we had eaten.*

Spanish uses the imperfect tense (see Unit 54) of **haber** (*to have*), with the corresponding past participle.

HABER había, habías, había, habíamos, habíais, habían

⚠ Remember not to use **tener** (*to have*) to form other tenses.

B The past participles are the same regular and irregular ones you met with the present perfect tense (Unit 59).

habíamos hablado	*we had spoken*
había vivido	*he/she had lived*
habías visto	*you had seen*
habían escrito	*they had written*

C As its name implies, the past perfect is used to describe a completed action in the past that happened before something else.

Como había recibido la carta, Juan sabía la verdad.	*As he had received the letter, Juan knew the truth.*
Julio no hablaba portugués porque nunca lo había estudiado.	*Julio didn't speak Portuguese, because he had never studied it.*
Yo me había levantado ya cuando mis amigos llegaron.	*I had already got up when my friends arrived.*
Cuando Isabel llegó a casa, los ladrones ya se habían escapado.	*When Isabel got home, the robbers had already escaped.*

D As with the present perfect (and other tenses formed with **haber**), do not split up the two parts of the verb. In negatives, the **no** comes in front of any object or reflexive pronouns but after any subject pronouns.

Nosotros no la habíamos visto. *We had not seen her.*

61 Exercises

1 Give the past perfect forms of the following.

E.g. yo (llegar = *arrive*) → yo había llegado

a yo (hablar = *speak*)
b ellos (comer = *eat*)
c nosotros (salir = *go out*)
d ella (ir = *to go*)
e vosotros (beber = *drink*)
f el ladrón se (escapar = *escape*)
g la policía (venir = *come*)
h tú (llamar = *call, phone*)
i ellas (contestar = *answer*)
j usted (buscar = *search*)

2 The same exercise, but with irregular past participles.

a Juan (escribir = *write*)
b nosotros (poner = *put*)
c ella (volver = *return*)
d vosotros (devolver = *give back*)
e ellos (morir = *die*)
f yo (ver = *see*)
g él (abrir = *open*)
h tú (decir = *say*)
i usted (romper = *break*)
h yo (hacer = *make, do*)

3 Make these sentences negative using *no*, *nunca* (never), *nada* (nothing) or *nadie* (no one) as necessary.

E.g. Julio lo había hecho. → Julio no lo había hecho.

a Nosotros nos habíamos levantado.
b Ellos siempre lo habían terminado puntualmente.
c Alguien los había visto en el pueblo.
d Yo siempre había querido comer algo.
e Usted se había levantado a las ocho.
f Ustedes los habían probado.
g Tú le habías escrito.
h Ella siempre se había puesto algo.
i Yo siempre me había acostado temprano.
j Juan y María se habían ido.

62 The conditional perfect tense

This compound tense with haber *describes an action or event in the past that would have happened in certain circumstances.*

A The conditional perfect is formed as in English, using the conditional tense of **haber** (*to have*) plus the past participle.

Habría hablado.   *He would have spoken.*

HABER   habría, habrías, habría, habríamos, habríais, habrían

B These are followed by the past participles we have already met in Unit 59.

Habríamos hablado español.	*We would have spoken Spanish.*
Julio habría comprado un coche.	*Julio would have bought a car.*
Habrías comido demasiado.	*You would have eaten too much.*
Probablemente Luisa habría salido contigo.	*Luisa would probably have gone out with you.*
En tu sitio habría dicho la verdad.	*In your place I would have told the truth.*
En ese caso habríamos llamado a la policía.	*In that case we would have called the police.*
Con mejor tiempo, Luisa se habría bañado en el mar.	*In better weather, Luisa would have bathed in the sea.*

C The conditional perfect can express probability or supposition about the past.

El rey habría muerto.	*The king would have died.*
A las ocho habría salido ya.	*At eight o'clock he would have already left.*

D The word order, as with the other compound tenses with **haber**, is subject + **no** + object/reflexive pronoun + **haber** + past participle.

Viviendo en el campo usted no lo habría sabido.	*Living in the country, you would not have known that.*
Con todos estos problemas tú te habrías vuelto loco también.	*With all these problems, you would have gone mad too.*

62 Exercises

1 Give the conditional perfect forms of the following.

E.g. él (comer = *eat*) → él habría comido

a nosotros (salir = *leave*)
b ellos (acostarse = *go to bed*)
c usted (beber = *drink*)
d yo (creer = *believe*)
e ella (leer = *read*)
f nosotros (casarse = *get married*)
g tú (ir = *go*)
h yo (dormir = *sleep*)
i ustedes (olvidar = *forget*)
j vosotros (pensar = *think*)

2 Do the same with the following which have irregular past participles.

a ella (morir = *die*)
b tú (escribir = *write*)
c nosotros (decir = *say*)
d ustedes (freír = *fry*)
e yo (hacer = *do, make*)
f ellos (poner = *put*)
g usted (ver = *see*)
h vosotros (romper = *break*)
i tú (volver = *return*)
j el (resolver = *solve*)

3 Use the conditional perfect to disassociate yourself from someone else's actions.

E.g. Julio compró un elefante. → Yo no lo habría comprado.

a Luisa se acostó tarde.
b Usted fumó muchos cigarrillos.
c Emilio y Juanita se casaron.
d Dormiste toda la tarde.
e Juan estudió inglés en la universidad.
f Lo creíste.
g Andrés se bañó en el mar.
h Ustedes dijeron la verdad.
i Julio se puso la mejor camisa.
j El prisionero se volvió loco.

4 Repeat exercise 3, but using the *nosotros* form instead.

E.g. Nosotros no lo habríamos comprado tampoco.

5 Speculate on what you might have done using the suggestions that follow.

E.g. comprar un coche nuevo → Habria comprado un coche nuevo.

a viajar por el mundo (*travel round the world*)
b vivir en un país exótico (*live in an exotic country*)
c casarme con Julia (*marry Julia*)
d visitar a mi abuela en Perú (*visit my grandmother in Peru*)

63 The passive

The passive is used to make the direct object of an action the subject of the sentence.

A The passive is not used as commonly in Spanish as in English; nevertheless it is used in fairly formal style.

(ACTIVE)

Mucha gente lee este periódico.

Many people read this newspaper.

(PASSIVE)

Este periódico es leído por mucha gente.

This newspaper is read by many people.

B The verb is made passive, as in English, by using the verb **ser** (*to be*) (see Unit 41) and a past participle (see Unit 59). The person bringing about the action is shown by **por** (*by*).

La puerta es cerrada por el profesor.

The door is closed by the teacher.

Los ladrones fueron cogidos por la policía.

The robbers were caught by the police.

In this construction after **ser**, the past participle agrees in gender and number with the subject, for example **la puerta, los ladrones**.

C Spanish tends to avoid the passive by either using the normal active subject + verb + object or by using a reflexive verb with **se**.

Aquí se habla español. *Spanish is spoken here.*

D The word order is fairly flexible, but the verb frequently comes in front of the subject: **se escondió el dinero** or **el dinero se escondió**. An article is required if a noun starts the expression: **Se habla inglés** but **el inglés se habla**.

Los libros se devolvieron a la biblioteca.

The books were returned to the library.

Se vende pan en la panadería pero las legumbres se venden solamente en el mercado.

Bread is sold in the baker's, but vegetables are sold only in the market.

⚠ If **por** is used to show the agent responsible, correct style requires the **ser** construction instead of **se**.

Los libros fueron devueltos por los estudiantes.

The books were returned by the students.

Las legumbres son vendidas por los granjeros solamente en el mercado.

Vegetables are sold by the farmers only in the market.

63 Exercises

1 Change the following into the passive.

E.g. La profesora lee el libro. → El libro es leído por la profesora.

a Juan bebe el vino.
b Julio escribió la carta.
c Los chicos vieron a Luisa en la calle.
d Nosotros pintamos la casa todos los años.
e La policía cogió al ladrón.
f Luisa y Emilio cogen las flores.
g Usted hizo la paella.
h Todo el mundo lee está revista.
i El mecánico reparó mi coche.
j Los animales comen la hierba.

2 The following sentences sound rather inelegant and unnatural in Spanish. Change the passive into the construction with *se*.

E.g. Este pan es vendido en todas las tiendas. → Se vende este pan en todas las tiendas.

a La paella es comida por toda España.
b El inglés es hablado en muchos países.
c Muchos cigarrillos son fumados en la calle.
d El vino tinto es bebido con frecuencia.
e Las cartas son escritas con lápiz.
f La puerta es abierta lentamente.
g Este periódico es leído mucho.
h La hierba es comida en el verano.
i Las flores son cogidas en el campo.
j El pueblo es conocido.

3 Change these passive sentences to the active.

E.g. El español es hablado por mucha gente. → Mucha gente habla español.

a El libro fue escrito por Juan López.
b Esta paella es hecha por las chicas.
c La puerta es abierta por un estudiante.
d La hierba es comida por las vacas.
e La catedral es visitada por muchos turistas.
f Mi dinero fue robado por un ladrón.
g Su coche será reparado por un mecánico.
h Mi pasaporte fue inspeccionado por un policía.

64 The subjunctive

Spanish uses a special set of verb endings in different tenses to denote actions which are connected with or depend on another person's attitude.

A Look at the present subjunctive of the following verbs.

HABLAR	COMER	ESCRIBIR
hable	coma	escriba
hables	comas	escribas
hable	coma	escriba
hablemos	comamos	escribamos
habléis	comáis	escribáis
hablen	coman	escriban

⚠ Note that -er and -ir verbs have the same endings.

You can see that in the present subjunctive verbs ending in -ar and -er/-ir have swapped endings compared with the ordinary present tense.

B Normally when one verb depends on another, you combine them using an infinitive, as in **quiero trabajar** (*I want to work*); **prefieres descansar** (*you prefer to rest*). However, the subjunctive is used after **que** if the subject changes.

Yo quiero trabajar.   *I want to work.*
(Yo) quiero que (tú) trabajes. *I want you to work.*
Julio prefiere escribir la carta. *Julio prefers to write the letter.*
Julio prefiere que nosotros   *Julio prefers us to write the*
escribamos la carta.   *letter.*

C When person B's (the second subject after **que**, known as the 'subordinate' clause) action is linked with person A's (the subject in the 'main' clause) attitude, replace the infinitive with **que** and a subjunctive.

No me gusta que usted   *I don't like you speaking*
hable inglés.   *English.*
Prohíben que comamos los   *They forbid us to eat the*
caramelos.   *sweets.*

⚠ Only use the subjunctive in the 'subordinate' clauses.

These verbs express emotion and opinion; they also need a subjunctive after **que**: **esperar** (*to hope*); **desear** (*to desire*); **me gusta** (*I like*); **preferir** (*to prefer*); **insistir (en)** (*to insist*); **mandar** (*to order*); **necesitar** (*to need*).

64 Exercises

1 Give the correct form of the present subjunctive.

E.g. tú (vivir = *to live*) → tú vivas

a tú (comer = *to eat*)
b nosotros (ganar = *to win*)
c usted (gritar = *to shout*)
d ellos (contestar = *to reply*)
e vosotros (beber = *to drink*)
f ella (lavarse = *get washed*)
g yo (descansar = *to rest*)
h ustedes (escribir = *to write*)
i tú (prometer = *to promise*)
j nosotros (fumar = *to smoke*)

2 Contrast the use of the infinitive or the subjunctive.

E.g. ¿Julio quiere trabajar? (nosotros) → Julio quiere que nosotros trabajemos.

a ¿Julio prefiere descansar? (nosotros)
b ¿Julio espera ganar la lotería? (Luisa)
c ¿Julio quiere comer? (usted)
d ¿Julio necesita contestar? (Juan y María)
e ¿Julio no quiere fumar? (tú)
f ¿Julio quiere lavarse? (los niños)
g ¿Julio necesita trabajar? (vosotros)
h ¿Julio no quiere gritar? (la gente)
i ¿Julio no quiere escribir? (yo)
j ¿Julio insiste en beber? (las chicas)

3 Use the subjunctive after an expression of liking with a change of subject.

E.g. No me gusta (tú; gritar). → No me gusta que grites.

a No me gusta (usted; fumar).
b No nos gusta (Luisa; cantar).
c ¿No te gusta (yo; descansar)?
d No les gusta (nosotros; beber).
e No le gusta a Luisa (Pedro; escribir).
f No me gusta (los niños; gritar).

4 Fill the gap with the appropriate subjunctive verb from the box.

a Juan necesita que nosotros _____ en su jardín.
b Luisa y Ana prefieren que los chicos no _____ .
c Deseamos que ustedes _____ la carta ahora.
d No me gusta que tú _____ en la casa.
e ¿Esperas que Luisa _____ ?
f Esperamos que vosotros _____ bien.

| cante descanséis escriban fumes griten trabajemos |

65 The subjunctive: more on formation

Verbs which show some irregularity in the ordinary present tense usually repeat that change in the subjunctive.

A The root (= the base) of the present subjunctive is the first person of the present tense. Look what happens with verbs whose first person present ends in -go, like **tengo** and **salgo**.

TENER (*to have*)   tenga, tengas, tenga, tengamos, tengáis, tengan
SALIR (*to go out*)   salga, salgas, salga, salgamos, salgáis, salgan

No me gusta que Juan   *I don't like Juan to have beer.*
  tenga cerveza.
Quiere que salgas.   *He wants you to go out.*

Verbs similarly affected include **oír** (*to hear*) → **oiga**; **venir** (*to come*) → **venga**; **hacer** (*to do, make*) → **haga**; **decir** (*to say, tell*) → **diga**; **poner** (*to put*) → **ponga**.

Necesito que digas la verdad. *I need you to tell the truth.*
Su madre quiere que se   *His mother wants him to*
  ponga un traje.   *put on a suit.*

B Most radical-changing verbs make the same changes in the present subjunctive as in the ordinary present tense.

CONTAR (*to count*)   cuente, cuentes, cuente, contemos, contéis, cuenten
PERDER (*to lose*)   pierda, pierdas, pierda, perdamos, perdáis, pierdan

C Now look at what happens to that group of radical-changing verbs in **-ir** like **pedir** (*to ask*); **divertirse** (*to have a good time*); **dormir** (*to sleep*).

PEDIR   pida, pidas, pida, pidamos, pidáis, pidan
DIVERTIRSE   me divierta, te diviertas, se divierta, nos divirtamos, os divirtáis, se diviertan
DORMIR   duerma, duermas, duerma, durmamos, durmáis, duerman

D **Ver** (*to see*) and **ser** (*to be*) have similar forms.

VER   vea, veas, vea, veamos, veáis, vean
SER   sea, seas, sea, seamos, seáis, sean

65 Exercises

1 **Change the present tenses to the corresponding person and forms of the subjunctive.**

E.g. pides → pidas

a tiene
b salimos
c vienes
d digo
e hacemos
f pone
g cuentan
h nos divertimos
i dormimos
j vemos

2 **Link the expressions, using a subjunctive with *que*.**

E.g. Juana quiere; Luisa tiene el dinero → Juana quiere que Luisa tenga el dinero.

a Nosotros no queremos; los niños salen.
b Julio prefiere; Luisa se pone el jersey azul.
c Me gusta; dices la verdad.
d Necesitan; hacemos una paella.
e La madre espera; el niño no cae.
f Insisto; usted pide permiso.
g Espero; os divertís.
h Al profesor no le gusta; dormimos en la clase.
i Mando; cuentas el dinero.
j No me gusta; hace frío.

3 **Fit the subjunctives in the grid. The clues are not necessarily in order!**

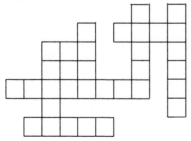

a Espero que el niño no (caer).
b Mi madre prefiere que Juan no (ver) la película.
c Espero que María y yo (tener) bastante dinero.
d Quiero que mi madre (hacer) una paella.
e Insisto en que tú (pedir) permiso.
f Luisa quiere que Julio (decir) la verdad.
g El profesor prohíbe que los niños (salir).
h Esperamos que Ana (viene).

66 The subjunctive: further uses

> *Spanish uses the subjunctive with a variety of expressions of attitude.*

A The subjunctive is used with verbs of wanting like **querer**. It is similarly used with verbs of not wanting and others with negative connotations, such as **prohibir** (*to forbid*); **odiar** (*to hate*); **impedir** (*to prevent*).

Prohíbo que fumes.	*I forbid to you to smoke.*
Odio que bebas tanto.	*I hate you drinking so much.*
Impedimos que entren.	*We prevent them entering.*

B Other expressions involving attitude, including **alegrarse de** (*to be glad*); **sentir** (*to regret, be sorry*); **temer/tener miedo de** (*to be afraid*) and **dudar** (*to doubt*) are followed by **que** and a subjunctive.

Me alegro de que vengas.	*I am glad you are coming.*
Siento que Julio no esté aquí.	*I am sorry that Julio is not here.*
Teme que los niños se caigan.	*He is afraid that the children may/will fall over.*
Dudo que podamos ir.	*I doubt that we can go.*

⚠ **Lo siento** (*I'm sorry*) drops the **lo** when followed by **que** and the subjunctive.

C Similarly **ser/estar** (*to be*) + adjective of emotion require a subjunctive.

Está contenta que no llueva.	*She is pleased it's not raining.*

D Almost any 'impersonal' expression introduced by **es** and followed by **que** requires a subjunctive.

Es imposible que vuelva.	*It's impossible for him to return.*
Es necesario que trabajemos.	*It's necessary (that) we work.*
Es imprescindible que sepa.	*It's essential that he knows.*
Es curioso que vayas.	*It's curious that you are going.*

Saber and **ir** have irregular subjunctives in **sepa** (etc.) and **vaya**.

66 Exercises

1 Give the full present subjunctive of the following verbs.

a ir   *(to go)*   **b** saber   *(to know)*

2 Complete these sentences with an appropriate expression requiring the subjunctive from the box.

E.g. _____ que visites al médico. → Es necesario que visites al médico.

a Juanita _____ que no puedas ir a la fiesta.
b _____ que llueva mañana.
c _____ que los estudiantes estudien mucho.
d _____ que ganemos la lotería.
e Julio _____ que el tigre se escape.
f El profesor _____ que los niños entren en la clase.
g _____ que mis padren vengan a vernos.
h _____ que aprobemos el examen.
i _____ que te laves sin agua.
j _____ que llame al médico.

> dudo   es importante   es imposible   es necesario
> es posible   es urgente   estamos alegres de   impide   siente   teme

3 The answers in this crossword are all subjunctive verbs.

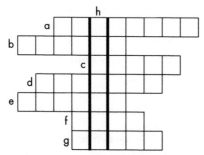

a Quiero que el niño (descansar).
b Es necesario que tú (hablar) español.
c Espero que Julio (poder) venir.
d Es necesario que nosotros (decir) la verdad.
e Ellos esperan que Luisa (dormir) bien.
f La madre quiere que el niño (comer) mucho.
g Me alegro que tú (estar) aquí.
h Es importante que nosotros (saber) nadar.

67 Subjunctive: expressions of futurity

> *Spanish uses the subjunctive in subordinate clauses when the event has not yet happened or is in doubt.*

A The subjunctive is often used after words such as **cuando** (*when*), **tan pronto como** (*as soon as*), **mientras** (*while*) and **hasta que** (*until*).

Iré a la playa cuando Julio venga.	*I shall go to the beach when Julio comes.*
Cuando termines el desayuno puedes salir.	*When you finish your breakfast you can go out.*
Tan pronto como usted me diga la verdad estaré contento.	*As soon as you tell me the truth I shall be happy.*
Cuando gane la lotería voy a comprar un coche.	*When I win the lottery I shall buy a car.*
Te miraré mientras subas.	*I'll watch you while you go up.*
Esperaremos aquí hasta que lleguen.	*We shall wait here until they arrive.*

In all the above examples the speaker does not know for certain if they will be told the truth or if they will win the lottery or not – the actions referred to are all sometime in the future.

⚠ Notice that verbs like **llegar** insert a **u** before the endings of the subjunctive to preserve the hard **g** sound. Verbs like **comenzar** and **empezar** change the **z** to **c**.

Jugaremos hasta que empiece a llover.	*We shall play until it starts raining.*

B The expression **antes (de) que** (*before*) always takes a subjunctive verb, as the event referred to has obviously not yet happened!

Vamos a salir antes (de) que nos vean.	*Let's leave before they see us (they have not seen us yet!)*

⚠ There does not need to be a change of subject for these expressions of futurity to require a subjunctive.

Trabajaré hasta que termine. *I shall work until I finish.*
Cantarán hasta que mueran. *They will sing until they die.*

⚠ It is also possible to use **hasta** + infinitive: **Trabajaré hasta terminar; cantarán hasta morir.**

1 Use the subjunctive after *cuando* (when).

> **E.g.** Dormiré cuando los niños (venir) → Dormiré cuando los niños vengan.

a Cuando (ganar) la lotería voy a comprar un coche.
b Cuando Julio (salir) comeremos.
c Saldré cuando (volver) los niños.
d Vamos a entrar cuando (empezar) a llover.
e Estaremos contentos cuando tú (decir) la verdad.

2 This time use the subjunctive with *antes (de) que* (the *de* is optional).

a Comeré antes que (llegar) los niños.
b Voy a salir antes de que (venir) mi padre.
c Quiero terminar antes que (llegar) el profesor.
d Tengo que trabajar mucho antes que (recibir) un salario bueno.
e Tenemos que ganar la lotería antes que (poder) comprar un coche.

3 Use *tan pronto como* (as soon as) or *hasta que* (until) to suit the context.

> **E.g.** Voy a esperar _____ el estudiante comience a escribir. → hasta que.

a Trabajaremos _____ terminemos.
b _____ llegue Julio vamos a salir.
c Compraré el libro _____ me des el dinero.
d Esperaré _____ salga el tren.
e Luisa va a trabajar _____ se case.
f ¡Creo que tú vas a trabajar _____ mueras!

4 Translate the following in to Spanish.

a We shall sing until the children leave.
b Luisa is going to rest until Julio comes.
c I shall buy a big house when I win the lottery.
d As soon as your father comes, we will eat.
e They will be happy when you tell the truth.
f We are going to swim until it starts raining.

68 Conditional sentences: clauses with *si*

Conditional sentences explain what someone would do or be if something happened. Spanish uses different constructions with si (if).

Spanish makes a distinction between a genuine possibility, (*If it rains, I'll go in*), and an imaginary or hypothetical situation (*If I were rich, I would buy a car*).

A Si with genuine possibilities.
Spanish uses the same construction as English. **Si** is usually followed by the ordinary present tense. The main clause may be in the present or future tense.

Si tengo tiempo, voy al cine.	*If I have time, I go to the cinema.*
Si tengo tiempo, iré al cine mañana.	*If I have time, I'll go to the cinema tomorrow.*
Yo trabajaré si tú trabajas también.	*I'll work if you work too.*
Voy a ver la televisión si hay un programa bueno.	*I'm going to watch television if there's a good programme.*

B When if refers to an imaginary situation or something which is contrary to fact, **si** is followed by a past subjunctive (typically the imperfect subjunctive) and the main clause is in the conditional tense.

Si (yo) viviese/viviera en Madrid hablaría español.	*If I lived in Madrid, I would speak Spanish.*
Si tú comieses/comieras pescado te daría sardinas.	*If you ate fish I would give you sardines.*
Compraríamos un coche nuevo si tuviésemos/tuviéramos dinero.	*We would buy a new car if we had the money.*

C The subjunctive is also used when the *if* refers to as yet unfulfilled conditions in the past.

Si yo fuese/fuera el profesor estaría muy enfadado.	*If I were the teacher I'd be very cross.*

⚠ Only use a past subjunctive, never the present subjunctive, after **si**.

D In literary or formal style it is possible to use the **-ra** form of the subjunctive in both parts of the sentence.

Si tuviera dinero comprara un coche.	*If I had the money I would buy a car.*

68 Exercises

1 Use *si* with the ordinary present tense to show these possible conditions.

E.g. (venir; Julio) iremos al cine → Si viene Julio, iremos al cine.

a (escribir; Luisa), contestaremos en seguida.
b (tener tiempo; yo) iré al médico.
c (sentir mal; tú) llamo al médico.
d (haber; película buena) iremos al cine.
e (invitarme; tú) iremos a un restaurante.
f (tener hambre; usted) le invito a comer.
g (llover) voy a leer un libro.
h (no quererme; tú) me voy.

2 Use an imperfect subjunctive after *si*.

E.g. ser rico → Si fuese/fuera rico compraría un coche.

a tener dinero
b vivir en el campo
c saber conducir
d ver bien
e visitar a mis amigos
f beber menos

3 Select the correct form according to the context.

E.g. Si tengo/tuviese tiempo, iría al cine. → tuviese

a Si Juan viene/viniese, vamos a nadar.
b Si tengo/tuviera hijos, compraré una casa más grande.
c Si tenemos/tuviésemos tiempo, visitaríamos a la familia.
d Si estoy/estuviera enfermo, llamaría al médico.
e Si estamos/estuviéramos enfermos, no vamos a trabajar.
f Si Julio tiene/tuviera dinero, compraría una casa.
g Si llueve/lloviese mañana, Luisa va a ver la televisión.
h Si llueve/lloviese, no podríamos comer en el jardín.

69 Perhaps, it's possible

Spanish has many ways of expressing possibility. This unit looks at the most important ones.

A **Es posible que** (*It's possible that, It may/might*) – like other 'impersonal expressions' – is followed by the subjunctive.

Es posible que llueva.   *It's possible it will rain/ it might rain.*

No es cierto que venga.   *It's not certain he'll come.*

Es dudoso que haya un tren.   *It's doubtful there's a train.*

B There are many ways of expressing *perhaps* in Spanish.

- **Puede ser que** + subjunctive (*perhaps, maybe*)

  Puede ser que no llegue   *Maybe he won't arrive in*
  a tiempo.   *time.*

- **Tal vez, acaso, quizás, quizá** (*perhaps*) are all usually followed by the subjunctive.

  Acaso no tengamos que   *Perhaps we don't/won't have*
  pagar.   *to pay.*

  Quizás haya una gasolinera   *Perhaps there is a petrol*
  por aquí.   *station round here.*

  Quizá el perro no muerda.   *Perhaps the dog won't bite.*

C These expressions are sometimes followed by a non-subjunctive verb to imply a greater degree of certainty.

Tal vez el profesor comprende   *Perhaps the teacher will*
– es un hombre simpático.   *understand – he's a nice man.*

Quizás te veremos a la hora   *Perhaps we'll see you at*
de comer.   *lunchtime.*

D You can avoid a subjunctive by putting the **quizá** (etc.) at the end of the sentence.

Te veremos pronto, quizá.   *We'll see you soon, perhaps.*

E **A lo mejor** (*perhaps*) is a useful expression which never takes the subjunctive. It is not as strong as **quizás**, etc. and can (but not necessarily) suggest optimism.

A lo mejor encontramos una   *Perhaps we'll get a room here.*
habitación aquí.

A lo mejor tendremos mejor   *Perhaps we'll have a better*
día mañana.   *day tomorrow.*

69 Exercises

1 **Complete the sentences using the expression in brackets with the present subjunctive.**

E.g. Hay un tren (Es dudoso) → Es dudoso que haya un tren.

a Tenemos bastante dinero (Es dudoso)
b El hombre comprende (Es posible)
c Hay un autobús (No es cierto)
d Hablamos con el profesor (Es probable)
d Encontramos una habitación (No es probable)

2 **Use *puede ser que* + present subjunctive in reply to the following questions.**

E.g. ¿Vienes, Julio? → Puede ser que venga.

a ¿Visitas al médico, Luisa?   d ¿Usted puede ayudarme?
b ¿Viene Juan con nosotros?   e ¿Tenemos que ir?
c ¿Pueden reparar el coche hoy?

3 **Put in *quizás* or *a lo mejor* as appropriate.**

a _____ trabaje en el jardín hoy.
b Juan dice que _____ haya una película buena hoy.
c _____ no hay clase hoy.
d _____ el profesor esté enfermo.
e Aquí _____ encontramos un hotel.

4 **Translate the following into Spanish.**

a It is possible it will rain today.
b It is probable that he won't come.
c Maybe Pedro will write soon.
d It's doubtful we have enough money.
e It is not certain that we can go.
f Perhaps he will arrive tomorrow.
g He will arrive tomorrow, perhaps.
h Perhaps the nice man will pay!
i Perhaps he understands Spanish.
j Perhaps you'll feel better soon.

70 Subjunctive – or not?

*Spanish can reflect certainty or uncertainty by choosing
to use the subjunctive or not in a variety of contexts.*

A **Aunque** (*although*, *even though*) is followed by the appropriate (non-subjunctive) tense when stating a fact.

Aunque es tarde, el sol brilla todavía.	*Although it is late, the sun is still shining.*
Bebe mucho aunque no tiene mucho dinero.	*He drinks a lot even though he does not have much money.*
Vamos a nadar aunque llueve mucho.	*We are going swimming even though it is raining hard.*

B **Aunque** (*even if*) is followed by a subjunctive verb.

Aunque llueva mucho, vamos a nadar.	*We are going swimming even if it rains hard.*
No les daré el dinero aunque tengan pistola.	*I shall not give them the money even if they have guns.*
Dijo que no saldría con Julio aunque la invitase/invitara.	*She said she would not go out with Julio even if he invited her.*

C Many other situations use the subjunctive rather than the ordinary ('indicative') tenses in a subordinate or secondary clause with an unknown or hypothetical subject.

Toma el libro que quieres.	Take the book (= specific book) you want.
Toma el libro que quieras.	Take the book (= whichever one) you want.
Buscamos al mecánico que repara coches.	*We are looking for the mechanic (a specific person) who repairs cars.*
Buscamos un mecánico que repare coches.	*We are looking for a mechanic (= any one) who repairs cars.*

D **Ojalá** (*if only*) is followed by a subjunctive. It refers to an event which is contrary to fact or not yet certain. In the present it is often followed by **que**.

Ojalá (que) gane la lotería esta vez.	*If only I win the lottery this time.*
Ojalá hablase/hablara inglés.	*If only I spoke English.*

Ojalá is also used as a one-word answer.

¿Estás de vacaciones? ¡Ojalá!	*Are you on holiday? If only!/I wish!/You must be joking!*, etc.

70 Exercises

1 Give the English to show the difference in meaning or emphasis in these pairs of expressions.

E.g. Aunque no tengo dinero voy al bar; Aunque tuviese dinero no iría al bar. → *Although I have no money, I'm going to the bar; even if I had money, I wouldn't go to the bar.*

a Aunque Julio viene no vamos a comer; Aunque Julio venga no vamos a comer.

b Aunque llovía mucho no veíamos la televisión; Aunque lloviese mucho decidimos no ver la televisión.

c Quiere estudiar el español aunque es difícil; Quiere estudiar el español aunque sea difícil.

d Luisa fue a Madrid aunque no le gustaba; Luisa iría a Madrid aunque no le gustara.

e Aunque me dices la verdad voy a la policía; Aunque me digas la verdad voy a la policía.

2 Practise using *aunque*: choose the indicative or subjunctive according to the context.

a Te comprendo aunque no hablas/hables español.

b Voy a continuar trabajando aunque gano/gane la lotería.

c Aunque es/sea difícil, nos gusta estudiar el latín.

d Aunque Madrid es/sea grande es muy bonito.

e No te daré el dinero aunque me lo pides/pidieses.

3 Choose the appropriate verb, subjunctive or not, according to the context.

a Estoy triste: quiero ver una película que es/sea divertida.

b ¿Conoces el café donde hay/haya paella típica?

c ¿Conoces un café donde no hay/haya café?

d Busco un banco que cambia/cambie euros – es urgente.

e Busco un banco que cambia/cambie euros – está cerca de aquí, creo.

4 Use *ojalá* and an imperfect subjunctive.

E.g. No hablo español. → Ojalá hablase/hablara español.

a No tengo dinero.   c Elena no me escribe.

b Julio no me visita.   d Mis padres no son ricos.

71 The subjunctive: commands

The subjunctive is used for all negative commands and for polite positive commands.

A You will often see polite commands on public transport, formal notices or in adverts. These use the **usted** (singular) and **ustedes** (plural) forms of the subjunctive.

Tenga cuidado.	*Take care.*
Suban y bajen rápidamente.	*Get on and off quickly.*
No pisen la hierba.	*Don't walk on the grass.*
Tiren; Empujen	*Pull; Push*

With strangers it is polite to add **usted** or **ustedes**.

Perdóneme usted.	*Excuse me.*

B The object or reflexive pronoun goes on the end of positive commands but before all negative commands.

Siéntese.	*Sit down.*
Quítese el abrigo.	*Take off your coat.*
Dígame/Diga.	*Hello?* (on the phone)
¡No me digas! ¡No me diga!	*You don't say!*
No se moleste usted.	*Don't bother yourself.*
No te preocupes/ No se preocupe.	*Don't worry.*

C You can also give a command by using the verb **querer** (*to want*) with an infinitive. This can sound less abrupt.

¿Quiere usted darme un kilo de patatas?	*Will you give me a kilo of potatoes?*

D There are also some rather formal expressions which use the polite commands of **tener** (*to have*) and **hacer** (*to do, make*): **tenga(n)** and **haga(n)** with an infinitive.

Tenga la bondad de pagar la cuenta.	*Have the goodness to pay the bill.*
Haga el favor de mantener silencio después de las once.	*Do the favour of observing silence after 11.*

E In instruction leaflets and notices, the infinitive is often used as a command.

Abrir el paquete y meter el contenido en una sartén.	*Open the packet and put the contents in a pan.*
No aparcar.	*No parking.*

71 Exercises

1 What do these polite (*usted*) commands mean?

E.g. Pise la hierba. → Walk on the grass.

a Hable español.
b Beba más agua.
c Pague la cuenta.
d Suba rápidamente.
e Tenga cuidado.
f Diga la verdad.

2 Make the commands in exercise 1 negative.

E.g. No pise la hierba.

3 Change the negative *usted* commands to the negative familiar (*tú*) commands by adding *-s*:

E.g. No pises la hierba.

4 Now change the positive commands to the *ustedes* plural form by adding *-n*.

E.g. Pisen la hierba.

5 Form commands using *¿Quiere usted?* and an infinitive to replace the subjunctive command forms.

E.g. Hable español. → ¿Quiere usted hablar español?

a Hable despacio.
b Abra la ventana.
c Cierre la puerta.
d Lave los platos.
e Diga la verdad.
f Pague la cuenta.
g Salga conmigo.
h Baje rápidamente.

6 Make these commands negative. Remember to change the word order and remove any unnecessary accents.

E.g. Preocúpese. → No se preocupe.

a Moléstese.
b Lávese.
c Ábrala.
d Ciérrela.
e Dígame.
f Págueme.
g Siéntense.
h Póngaselo.
i Quítenselo.

7 Rewrite the infinitives of these instructions using the *ustedes* (polite plural) commands.

E.g. Cortar el papel. → Corten el papel.
Beber más leche. → Beban más leche.

a Abrir el paquete.
b Llenar el depósito con aqua.
c No aparcar.
d Pagar la cuenta al salir.
e No pisar la hierba.
f No cantar en el bar.

72 Familiar commands: the true imperative

Tú and vosotros, the familiar forms singular and plural for you, form their positive commands using the 'true imperative'.

A **Tú** positive commands are usually formed by dropping the final -**s** from the **tú** form of the present tense.

hablar → habla; comer → come; escribir → escribe

Habla español.	*Speak Spanish.*
Come más.	*Eat more.*
Escribe una carta.	*Write a letter.*

B As with formal positive commands, any object or reflexive pronouns join on the end, adding an accent on the stressed syllable.

Levántate.	*Get up.*
Escríbeme pronto.	*Write to me soon.*

C A few verbs have irregular short **tú** imperatives.

poner (*to put*) → pon; hacer (*to do, make*) → haz; decir (*to say*) → di; salir (*to go out*) → sal; ser (*to be*) → sé; tener (*to have*) → ten; venir (*to come*) → ven; ir (*to go*) → ve.

Ven conmigo.	*Come with me.*
Ten cuidado.	*Take care.*
Pon la mesa.	*Lay the table.*
Dime la verdad.	*Tell me the truth.*

⚠ **Ve** is also the regular **tú** imperative from **ver** (*to see*).

An accent is only required with more than one object pronoun.

Póntelo. *Put it on.*   Dímelo. *Tell me it.*

D The **vosotros** (familiar plural) imperative is even simpler. Just change the final -**r** of the infinitive to -**d**.

hablar → hablad	decir → decid	hacer → haced
escribir → escribid	comer → comed	tener → tened

⚠ There are no exceptions, so ir (*to go*) → **id**; ser (*to be*) → **sed**.

E Reflexive verbs, however, drop the **d** in front of the reflexive pronoun **os**, except with **irse** (*to go away*): **lavaos** (*get washed*); **levantaos** (*get up*); **vestíos** (*get dressed*) (from **vestir**); **divertíos** (*have a good time*) (from **divertirse**), but **idos** (*go away*).

⚠ Remember all *negative* commands are formed from the subjunctive, see Unit 71.

72 Exercises

1 Give the *tú* imperative of the following verbs.

E.g. comer → come

a beber   d vivir

b hablar   e correr

c escribir

2 Give the *vosotros* imperative of the same verbs.

E.g. comer → comed

3 Give the *tú* imperative of these reflexive verbs. Don't forget to add any necessary accent.

E.g. lavarse → lávate

a levantarse (*to get up*)   d dormirse (*to fall asleep*)

b acostarse (*to go to bed*)   e esconderse (*to hide*)

c vestirse (*to get dressed*)

4 Give the *vosotros* imperative of the same reflexive verbs.

E.g. lavarse → lavaos

5 Give the *tú* and *vosotros* imperatives of the following verbs.

E.g. hacer → haz, haced

a decir   c salir   e venir

b poner   d tener

6 Translate the following into Spanish using the *tú* or *vosotros* imperative as necessary.

a Lay the table, children.   e Make a paella, mother.

b Tell the truth, Julio.   f Get dressed, children.

c Go out with me, Luisa.   g Have a good time, girls.

d Come to the cinema, boys.   h Go away, boys.

73 The subjunctive: past tenses

The subjunctive is used in past tenses as well as the present. This unit explains the most commonly used past tense, the imperfect subjunctive.

A The present subjunctive is used in a subordinate clause when the main clause refers to present or future time. If the main clause is in the past, the subjunctive will also be in the past.

No quiero que trabajes.   *I don't want you to work.*
No quería que trabajases.   *I didn't want you to work.*

In this sentence, **trabajases** is a past subjunctive.

B The good news is that one past tense of the subjunctive – the imperfect – serves a number of contexts. Even better news is that all verbs form this tense in the same way. The bad news is that, in modern Spanish, there are two alternative sets of endings. In practice, you use either!

The imperfect subjunctive is formed from the **ellos/ellas** form of the preterite (**hablaron, comieron** etc.): take off the **-ron** and add either a **-se** or a **-ra** set of endings.

HABLAR		COMER	
hablase	hablara	comiese	comiera
hablases	hablaras	comieses	comieras
hablase	hablara	comiese	comiera
hablásemos	habláramos	comiésemos	comiéramos
hablaseis	hablarais	comieseis	comierais
hablasen	hablaran	comiesen	comieran

⚠ All the **nosotros** forms have an accent: **hablásemos**, etc.

Mi madre quería que   *My mother wanted the*
  los niños comieran/comiesen *children to eat the*
  las legumbres.   *vegetables.*

C There are no irregular endings; all verbs form their imperfect subjunctives in the same way, from the preterite.

ir/ser (fueron) → fuese/fuera, ...
decir (dijeron) → dijese/dijera, ...
hacer (hicieron) → hiciese/hiciera, ...

73 Exercises

1 Give the imperfect subjunctive of the verbs.

> *E.g.* nosotros; hablar → hablásemos/habláramos

a nosotros; comer
b ellos; salir
c yo; escribir
d tú; comer
e nosotros; ir

f ella; trabajar
g ustedes; estudiar
h yo; hacer
i vosotros; hablar
j ellos; decir

2 Give the alternative form for the imperfect subjunctive.

> *E.g.* hablases → hablaras
> comiéramos → comiésemos

a hablases
b comieras
c fuera
d fuésemos
e saliera

f bebiesen
g hablarais
h dijese
i hicieses
j bebieras

3 Give the *nosotros* forms of the following verbs (both endings!).
Don't forget the accent.

a hablar
b comer
c salir

d decir
e hacer

4 Put these sentences into the past, using the imperfect
subjunctive after *que*.

> *E.g.* Juan quiere que Luisa hable. → Juan quería que Luisa
> hablase/ hablara.

a Juan quiere que Luisa coma. Juan quería …
b Queremos que los niños trabajen. Queríamos …
c El profesor prohíbe que el estudiante entre. El profesor
  prohibió …
d Los estudiantes quieren que el profesor salga. Los estudiantes
  querían …
e Prefiero que usted no fume. Prefería …
f Es imposible que Julio llegue. Era imposible …
g Me gusta que cante. Me gustaba …
h Preferimos que no bebáis. Preferíamos …

74 Putting verbs together

Sometimes we need to put two verbs together.
This and following units show how this is done.

A How Spanish verbs are joined depends on the verb being used. Many verbs combine simply as in English, with the first verb being directly followed by an infinitive.

Quiero descansar.	*I want to rest.*
Deben decidir.	*They must decide.*
No puedes salir mañana.	*You cannot go out tomorrow.*

B Common verbs followed directly by the infinitive include:

conseguir/lograr (*to succeed, manage*); deber (*must, should*); decidir (*to decide*); dejar/permitir (*to allow*); desear/querer (*to want, desire*); esperar (*to expect, hope, wait*); hacer (*to make*); impedir (*to prevent*); intentar (*to try*); mandar (*to order*); necesitar (*to need*); ofrecer (*to offer*); olvidar (*to forget*); pensar (*to intend*); poder (*to be able*); preferir (*to prefer*); prohibir (*to forbid*); prometer (*to promise*); recordar (*to remember, remind*); rehusar (*to refuse*); saber (*to know how*); soler (*to be accustomed*); temer (*to be afraid*)

Conseguí entrar por la ventana.	*I managed to get in through the window.*
Nos prohíben ver la película.	*They forbid us to see the film.*
Prefiero quedarme en casa.	*I prefer to stay at home.*
Has olvidado enviar la carta.	*You have forgotten to send the letter.*

C Verbs of perception such as **oír** (*to hear*), **ver** (*to see*) and **sentir** (*to feel, hear*) are also followed by the infinitive, whereas English uses **-ing**.

Los oímos jugar en el patio.	*We heard them playing in the yard.*
La veo tocar el piano.	*I see her playing the piano.*
Te siento correr por el pasillo.	*I hear/perceive you running down the corridor.*

1 Practise linking with *querer* (to want), *deber* (must, should), *poder* (can, be able), *pensar* (to intend), *preferir* (to prefer), *olvidar* (to forget), *decidir* (to decide).

> *E.g.* I want to read (leer). → Quiero leer.

a He wants to eat (**comer**).
b I prefer to rest (**descansar**).
c They decide to buy (**comprar**).
d You cannot go out today (**salir hoy**).
e We must study (**estudiar**).
f They forget to write (**escribir**).
g Do you intend to go (**ir**)?

2 Put verbs together using the infinitive.

> *E.g.* Visito España (quiero). → Quiero visitar España.

a Leo un libro (prefiero).
b Juan come pescado (rehúsa).
c Visitamos al médico (necesitamos).
d Lavas los platos (prometes).
e Sales por la noche (temes).
f Voy a Madrid (espero).
g Compré un coche (logré).
h Hablamos portugués (sabemos).
i Duermen bien (no pueden).
j Pago la cuenta (he olvidado).

3 Practise using these verbs of perception with an infinitive.

> *E.g.* Llamas; te oigo → Te oigo llamar.

a Juegan en el jardín; los oímos
b Toca el piano; le oigo a Julio
c Preparamos la comida; nos ven
d Sales por la ventana; te veo
e Entra por la noche; sentimos al ladrón

4 Translate the following into Spanish.

a I hear you knocking but you can't come in.
b We refuse to pay the bill.
c I don't know how to make a paella.
d He makes me come in through the window.
e They don't manage to sleep.

75 Putting verbs together with a

Some verbs are not linked directly. This unit deals with verbs that are joined with a.

A All verbs of motion take **a** before an infinitive.

Voy a comer pan.	*I'm going to eat bread.*
Corrieron a ayudarme.	*They ran to help me.*
¿Salimos a pasear?	*Are we going out for a walk?*
Julio viene a cenar.	*Julio is coming to have supper.*

Similarly **bajar** (*to go down(stairs)*), **subir** (*to go up(stairs)*), **entrar** (*to go in*), **llegar** (*to arrive*), etc.

B **A** may be changed to **para** if you want to emphasise the purpose.

Salieron para ayudarle.   *They went out (in order) to help him.*

C Verbs of beginning, such as **empezar, comenzar, ponerse** and **echar(se)**, are also followed by **a**.

Empiezo a estudiar.	*I begin to study.*
Comienzo a leer.	*I start to read.*
Me pongo a escribir.	*I start to write.*
(Me) echo a reír.	*I start to laugh.*

D Verbs which may be considered as equivalent to beginning or causing to begin are usually followed by **a**.

aprender (*to learn*); atreverse (*to dare*); acostumbrarse (*to get accustomed*); animar (*to encourage*); dedicarse (*to go in for, devote oneself*); enseñar (*to show, teach*); invitar (*to invite*); obligar (*to force*); persuadir (*to persuade*); prepararse (*to get ready*); volver (*to do again, to re-*)

Aprendieron a nadar.	*They learned to swim.*
Julio la invita a salir.	*Julio invites her to go out.*
Volvimos a leer el libro.	*We re-read the book.*

⚠ Although **decidir** (*to decide*) is followed by a direct infinitive (see Unit 74), **decidirse** is followed by **a** and tends to show greater emphasis.

Me decidí a aprender a conducir.   *I made up my mind to learn to drive.*

75 Exercises

1 Practise using verbs of motion.

> *E.g.* Escribo una carta (ir). → Voy a escribir una carta.

a Tocamos el piano (ir).
b Paseo en el parque (salir).
c Mi madre prepara la comida (bajar).
d Duermen (subir).
e Tú ves la televisión (entrar).
f Encuentran a papá (correr).

2 Use *a* with verbs of beginning.

> *E.g.* I begin to read (ponerse). → Me pongo a leer.

a He begins to read (**comenzar**).
b We start to write (**empezar**).
c They start to laugh (**echar**).
d You start to study (**ponerse**).
e She begins to swim (**empezar**).
f We start to run (**ponerse**).

3 Use *a* with verbs of learning and teaching.

> *E.g.* I'm learning to swim (aprender). → Aprendo a nadar.

a Luisa is learning to swim (**aprender**).
b Julio is studying to be a mechanic (**estudiar**).
c The children are learning to write (**aprender**).
d I teach you to read (**enseñar**).
e I am learning to play the piano (**aprender**).
f They are studying to speak English (**estudiar**).

4 Use *a* with verbs of getting things done.

> *E.g.* He forces me to work (obligar). → Me obliga a trabajar.

a He forces us to rest (**obligar**).
b We invite you to eat (**invitar**).
c They help us to read (**ayudar**).
d You encourage me to swim (**animar**).
e They persuade him to talk (**persuadir**).
f She gets ready to go out (**prepararse**).

76 Putting verbs together with *de*

This unit looks at verbs that require de *before an infinitive.*

A Verbs suggesting the end of an action or an event all tend to require **de** before an infinitive. These include **terminar** (*to finish*) and **dejar** (*to stop, give up*).

Terminó de leer.	He stopped reading.
He dejado de fumar.	I have given up smoking.

⚠️ **Acabar**, literally *to bring to an end*, followed by **de** means *to have just* + infinitive (see Unit 79).

Acabo de recibir la carta.   *I have just received the letter.*

B Similarly, verbs looking back on an action or event are often followed by **de**.

arrepentirse (*to repent, regret*); avergonzarse (*to be ashamed*); jactarse (*to boast*); presumir (*to show off, make a show*); preocuparse (*to worry*); cuidar (*to take care*); encargarse (*to take charge*); tratar (*to try*)

Me arrepiento de comprarlo.	I regret buying it.
Se avergüenza de reír.	He is ashamed of laughing.
Nos jactamos de ganar el premio.	We boast of winning the prize.
Luisa presume de conducir su coche nuevo.	Luisa makes a show of driving her new car.
Siempre me preocupo de conocer a gente nueva.	I always worry about meeting new people.
El portero se cuidó de aparcar el coche.	The doorman took care of parking the car.
Me encargué de escoger el vino.	I took charge of choosing the wine.
Tratamos de dormir, pero sin éxito.	We tried to sleep, but without success.

C Although **recordar** (*to remember*) is followed by a direct infinitive, **acordarse** (*to remember*) is followed by **de**.

Similarly, **olvidarse** (*to forget*) requires **de**.

Julio nunca se acuerda de cerrar los grifos.	Julio never remembers to turn off the taps.
No se olvide de despertarnos.	Don't forget to wake us.

76 Exercises

1 **Practise using verbs of finishing: *terminar*, *dejar*.**

E.g. Escribo la carta (terminar). → Termino de escribir la carta.
a Los niños juegan al fútbol (terminar).
b Fumo cigarrillos (dejar).
c Julio canta canciones románticas (terminar).
d El autor escribe novelas históricas (dejar).
e Luisa quiere fumar (dejar).
f Hablamos (terminar).

2 **Use *terminar de* with an infinitive.**

E.g. ¿Lees todavía? → Ahora mismo termino de leer.
a ¿Bebes todavía?
b ¿Luisa prepara la comida todavía?
c ¿El mecánico repara el coche todavía?
d ¿Ustedes comen todavía?
e ¿Tomas la foto todavía?
f ¿Los estudiantes escriben todavía?

3 **Use *dejar de* with an infinitive.**

E.g. ¿Por qué fumas mucho? → No puedo dejar de fumar.
a ¿Por qué comes chocolate?
b ¿Por qué bebe tanto Julio?
c ¿Por qué hablas tanto?
d ¿Por qué fuman mucho?
e ¿Por qué compras billetes de lotería?
f ¿Por qué ríe usted?

4 **Fill the gaps with the appropriate verb with *de* from the box.**

a El portero _____ de abrir la puerta.
b Julio no _____ de llamarme por teléfono.
c Yo _____ de comprar un coche.
d Siempre _____ de estudiar pero no puedo.
e Los niños _____ de ganar el partido de fútbol.
f Luisa _____ de conducir su coche rápido.
g No gracias, _____ de fumar.
h ¡Ay! ¡_____ de cerrar los grifos!

he dejado	me arrepentí	me he olvidado	presume
se acordó	se encargó	se jactaron	trato

77 Putting verbs together: other constructions

Although a and de are the most common linking prepositions with an infinitive, some verbs take other prepositions.

A Verbs of struggling, such as **luchar** (*to fight, struggle*) and **esforzarse** (*to make an effort, strive*), are followed by **por**.

Luchamos por conseguir una entrada.	*We fought to get a ticket.*
Me esfuerzo por aprobar el examen.	*I make an effort to pass the exam.*

B Some verbs are used with **en** before an infinitive.

consentir (*to consent, agree*); dudar/vacilar (*to hesitate*); empeñarse (*to be determined*); insistir (*to insist*); interesarse (*to be interested*); quedar (*to agree, arrange*); tardar (*to take time*)

Consentimos en prestarle el dinero.	*We agreed to lend him the money.*
Dudó en contestar.	*He hesitated to reply.*
Me empeño en terminar el libro.	*I'm determined to finish the book.*
Los amigos quedaron en reunirse a las seis.	*The friends agreed/arranged to meet at six.*
El tren tarda dos horas en llegar a Madrid.	*The train takes two hours to get to Madrid.*

⚠ Interesarse can also be followed by **por**.

C A few verbs are followed by **con**.

amenazar (*to threaten*); contar (*to rely, count on*); soñar (*to dream*)

Los vecinos amenazaron con llamar a la policía.	*The neighbours threatened to call the police.*
Siempre cuenta con encontrar trabajo.	*He always relies on finding work.*
Sueño con ganar la lotería.	*I dream of winning the lottery.*

⚠ Verbs of continuing, **continuar** and **seguir**, do not take an infinitive, unlike English, but are followed by the gerund.

Continúa leyendo.	*He continues to read.*

77 Exercises

1 Practise using *por*.

E.g. ¿Por qué luchas? (librar el país) → Lucho por librar el país.

a ¿Por qué luchan los soldados? (ganar la batalla)
b ¿Por qué se esfuerza usted? (llegar a tiempo)
c ¿Por qué se esfuerzan los estudiantes? (aprobar los exámenes).
d ¿Por qué lucha el dictador? (ganar las elecciones)

2 Practise using *en*.

E.g. Tú; dudar; contestar → Tú dudas en contestar.

a Los padres; consentir; comprar un coche
b Julio; insistir; venir
c Luisa; tardar dos horas; prepararse
d Nosotros; quedar; ir al cine
e Yo; interesarse; ver la televisión
f Los estudiantes; empeñarse; aprobar los exámenes
g Luisa y María; vacilar; salir con Julio
h ¿Tú; consentir; venir conmigo?

3 Practise using *con*.

E.g. El ladrón; amenazó; tirar → El ladrón amenazó con tirar.

a Los ladrones; amenazaron; robar el dinero
b La chica; sueña; salir con el chico
c Julio y Elena; sueñan; ganar la lotería
d La policía; cuenta; capturar a los criminales
e Nosotros; contamos; encontrar un hotel
f El vecino; amenaza; llamar a la policía

4 Fill the gaps with the appropriate preposition.

a El cantante consiente _____ cantar.
b El público se esfuerza _____ oír.
c Luchamos _____ ganar la victoria.
d Dudamos _____ pagar la cuenta.
e Los ladrones siempre cuentan _____ encontrar dinero.
f Insisto _____ pagar el vino.
g ¿Cuánto tiempo tardas _____ leer un libro?
h Los ingleses sueñan _____ tomar el sol.

78 Uses of *haber*: *hay* (*there is/are*)

This unit looks at haber *(to have) used in a special way.*

A The verb *to have* (*possess*) is **tener**.

Tengo dos hijos.	*I have two children.*
No tenemos tiempo para hacerlo.	*We haven't got time to do it.*

Haber (*to have*) is not used in the sense of *to possess*, but has two other main uses.

- To form compound tenses as in English.
  He comprado un coche.   *I have bought a car.*
  ¿Habías bebido todo el vino? *Had you drunk all the wine?*

- As an expression corresponding to the English *there is* or *there are*, when describing a scene or a situation. In this use, **haber** is only used in the third person singular. In the present tense alone, it adds **y** (**hay**).

hay (present) *there is/are*	**¿Hay servicios por aquí?** *Are there any toilets round here?*
había (imperfect) *there was/were/used to be*	**En España había muchos burros.** *In Spain there used to be a lot of donkeys.*
hubo (preterite) *there was*	**De repente hubo una llamada en la puerta.** *Suddenly there was a knock at the door.*
ha habido (present perfect) *there has/have been*	**Ha habido muchas huelgas recientemente.** *There have been a lot of strikes lately.*
había habido (past perfect) *there had been*	**Había habido un accidente.** *There had been an accident.*
habrá (future) *there will be*	**Mañana habrá una corrida.** *There will be a bullfight tomorrow.*
va a haber (future) *there is going to be*	**Va a haber una guerra.** *There is going to be a war.*
habría (conditional) *there would be*	**Habría muchos candidatos para el trabajo.** *There would be many candidates for the job.*

B Purists avoid **hay** with the definite article, preferring **existe** instead.

Existe la posibilidad de lluvia. *There is the possibility of rain.*

C **Hay que** plus an infinitive suggests a general requirement for action.

Para ganar hay que jugar.	*You've got to play in order to win.*
Hay que trabajar mucho aquí.	*One has to work hard here.*

78 Exercises

1 Use *tener* (to have) to translate the following.

a I have three children.
b You don't have time.
c We don't have money.
d Do you have sons or daughters?
e I do not have a car.

2 Use *haber* (to have) to express the following.

a I have bought a car.
b I have drunk the wine.
c Had you bought the house?
d They had bought a car.

3 Use *haber* with the meaning of *there is/are*.

E.g. There is a car in the garage. → Hay un coche en el garaje.

a There is wine on the table.
b There are children on the beach.
c Are there toilets round here?
d Is there a hotel in the town?
e There is a bullfight today.

4 Use *haber* in the appropriate tense to translate *there is/has been/will be*, etc.

E.g. There had been a bullfight. → Había habido una corrida.

a There used to be lots of donkeys on the beach.
b There has been an accident.
c There is going to be a bullfight.
d There will be many candidates for the job.
e Without money there would be a strike.
f There had been a car in the garage.
g Suddenly there was a knock on the door.
h There aren't any toilets in the bar.

79 Two useful verbs: *acabar* and *volver*

Spanish has two useful idiomatic constructions to express past and future actions using acabar *and* volver.

A **Acabar** on its own means *to finish* or *to be over*.

La palabra acaba por s.	*The word ends in s.*
Ha acabado la tarea.	*He has finished the task.*
La fiesta acabó.	*The party was over.*

B **Acabar de** plus an infinitive means *to have just ...*

Acabo de leer la carta.	*I have just read the letter.*
Juan acaba de salir.	*Juan has just left.*
Acabamos de ver el dinero.	*We have just seen the money.*

Acabar de is used in the present tense when it refers to an action that has just happened. If you refer to a past event, **acabar de** is put in the imperfect tense (see Unit 54).

Acababa de leer la carta.	*I had just read the letter.*
Juan acababa de salir.	*Juan had just left.*
Acabábamos de ver el dinero.	*We had just seen the money.*

⚠ It is unlikely that you will use **acabar de** in any tense other than the present or imperfect.

C **Volver** on its own means *to return*.

| Mañana volvemos a Madrid. | *Tomorrow we are returning to Madrid.* |
| Julio volvió al día siguiente. | *Julio came back the following day.* |

⚠ Remember that *return (give back)* is **devolver**.

| Julio devolvió el dinero. | *Julio gave back the money.* |

D **Volver a** plus an infinitive means *to (do) again*.

Vuelvo a leer la carta.	*I'm reading the letter again.*
Julio volvió a llamar.	*Julio called again.*
La besé y luego la volví a besar.	*I kissed her then kissed her again.*

Volver can be used in any tense the context demands.

| Todos los días volvía a tocar el disco. | *Every day I would play the record again.* |
| Después de media hora volvió a llover. | *Half an hour later it rained again.* |

79 Exercises

1 Use the present tense of *acabar de* with the infinitive to say you have just done the action referred to.

E.g. ¿Vas a salir? → No, acabo de salir.

a ¿Vas a comer?
b ¿Vas a dormir?
c ¿Vas a tocar el disco?
d ¿Vas a hacer una tortilla?
e ¿Vas a llamar a Luisa?

f ¿Vas a salir con el perro?
g ¿Vas a ver la televisión?
h ¿Vas a trabajar en el jardín?
i ¿Vas a ir al cine?
j ¿Vas a lavar los platos?

2 Use *acabar de* in the imperfect tense to say what the subject of the sentence had just been doing.

E.g. nosotros (comer) → Acabábamos de comer

a Juan (leer)
b Luisa y Pedro (cantar)
c Yo (levantarme)
d Sus padres (salir)
e Vosotros (recibir la carta)

f Nosotros (servir el café)
g Tú (dormir)
h Usted (ver la televisión)
i Ellos (hacer una paella)
j Yo (telefonear)

3 Express the person's enthusiasm for the action which follows, using *acabar de* and *volver a* plus infinitives.

E.g. yo (cantar) → Yo acabo de cantar pero vuelvo a cantar en seguida.

a yo (comer)
b usted (nadar)
c Julio (cantar)
d nosotros (leer)
e ellos (jugar al tenis)

f tú (salir)
g los señores García (llamar)
h tú (hacer una paella)
i nosotros (ir a la ciudad)
j ustedes (escribir)

4 Complete the sentences with the correct form of acabar de or volver a as necessary.

a Juan tiene hambre pero _____ comer mucho.
b Me gusta este libro, por eso lo _____ leer.
c Su padre está furioso porque Juanito _____ romper la ventana.
d Este ejercicio es malo – tienes que _____ hacerlo.
e Este programa es muy interesante. Quiero _____ verlo.
f No voy al cine porque _____ ver la película en la televisión.
g Luisa está contenta porque Julio _____ besarla.
h Vamos a estar contentos porque la orquesta _____ tocar.
i No hay problema – la policía _____ llegar.
j ¡Qué pena! _____ a llover.

80 To know: *saber* and *conocer*

Spanish has two principal ways of saying *to know*.

SABER (*to know (have learned)*)	CONOCER (*to know, be acquainted with*)
sé	conozco
sabes	conoces
sabe	conoce
sabemos	conocemos
sabéis	conocéis
saben	conocen

A **Saber** is used to know about something.

| Sabemos que España es muy bonita. | *We know that Spain is very pretty.* |
| No sé dónde está el banco. | *I don't know where the bank is.* |

B **Conocer** is used to express familiarity. **Reconocer** means *to recognize* (i.e. come across again).

| ¿Quién es Luisa? No la conozce. | *Who is Luisa? I don't know her (i.e. I have never met her).* |
| Este verano esperamos conocer Extremadura. ¿La conoces? | *This summer we are hoping to get to know Extremadura. Do you know (of) it?* |

BUT

| ¿Tú sabes algo de Extremadura? | *Do you know anything about Extremadura? (Is it big, hot, fertile?, etc.)* |

⚠ Never follow **conocer** with **que**: use **saber** in such cases.

| Sí, sé que Extremadura es una región en el oeste de España. | *Yes, I know (that) Extremadura is a region in the west of Spain.* |

C In the preterite tense (see Unit 51), **conocer** has the force of *to have met*.

| Conocí a Julio en Madrid. | *I met (= made the acquaintance of) Julio in Madrid.* |

⚠ The adjective/past participle **conocido** means *famous*.

| La paella valenciana es conocida por su riqueza. | *The paella they make in Valencia is famous for being tasty.* |

80 Exercises

1 **Fill the gaps with the correct form of either *saber* or *conocer*.**

a Julio _____ Granada porque su familia vive allí.
b Luisa _____ que Granada es una ciudad muy histórica.
c Julio _____ a Luisa: son colegas.
d Yo no _____ a Luisa, pero es una escritora conocida.
e Yo no _____ nada de Julio. ¿Es conocido?
f Claro que sí. Tú le _____ desde niño.

2 **Translate the following into Spanish.**

a I know Madrid well.
b We know that Madrid is the capital of Spain.
c Do you know that Luisa is Spanish?
d Do you know Luisa?
e I met her in Barcelona.
f Luisa's family is very well known in Barcelona.

3 **This puzzle revises *saber*, *conocer* and *poder* (from Unit 81). The ten missing verbs are in the word grid. Three are upside down.**

S	P	O	C	E	S	A
C	O	N	O	C	E	S
O	D	E	N	O	D	A
N	E	B	O	N	E	B
O	M	A	C	O	U	E
C	O	S	E	C	P	I
E	S	A	B	E	I	S

a Nosotros _____ salir esta tarde.
b ¿Tú _____ a María?
c Pedro no _____ Granada.
d Vosotros _____ hablar español.
e Usted _____ Madrid.
f Luisa no _____ a Julio.
g Tú no _____ ir al cine.
h Yo _____ tocar la guitarra bien.
i María y Luisa no _____ que Julio está aquí.
j Vosotros no _____ nada de mi trabajo.

81 *Poder* and *saber*

> *Spanish makes a distinction between* can *when it means ability, knowledge or permission.*

In English we use *can* in a variety of ways, for example, *I can swim; You can't swim because you have not brought your costume; Can you park here?; Can you speak Spanish?*

PODER (to be able, can)	SABER (to know (how), can)
puedo	sé
puedes	sabes
puede	sabe
podemos	sabemos
podéis	sabéis
pueden	saben

A *To be able* can be expressed by **poder** or **saber**. Both verbs have some points to note in their present tenses.

B **Poder** is used for a practical or physical possibility.

Puedo comprar un coche porque tengo mucho dinero. *I can buy a car because I have a lot of money.*

No podemos nadar hoy porque la piscina está cerrada. *We can't swim today because the pool is closed.*

Luis no puede hablar porque tiene la boca llena. *Luis can't speak because his mouth is full.*

For a general statement of permission, use **se puede**.

¿Se puede fumar aquí? *Can you/one smoke here?*

C **Saber** (= *to know*) is used if the ability depends on experience or learning.

¡Socorro! ¡No sé nadar! *Help! I can't swim!*

¿Sabes hablar español? *Can you speak Spanish?*

Compare:

Este pobre muchacho no sabe escribir. *This poor boy can't write (i.e. he's illiterate).*

Este pobre muchacho no puede escribir. *This poor boy can't write (i.e. he doesn't have pencil and paper)*

81 Exercises

1 **Insert the correct form of *poder* or *saber* as required.**

a Estoy perdido. ¿_____ usted ayudarme?

b No _____ abrir la puerta. Está cerrada.

c Luisa, ¿tú _____ nadar esta tarde?

d Me gusta mucho estar en la playa, pero no _____ nadar.

e No se _____ aparcar en el centro de la ciudad.

f No _____ leer este libro porque no tengo mis gafas.

g No comprendo los periódicos porque no _____ leer.

h Mi hermana _____ tocar el piano. En casa _____ practicar todos los días, pero en el colegio no _____ .

2 **Translate the following into Spanish.**

a Can you swim?

b Can you swim if your leg hurts?

c I can speak Spanish.

d Here you can speak Spanish or English.

e Can you smoke here?

f The poor child cannot read without his glasses.

g The poor child cannot read.

h Can you read a newspaper?

i Can you read a Spanish newspaper?

j I cannot go out today because I have to study.

82 Idioms with *tener*

The verb tener (to have) is used in a number of important expressions.

TENER (*to have*)   tengo, tienes, tiene, tenemos, tenéis, tienen

A The principal use of **tener** is to show possession.

Tenemos una casa en Madrid. *We have a house in Madrid.*

No tengo tiempo para estudiar. *I haven't got time to study.*

B Tener que followed by an infinitive indicates obligation.

Tengo que estudiar.   *I have to study.*

No tienes que trabajar hoy.   *You don't have to work today.*

C Tener is also used to form several idiomatic expressions.

- **tener frío/calor** = *to be cold/hot*
  Tengo mucho frío/tengo mucho calor. *I am very cold/hot.*
- **(no) tener razón** = *to be right/wrong*
  Usted no tiene razón.   *You are wrong.*
- **tengo hambre/sed** = *to be hungry/thirsty*
  Tengo mucha hambre.   *I am very hungry.*
  Julio tiene mucha sed.   *Julio is very thirsty.*
- **tener prisa** = *to be in a hurry*
  Tengo (mucha) prisa.   *I am in a (great) hurry.*
- **tener cuidado** = *to be careful*
  Tengo (mucho) cuidado.   *I am (very) careful.*
- **tener éxito** = *to be successful*
  Tengo (mucho) éxito.   *I am (very) successful.*
- **tener miedo (de)** = *to be afraid (of)*
  Tengo (mucho) miedo de   *I am (very) afraid of bears.*
  los osos.
- **(no) tener suerte** = *to be (un)lucky*
  Tengo (mucha) suerte en mis *I am (very) lucky in my studies.*
  estudios.
- **tener sueño** = *to be sleepy*
  Tengo (mucho) sueño.   *I am (very) sleepy.*
- **tener ganas de** = *to feel like*
  Tengo (muchas) ganas   *I (really) feel like dancing.*
  de bailar.
- **no tener nada que ver con** = *to have nothing to do with*
  Eso no tiene nada que ver   *That's got nothing to do with*
  con (Julio).   *(Julio)/It's none of (Julio's)*
                              business.

82 Exercises

1 Reply to the following statements or questions by using an idiom with *tener*.

> *E.g.* ¿Quieres una copa? → No, no tengo sed.

a ¿Quiere usted una hamburguesa?
b ¿Puedes venir al cine?
c ¿Por qué tomas un taxi?
d ¿Por qué lleva Julio tres jerseys y un poncho?
e ¿Has ganado la lotería?
f ¿Por qué no le hablas a Julio de tu problema?
g Madrid está en Portugal, ¿no?
h ¿Por qué tienes los ojos cerrados?
i ¡Ciudado!, ¡Hay una serpiente boa en el jardin!
j Mañana hay exámenes.

2 Match the English idioms with their *opposites* in Spanish.

a to be hot	1 tener éxito
b to be thirsty	2 tener frío
c to be unafraid	3 tener ganas
d to be unlucky	4 tener hambre
e to be unwilling	5 tener miedo
f to be wide awake	6 tener prisa
g to be wrong	7 tener que ver con
h not to concern	8 tener razón
i to fail	9 tener sueño
j to have plenty of time	10 tener suerte

3 Complete the sentences with the correct agreement of *mucho*.

a Julio tiene _____ sed.
b María tiene _____ ganas de ir al cine.
c Yo no tengo _____ hambre.
d Siempre tienes _____ suerte.
e Julia y Luisa no tienen _____ tiempo para estudiar.
f Luisa tiene _____ frío pero Julio tiene _____ calor.
g Tenemos _____ miedo porque hay serpientes y osos en el bosque.
h Paquita, tienes que tener _____ cuidado con el tráfico.

83 Verbs of taking

Spanish uses different verbs for to take *according to the context.*

A In most contexts **tomar** can be used.

Voy a tomar esto.	*I'll take this (in a shop).*
Tome dos pastillas tres veces al día.	*Take two tablets three times a day.*
Tome la tercera calle a la derecha.	*Take the third street on the right.*

Tomar frequently translates *to have* with food or drink.

Vamos a tomar una copa aquí. *Let's have a drink here.*

Tomar can be used with transport.

Vamos a tomar el autobús. *Let's get the bus.*

B **Coger** can also be used.

Cojo el autobús aquí. *I catch the bus here.*

Coger usually means *to gather, pick (up), collect.*

A Luisa le gusta coger las flores.	*Luisa likes picking flowers.*
Coge tu sombrero y póntelo.	*Grab your hat and put it on.*
Cogí un resfriado.	*I caught a cold.*

⚠ **Coger** should be used with care in American Spanish – it frequently has obscene overtones. Use **tomar** instead.

C **Llevar** is used when taking people or animals somewhere.

Voy a llevar a mi novia a Acapulco.	*I'm taking my girlfriend to Acapulco.*
¿Adónde me lleva usted?	*Where are you taking me?*

Llevar also means *to wear* or *to carry.*

Mi amigo lleva un jersey rayado.	*My friend is wearing a striped jersey.*

D **Sacar** is used with the idea of *taking out.*

Saqué este libro de la biblioteca. *I got this book out of the library.*

E With time, use **tardar en**.

Tardamos cinco horas en llegar.	*It took us five hours to get there.*

83 Exercises

1 Complete the sentences with the appropriate verb *to take*.

E.g. Mi amigo _____ chocolate con churros. → **Mi amigo toma chocolate con churros.**

a Es tarde. Vamos a _____ un taxi.

b Mira, el autobús viene. No lo vamos a _____ .

c ¿Dónde hay un banco? Necesito _____ dinero.

d La ciudad está muy lejos. Vamos a _____ mucho en llegar.

e ¿Qué quieres _____ ? ¿Cerveza o vino?

f Vamos a la taquilla a _____ las entradas para el concierto.

g Es muy difícil _____ un autobús en Argentina.

h Juan quiere _____ a Isabel al concierto.

i ¡Por fin mi marido me va a _____ de la casa!

j ¿Cuántas aspirinas debo _____ ?

2 Complete this account with the correct form of *to take* from the box.

Cuando voy a la ciudad, normalmente **a** _____ el autobús, pero esta mañana **b** _____ un taxi porque estaba lloviendo. También tuve que **c** _____ a los niños porque hoy no hay colegio. En la ciudad entramos en la biblioteca y **d** _____ libros. Luego visitamos el banco donde **e** _____ dinero. En la cafetería **f** _____ café o limonada. Después, en el parque, **g** _____ fotos de las flores, pero, claro, ¡no las **h** _____ ! A las tres **i** _____ el autobús a casa, pero **j** _____ mucho tiempo en llegar. Una vez en casa, **k** _____ la botella de aspirinas del armario y **l** _____ dos pastillas.

> cogimos   cogimos   cojo   llevar   sacamos   sacamos
> sacamos   saqué   tardamos   tomamos   tomé   tomé

84 Prepositions: *para*

This unit explains how to say *for* in Spanish.

A The bad news is that Spanish has two common words for *for*: **para** and **por**. The good news is that they have a difference in meaning and avoid ambiguity.

¿Quiere usted darme gasolina para mi coche?	*Would you give me some petrol for my car?*
¿Quiere usted darme cien libras por mi coche?	*Would you give me a hundred pounds for my car?*

In the first example, *for* means *to go into* and is translated by **para**; in the second example, *for* means *in exchange for* and is translated by **por**. This unit deals with **para**; see Unit 85 for the uses of **por**.

B **Para** = *for* (stresses destination, purpose, aim, achievement).

Salimos para Madrid.	*We are leaving for Madrid.*
Este regalo es para usted.	*This present is for you.*
Necesito una pieza para mi coche.	*I need a part for my car.*
Estudia para profesora.	*She's studying to be a teacher.*

C **Para** is used with an infinitive to mean *in order to*.

Trabajamos para comer.	*We work (in order) to eat.*

D **Para** tells when something is required.

Este ejercicio es para el lunes.	*This exercise is for Monday.*
¿Tiene usted una habitación para esta noche?	*Do you have a room for tonight?*

E **Para** is used with words like **siempre** and **entonces**.

Adiós para siempre.	*Goodbye for ever.*
Para entonces el tren había salido.	*By that time the train had left.*

F **Para** identifies a standard.

Para médico no sabe mucho.	*For a doctor he doesn't know very much.*

G **Para** also identifies someone's opinion.

Para mí, la corrida es cruel.	*The bullfight is cruel, as far as I'm concerned.*

84 Exercises

1 Translate the following into Spanish.

a This present is for my father.
b The train is leaving for Barcelona.
c Is the wine for me?
d I need a part for my radio.
e Do you have two rooms for the night?
f I think the book is interesting.
g Luisa is studying to be a doctor.
h She only lives to study.
i For a singer he has a terrible voice.
j We are forever friends.

2 Revise the disjunctive pronouns (see Unit 27) and give the correct forms after *para*.

E.g. Tenemos una carta para (*her*). → Tenemos una carta para ella.

a Tengo un regalo para (*you*), hijo.
b ¿Esta revista es para (*us*)?
c ¿Tienen ustedes una carta para (*me*)?
d Necesito una habitación para (*them*).
e Este paquete es para (*you*), señor.

3 Translate the following into English.

a Para padre no juega mucho con los hijos.
b Para él esta carta no significa nada.
c Juan estudia para mecánico.
d ¿Tiene usted un neumático para mi coche?
e Es un gran honor para nosotros.
f El avión había llegado para entonces.
g Necesito la reparación para mañana.
h Compramos un regalo para mi madre.
i Trabajamos mucho para vivir bien.
j Mi hermano ha salido para el colegio.

85 Prepositions: *por*

A Whereas **para** suggests aim or purpose, **por** stresses the reason or motivation behind an action.

Lo hizo por envidia.	*He did it for (= out of) spite.*
Gracias por el regalo.	*Thank you for the present.*
Te felicito por el resultado.	*I congratulate you for (= because of) the result.*
No pudimos salir por la lluvia.	*We couldn't go out for (= owing to) the rain.*
Lo hizo por su familia.	*He did it for (= for the sake of) his family.*
Se quejan por cualquier razón.	*They complain for any reason.*
¿Por qué no viniste?	*Why (= what for) didn't you come?*
Porque no tenía bastante dinero.	*Because I didn't have enough money.*
Fuimos al pueblo por pan.	*We went to the town for (= because we needed) bread.*

B **Por** is also used to express the means by which something is done.

Les mandé una carta por fax.	*I sent them a letter by fax.*
Tienes que ir por Madrid.	*You have to go by (= via) Madrid.*
No salgas por esas escaleras.	*Don't leave by those stairs.*

C **Por** suggests a vague location or time.

Por aquí no hay servicios públicos.	*There are no public toilets round here.*
La buscábamos por todas partes.	*We were looking for her everywhere.*
Trabajo por la tarde.	*I work in the afternoon.*

⚠ But **trabajo a las dos de la tarde** (*I work at 2 o'clock in the afternoon*) (precise time).

D **Por** is used for exchange or substitution.

Necesito euros por estas libras esterlinas.	*I need euro for these pounds.*
Preparé la comida por mi madre.	*I prepared the meal for (= instead of) my mother.*

85 Exercises

1 Use *por* to say who you did something for.

E.g. Preparé la comida (*for my mother*) → preparé la comida por mi madre.

a Lavé los platos (*for my mother*).
b Trabajamos en el jardín (*for my uncle*).
c Recogí las cartas (*for my neighbours*).
d Tomé la clase (*for the ill teacher*).
e Escribí la carta (*for the illiterate man* (**el analfabeto**)).

2 Translate the English expressions using *por*.

a El tren sale para Lisboa (*via Madrid*).
b Cambiamos el jersey (*for a shirt*).
c (*Round here*) hay muchos bares.
d Pagamos mucho dinero (*for the car*).
e Te buscaba (*everywhere*).
f Te mandaré una carta (*by fax*).
g No pudimos salir (*because of the sun*).
h Lo hicimos todo (*for the children*).
i Gracias (*for the present*).
j Fui a la ciudad (*for bread*).

3 *Por* and *para* contrasted. Revise *para* (see Unit 91) and translate the following into Spanish.

a I am studying for the exams.
b I am studying because of the exams.
c I am preparing the meal for my mother (she's hungry).
d I am preparing the meal for my mother (she's ill).
e I need this repair by today.
f That's all for today.
g I want petrol for my car.
h I want a bicycle for my car.
i He is working to become a doctor.
j He is working instead of the doctor.

86 Prepositions: *with* and *without*

This unit tells you how to order coffee with or without sugar.

A Con = *with*

¿Quieres salir con Julio? — *Do you want to go out with Julio?*

Prefiero café con leche. — *I prefer coffee with milk.*

Una botella de agua con gas, por favor. — *A bottle of fizzy water, please.*

B Con is also used to say what you use.

Abrí la caja con una llave. — *I opened the box with a key.*

C Con may be used with an infinitive.

Con pulsar este botón, puede llamar a la criada. — *By pressing this button you can call the maid.*

D Con also expresses attitude or behaviour.

Ana era muy simpática con nosotros. — *Ana was very kind to us.*

Eres descortés conmigo. — *You are rude to me.*

⚠ Remember special personal pronouns **conmigo** (*with me*) and **contigo** (*with you*) (see Unit 27).

E Con is used with some expressions of clothing and appearance.

¡Qué guapa estás con esa falda! — *How pretty you look in that skirt!*

F Con also translates **a pesar de** (*in spite of*).

Con tantas dificultades pudimos llegar a tiempo. — *With (= in spite of) all the difficulties, we managed to arrive on time.*

G Sin = *without*

Prefiero café sin azúcar. — *I prefer coffee without sugar.*

agua sin gas — *still mineral water*

H After sin, the article is frequently omitted.

Quisiera una habitación sin ducha. — *I'd like a room without a shower.*

I Sin needs to be followed by a negative expression, such as **nada** (*nothing*), **nadie** (*no one*) (see Unit 31).

Se fue sin nada. — *He went away without anything.*

86 Exercises

1 Put *con* or *sin* in the gaps to complete the sense.

a Soy vegetariano, necesito algo _____ carne.

b ¿Puede usted ayudarme? He salido _____ dinero.

c Prefiero té _____ limón porque me gusta la fruta.

d Café _____ azúcar, por favor. Tengo que guardar la línea.

e El estudiante salió _____ decir nada al profesor.

f No puedes ir _____ mí porque tengo las entradas.

g ¡No puedes abrir la botella _____ una cuchara!

h Para mí pescado _____ patatas. Muchas por favor.

i ¿Quieres venir _____ migo?

j _____ todos sus problemas tiene mucha paciencia.

2 Translate the following into English.

a ¿Tiene usted una habitación con baño?

b Con pulsar el botón, la puerta se abre.

c Salió sin decir nada a sus amigos.

d ¿Por qué estás enfadado conmigo?

e ¿Quiere usted carne con patatas o sin patatas?

f No quiere ir contigo, prefiere ir con ella.

g ¿Hay gasolina sin plomo?

h La caja está cerrada con llave.

3 Translate the following into Spanish.

a Still mineral water, please.

b Tea with lemon but without sugar.

c He is very kind to us.

d She looks elegant in that black dress.

e In spite of all his problems he studies a lot.

f You must tie the parcel with string.

g He always goes out without a key.

h Do you want a room with or without a bath?

i Twenty litres of unleaded petrol, please.

j He left without stealing anything.

87 Three common prepositions: *a, de, en*

A, de and en are three words which you will use over and over again to show directions, position or movement.

A **En** shows where something or someone is and usually translates *in, on* or *at*. It is frequently used with the verb **estar**.

Madrid está en España.	*Madrid is in Spain.*
Mi madre está en casa.	*My mother is at home.*
El libro está en la mesa.	*The book is on the table.*

B If there is likely to be any ambiguity, use **sobre** to translate *on* and **dentro de** to emphasise *inside*.

El periódico está sobre la mesa. *The newspaper is on the table.*
El pájaro está dentro de la casa. *The bird is inside the house.*

C **A** expresses movement. It is used with verbs of motion like **ir** (*to go*).

Vamos a Madrid, a España.	*Let's go to Madrid, to Spain.*
Mi madre va a casa.	*My mother is going home.*
Voy al trabajo.	*I'm going to work.*

⚠ Don't forget that **a** + **el** becomes **al**.

D A common exception is the verb **entrar** (*to go in*). This is usually followed by **en** in Spain (though American Spanish prefers the more logical **a**).

Todos los días entro en la clase.	*Everyday I go into the classroom.*

E **A** is sometimes used to show position, when **en** would invite ambiguity.

Estamos sentados al sol. *We're sitting in the sun (= shine).*

F Notice these expressions of transport.

en (el) coche (*by car*); en (el) autobús (*by bus*); en (el) tren (*by train*); en (el) avión (*by plane*); a pie (*on foot*); a caballo (*riding, on horseback*)

A is also used after **llegar** (*to arrive*).

El tren llega a la estación. *The train arrives at the station.*

G **A** is used without a specific meaning but to indicate a direct object which is a specific person or people.

Quiero a Julio. *I love Julio.*

H **De** shows either origin, possession or movement from.

Es el coche de mi padre.	*It's my father's car.*
Salgo del trabajo a las seis.	*I leave work at six.*
He recibido una carta de mi amigo.	*I've received a letter from my friend.*

⚠ Remember that **de** + **el** becomes **del**.

87 Exercises

1 Complete the sentences with *a*, *en*, *de* as necessary.

a Mi amigo trabaja _____ la fábrica _____ la ciudad.
b Mi amigo va _____ la fábrica _____ su coche.
c Sale _____ la fábrica _____ las seis y media y vuelve _____ casa.
d _____ casa prefiere sentarse _____ sol para leer.
e Pero _____ el jardín prefiere trabajar _____ la sombra.

2 Give the Spanish for the following.

a in the morning.
b on the beach.
c at work.
d at home.
e I'm going to church.
f I'm going home.
g I'm entering the room.
h They are arriving at the factory.
i I am leaving the house.
j He is leaving the office.

3 Decipher this message by putting in the missing *a, al, de, del* or *en*.

Julio, estoy **a** _____ la ciudad. Quiero ir **b** _____ mercado que está **c** _____ el centro cerca **d** _____ la plaza mayor. No puedo volver **e** _____ el autobús porque tengo que estar **f** _____ la casa **g** _____ mi amiga **h** _____ las cinco **i** _____ la tarde. Queremos sentarnos **j** _____ el balcón para criticar a los vecinos que están **k** _____ la costa **l** _____ vacaciones. Pero nosotras preferimos estar **m** _____ la sombra. ¿Quieres venir **n** _____ la ciudad **o** _____ tu coche para llevarme **p** _____ mercado **q** _____ la casa **r** _____ Luisa? No quiero ir **s** _____ pie. Gracias. Besos, Julia.

88 Compound prepositions of place

This unit summarizes prepositions that show location.

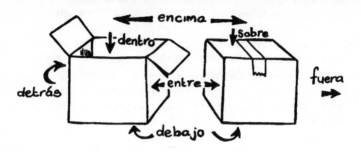

A Compound prepositions are followed by **de**.

encima (*over, above*); **debajo** (*under, below*); **detrás** (*behind*);
delante (*in front*); **dentro** (*inside*); **fuera** (*outside, away from*);
cerca (*near*); **lejos** (*far from*); **al lado** (*next to*); **más allá** (*beyond*)

Encima de las casas los pájaros volaban.	*Birds were flying over the houses.*
Debajo de la tierra había minas.	*Under the ground there used to be mines.*
Dentro de la casa todo estaba tranquilo.	*Inside the house, all was quiet.*
Ahora vivimos fuera de la ciudad, lejos del centro.	*Now we live out of town, far from the centre.*

B These prepositions can be used as adverbs by dropping the **de**.
¿Dónde está Luisa? Dentro.   *Where is Luisa? Inside.*

C They can be intensified by adding **por**.
Había basura por dentro   *There was rubbish inside*
y por fuera.   *and out.*

D Simple prepositions include: **entre** (*between*), **en** (*in*), **de** (*from*)
and **desde** (*from*).

Estaba sentada entre Juan y Julio.	*She was sitting between Juan and Julio.*
Hay un buen panorama desde la ventana.	*There's a good view from the window.*

⚠ These prepositions cannot be used as adverbs.

88 Exercises

1 Translate the following expressions.

a entre tú y yo
b desde el balcón
c en mi habitación
d fuera del restaurante
e encima de la casa
f debajo de la calle
g más allá del horizonte
h dentro de la mina

2 Give the Spanish for the following.

a inside the cinema
b outside the house
c near the school
d far from the city
e between the houses
f from my window

3 Fill in the gaps in this account of a deserted town using the words in the box.

a _____ el oeste, b _____ de la civilización, c _____ del desierto, hay un pueblo misterioso. Nadie vive d _____ las casas; pájaros negros vuelan e _____ de los techos arruinados y algunos animales viven ahora f _____ de las habitaciones abandonadas. g _____ del pueblo, h _____ de la iglesia, hay un cementerio, donde los cadáveres de los habitantes muertos duermen i _____ de la tierra. A veces, por las noches, se oyen gritos y unas figuras blancas caminan j _____ las ruinas. Nadie sabe la historia de este pueblo – ni su secreto.

> al lado   debajo   dentro   en   en   encima   entre
> fuera   lejos   más allá

4 This word puzzle uses prepositions. When you have completed it, you will find another preposition in the shaded boxes

a Hay una farmacia cerca _____ mi casa.
b No hay cine _____ este pueblo.
c El hotel está _____ la panadería y el restaurante.
d Hay algo duro _____ del paquete.
e Tenemos un jardín _____ de la casa.
f Hay un panorama magnífico _____ el balcón.

89 Prepositions: *before*

This unit looks at the different ways of expressing before.

A Antes de = *before* (time)

Antes de is a compound preposition used with a noun or an infinitive in expressions of time.

Antes de las nueve	*before nine o' clock*
Antes de Navidad	*before Christmas*
Antes de salir vamos a comer.	*Let's eat before we go out.*

B With **antes de** + infinitive, the subject of the two parts of the expression should be the same: *We go out, we eat.*

⚠ If the subjects are not the same, **antes de** becomes a conjunction **antes (de) que** and requires a subjunctive verb (see Unit 64).

Tenemos que hacerlo antes de que venga Juan.	*We must do it before Juan comes.*

C Ante (*before*) is used in figurative expressions. It is not followed by **de**.

Ante todo, tenemos que trabajar.	*First of all we must work.*
¿Qué podemos hacer ante tantos problemas?	*What can we do faced with (= before) such problems?*
Julio compareció ante el juez.	*Julio came up before the judge.*

D Delante de = *before, in front of* (used for position).

Hay un parque delante de la plaza.	*There's a park in front of the square.*
Mi coche está delante de la casa.	*My car is in front of the house.*

E Enfrente de means *facing* or *opposite*.

La farmacia está enfrente del hotel.	*The chemist's is opposite the hotel.*
Hay que hacer cola enfrente del letrero.	*We must queue up in front of (= facing) the notice.*

Frente a can also be used for *facing*.

La parada está frente a nuestra casa.	*The (bus) stop is opposite our house.*

1 Describe the pictures using *antes de, ante, delante de, enfrente de* or as appropriate.

2 Put *ante, antes de, delante de, enfrente de* as appropriate in the gaps. Remember that *de + el* becomes del!

a Por favor, lava los platos _____ salir.

b Mira, la leche está _____ la cafetera.

c Creo que hay un hotel _____ el parque.

d Es difícil dormir bien _____ estos problemas.

e Paco tuvo que comparecer _____ el director porque no había estudiado bien.

f Tenemos un jardín pequeño _____ nuestra casa.

g El profesor estaba _____ de la clase, hablando con los estudiantes.

h Juanito, por favor, tienes que terminarlo _____ las seis.

i Vamos a sentarnos aquí, _____ la otra gente.

j Luisa va a volver _____ septiembre.

3 Translate the following into Spanish.

a There is a café opposite the chemist's.

b We must arrive before eight.

c The singer appeared before his public.

d There is a car in front of our garage.

e The bus stop is opposite the school.

f Will you pay the bill before you leave?

g What can Pedro do faced with the bill?

h The square is in front of the hotel.

i I am going to Spain before September.

j Will you repair my car before Saturday?

90 Miscellaneous prepositions

This unit summarizes a number of useful prepositions.

A Hasta = *until*

| Vivimos aquí hasta septiembre. | *We are living here until September.* |
| Hasta la vista. | *Until we meet again, au revoir.* |

B Desde = *since* (of time)

| Vivimos aquí desde septiembre. | *We have been living here since September.* |

⚠ **Desde** also means *from* (see Unit 88).

| Hay una vista maravillosa desde la terraza. | *There's a wonderful view from the terrace.* |

C Sobre = *about, concerning*

| Es un libro sobre España. | *It's a book about Spain.* |

D Hacia = *towards*

| Caminaba hacia el pueblo. | *He was walking towards the town.* |

E Según = *according to*

| Según Julio, hay una fiesta mañana. | *According to Julio, there is a party tomorrow.* |

F Durante = *during*

| Trabajo durante las vacaciones. | *I work during the holidays.* |

G Excepto, menos, salvo = *except*

| Todos salieron, menos Luisa. | *They all left, except Luisa.* |

H Debajo de (*under*) is a compound preposition referring to physical location.

| Hay una moneda debajo de la mesa. | *There's a coin under the table.* |

I Bajo is used for *under* in figurative contexts. It is not followed by **de**.

| La vida bajo el dictador era difícil. | *Life under the dictator was difficult.* |

J Detrás de (*behind*) is a compound preposition used to show position.

| Hay un jardín detrás de la casa. | *There is a garden behind the house.* |

K Tras means *behind*, *after* in figurative expressions.

| día tras día, año tras año | *day after day, year after year* |

L Después de is the usual compound preposition meaning *after*.

| Estoy en casa después de las dos. | *I'm at home after two.* |

90 Exercises

1 Give the Spanish, for the following expressions.

a until tomorrow
b since yesterday
c since August
d until then
e a book about Madrid

f towards the park
g according to Luisa
h during the week
i on the table
j my attitude towards you

2 Complete the sentences with the appropriate preposition.

a Vamos a continuar aquí _____ octubre.
b Viven en Málaga _____ el año pasado.
c Hay una vista magnífica _____ nuestro balcón.
d Su actitud _____ su mujer es algo rara.
e Caminamos lentamente _____ el río.
f Todos _____ Julio jugaban al fútbol.
g Tengo que estudiar _____ la semana.
h _____ Pedro, hay una película buena hoy.
i ¿Tiene usted un libro _____ la cocina española?
j Por favor, no hablen _____ la película.

3 Pick the correct preposition.

a Necesito un libro de/sobre/durante los deportes.
b Vamos hacia/sobre/desde el mar.
c Julia tiene una actitud muy rara sobre/desde/hacia él.
d Los chicos comen caramelos durante/desde/sobre el programa.
e No trabajo desde/hacia/durante agosto – hay vacaciones.
f Estoy aquí hasta/desde/hacia las seis – ¿Por qué llegas tan tarde?
g Sobre/Hasta/Según mi profesor, el español es fácil.
h Todos los estudiantes según/salvo/sobre nosotros aprenden mucho.
i ¿Quieres acompañarme hasta/desde/sobre la plaza?
j Tengo un panorama estupendo desde/hacia/según mi habitación.

4 Give the Spanish for the following.

a under the table
b under the influence of the wine
c under the Liberals

d under the book
e under lock and key
f under the house.

5 Give the Spanish for the following.

a day after day
b after the war
c behind the house
d after lessons

e letter after letter
f behind the school
g after school
h after your problems

key to exercises

Unit 1: **1 a** eme a de ere i de **b** ese e uve i elle a **c** ge ere a ene a de a **d** be a ere ce e ele o ene a **e** te o ele e de o **f** ese i te ge e ese **g** a ere a ene jota u e zeta **2 a** profesor **b** posible **c** cero **d** millón **e** gorila **3 a** equator **b** LP **c** whisky **d** train **e** emphasis **f** symbol **4 a** suéter **b** fútbol **c** quiosco **d** champú **e** chófer **f** tenis **g** ¡gol! **h** cebra **5 a** be ce che de e efe ge ache i jota ka ele elle eme ene eñe o pe cu ere ese te u uve uve doble equis i griega zeta

Unit 2: **1 a** sí **b** si **c** mi **d** mí **e** tú **f** tu **g** como **h** cómo **2 a** ¿Dónde? **b** ¿Cuándo? **c** ¿Cómo? **d** ¿Qué? **e** ¿Por qué? **f** ¿Quién? **3 a** Madrid **b** Barcelona **c** Pedro **d** Elena **e** España **f** casa **g** hospital **h** universidad **i** ocupado **j** hablar **4 a** lámina **b** Dalí **c** Perú **d** Bogotá **e** límite **f** café **g** fútbol **h** médico **i** vídeo **j** récord **5 a** feroces; **b** francés; **c** posición; **d** resúmenes; **e** sigues; **f** hizo; **g** Paquita.

Unit 3: **1 a** el vino **b** la cerveza **c** la casa **d** el colegio **e** el chico **f** la chica **g** el periódico **h** la revista **i** la niña **j** el niño **2 a** la clase **b** la llave **c** el aceite **d** la gente **e** el cine **f** el garaje **g** la madre **h** el té **i** el café **j** el equipaje **k** la torre **3 a** la mujer **b** la niña **c** la madre **d** la chica **e** la cantante **4 a** el profesor **b** el señor **c** el cantante **d** el director **e** el padre **5 a** la tía **b** el hijo **c** la hermana **d** el tío **e** la hija **f** el hermano **g** la enfermera **h** la secretaria **i** el actor **j** la abuela **k** el marido **l** el abuelo **6 a** la italiana **b** el ruso **c** el secretario **d** la ministra **e** la camarera

Unit 4: **1 a** la luz **b** el arroz **c** la ciudad **d** la piel **e** el cartel **f** el papel **g** el andaluz **h** la habitación **i** el lápiz **j** la catedral **2 a** una luz **b** un arroz **c** una ciudad **d** una piel **e** un cartel **f** un papel **g** un andaluz **h** una habitación **i** un lápiz **j** una catedral **3 a** las luces **b** los arroces **c** las ciudades **d** las pieles **e** los carteles **f** los papeles **g** los andaluces **h** las habitaciones **i** los lápices **j** las catedrales **4 a** la casa **b** el lápiz **c** la ciudad **d** el cartel **e** la universidad **f** el papel **g** la luz **h** la habitación **i** el andaluz **j** la piel **5 a** los hijos y las hijas **b** los abuelos y las abuelas **c** los niños y las niñas **d** los hermanos y las hermanas **e** los sobrinos y las sobrinas **f** los nietos y las nietas **g** los padres y las madres

Unit 5: **1 a** la mano **b** la radio **c** la foto **d** la moto **e** la disco
2 a las manos **b** las radios **c** las fotos **d** las motos **e** las discos
3 a una mano **b** una radio **c** una foto **d** una moto **e** una disco
4 a Tengo una radio buena. **b** La foto de los niños es fantástica.
c La moto de Julio es rápida. **d** María es una modelo hermosa.
e la casa a la derecha. **f** la puerta a la izquierda. **g** Vamos a la disco.
h Hay muchas discos aquí. **i** Tengo un coche de segunda mano. **j** Dame
las manos.

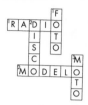

Unit 6: **1 a** una **b** un; la **c** una **d** una; un/el **e** el **f** un **g** el
h la; la **i** una/la **j** el **2 a** las modelos; **b** las discos; **c** los tranvías; **d** las
manos; **e** las motos; **f** los cometas **3 a** una **b** un **c** el
d el **e** el/un **f** la **g** el;la **h** la **i** el **j** la

Unit 7: **1 a** el valor **b** el champú **c** el lunes **d** el rubí **e** el amor **f** la
muchedumbre **g** la multitud **h** la crisis **i** la reunión **j** la serie **2 a** el
lavaplatos **b** el paraguas **c** el limpiacristales **d** el cumpleaños **3 a** los
lavaplatos **b** los paraguas **c** los limpiacristales **d** los cumpleaños
4 a Cuba (feminine) **b** Australia (feminine) **c** China (feminine) **d** España
(feminine) **5 a** un hacha **b** un agua **c** un harpa **d** un águila
6 a el
hacha **b** el agua **c** el harpa **d** el águila **7 a** las hachas **b** las aguas
c las harpas **d** las águilas.

Unit 8: **1 a** No me gustan los tomates. **b** El pan francés es muy bueno.
c ¿Te gusta el vino? **d** No bebo vino. **e** ¿Hay pan? **f** El español es difícil.
g Agua, por favor. **h** ¿Dónde vive el señor López? **i** ¿Qué quieres, vino o
café? **j** España es diferente. **k** La España de los turistas es
diferente.(feminine) **2 a** Spain is pretty. **b** Spanish is pretty. **c** Teresa
does not speak Spanish. **4.** We live in India. **e** I don't like Mr Gómez.
f Good morning, Mrs García. **3 a** Hablo español. **b** El señor Ortega no
habla inglés. **c** La Inglaterra del señor Blair es muy diferente. **d** No me
gusta el café. **e** No tengo vino. **f** No tengo el vino. **g** Vivimos en España.
h Vivimos en la España de los turistas. **i** ¿Dónde está la señorita García?
j Buenos días, señorita García.

Unit 9: **1 a** una naranja **b** un plátano **c** una manzana **d** un chico
e una niña **f** una mesa **g** un coche **h** una luz **i** una ciudad **j** un libro
2 a una habitación **b** un hospital **c** un hacha **d** una aldea **e** un arpa
f una autora **g** una actriz **h** un ala **3 a** unas casas **b** unos hombres
c unas tijeras **d** unos tirantes **e** unas legumbres **f** unos euros **g** unos
chicos **h** unas habitaciones **4 a** otra habitación **b** otro hombre
c otro coche **d** cierta chica **e** tal actriz **f** tales estudiantes **g** sin libro
h sin llave **5 a** Soy estudiante. **b** Somos mecánicos. **c** Tengo un libro.
d No tengo libro. **e** Tenemos una casa. **f** No tenemos coche.

Unit 10: **1 a** dieciséis años **b** un euro **c** cuatro casas **d** nueve meses **e**
diez chicas **f** veintiocho días **g** veintiún hombres **h** un águila **i** dos cervezas

2 a Una limonada, por favor. **b** Tres cervezas, por favor. **c** Dos cafés, uno con leche y un solo. **d** ¿Hay una mesa para cuatro? **e** Tres botellas de vino, una de blanco y dos de tinto. **3 a** tres más cuatro más dos son nueve **b** diez menos tres más cuatro son once **c** nueve más nueve más ocho son veintiséis **d** veintiuno menos diecisiete menos dos son dos **e** once más trece más cinco son veintinueve **4 a** veintiún euros **b** ciento veintiún libros **c** ciento treinta y una casa **d** cincuenta y un hombres **e** ochenta y una revistas **f** ciento una chicas **g** treinta y un niños **h** ciento sesenta y un cigarrillos **i** ciento noventa y una botellas **j** setenta y un estudiantes **5 a** La ciento sesenta y cuatro, por favor. **b** La cuarenta y cuatro, por favor. **c** La noventa y siete, por favor. **d** La cincuenta y seis, por favor. **e** La ciento uno, por favor. **f** La ciento cincuenta y ocho, por favor.

Unit 11: 1 a mil sesenta y seis **b** mil doscientos quince **c** mil cuatrocientos noventa y dos **d** mil quinientos ochenta y ocho **e** mil setecientos ochenta y nueve **f** mil ochocientos noventa y ocho **g** mil novecientos treinta y seis **h** mil novecientos cuarenta y cinco **i** dos mil **j** dos mil uno **2** Policía: ciento diecinueve; Hospital: ciento treinta y uno treinta y cuatro treinta y tres treinta y dos; Médico: cuatrocientos cincuenta y seis once doce trece; Dentista: doscientos treinta y cinco noventa y nueve ochenta y ocho setenta y siete; Garaje: setecientos setenta y nueve sesenta y cuatro cero seis cero cero; Restaurante: novecientos cuarenta y tres sesenta y siete quince ochenta y uno **3 a** Motor: mil novecientos ochenta y cuatro centímetros cuadrados **b** Potencia: ciento cincuenta caballos a seis mil revoluciones; **c** Neumáticos: ciento noventa y cinco **d** Dimensiones exteriores: tres coma ochenta y cinco/uno coma sesenta y cuatro/uno coma cuarenta y un metros **e** Velocidad máxima: doscientos dieciséis kilómetros por hora **f** Aceleración cero a un kilómetro: treinta coma cuatro segundos **g** Consumo: nueve litros en cien kilómetros **h** Precio: dieciocho mil quinientos euros

Unit 12: 1 a veintidós de mayo **b** dieciocho de enero **c** cinco de agosto **d** seis de marzo **e** ocho de abril **f** treinta de septiembre **g** quince de febrero **h** nueve de diciembre **2** Aries: veintiuno de marzo – veintiuno de abril **b** Tauro: veintidós de abril – veintiuno de mayo **c** Géminis: veintidós de mayo – veintiuno de junio **d** Cáncer: veintidós de junio – veintidós de julio **e** Leo: veintitrés de julio – veintidós de agosto **f** Virgo: veintitrés de agosto – veintidós de septiembre **g** Libra: veintitrés de septiembre – veintidós de octubre **h** Escorpio: veintitrés de octubre – veintidós de noviembre **i** Sagitario: veintitrés de noviembre – veintidós de diciembre **j** Capricornio: veintitrés de diciembre – veinte de enero **k** Acuario: veintiuno de enero – diecinueve de febrero **l** Piscis: veinte de febrero – veinte de marzo **3 a** enero **b** mayo **c** junio **d** febrero **e** abril **f** noviembre **g** diciembre **h** agosto **4 a** primavera **b** abril **c** diciembre **d** mayo **e** invierno **f** julio **5** invierno = *winter*, infierno = *hell* (junio, julio, agosto)

Unit 13: 1 a Son las diez y veinte de la mañana. **b** Son las dos y cinco de la tarde. **c** Son las nueve menos cuarto de la mañana. **d** Son las once y media de la mañana. **e** Es la una y pico de la tarde. **f** Son las nueve menos algo de la tarde. **g** Es la una y media de la madrugada. **h** Es la una menos cuarto la madrugada. **i** Son las dos en punto de la madrugada. **2 a** El tren sale a las diez de la mañana. **b** La película empieza a las cinco en punto. **c** Julio viene a las nueve y media. **d** Son las seis pasadas. **e** Mi reloj está atrasado. **f** Voy a salir a las diez menos algo. **g** Silencio – son las cinco de la madrugada. **h** ¿Tu reloj está adelantado? **i** Son las cuatro menos cuarto. **j** Son las tres y pico.

Unit 14: **1 a** Enrique octavo **b** Carlos quinto **c** Juan veintitrés
d Alfonso trece **e** Juan Carlos primero **f** el piso primero **g** el piso tercero
h el siglo séptimo **i** el piso once **j** el siglo veinte **2 a** El tercer tren sale
de Madrid a las diez veinticinco y llega a Pinto a las diez cuarenta y seis.
b El quinto tren sale de Villaverde Bajo a las catorce treinta y tres y llega a
Toledo a las quince cuarenta. **c** El primer tren sale de Aranjuez a las siete
cincuenta y uno y llega a Toledo a las ocho veinticinco. **d** El segundo tren de
la tarde sale de Madrid a las catorce veinticinco y llega a Aranjuez a las quince
siete. **e** El octavo tren sale de Valdemoro a las dieciocho cincuenta y dos y
llega a Aranjuez a las diecisiete ocho. **f** El último tren sale de Madrid a las
veinte cuarenta y tres y llega a Toledo a las veintiuno cuarenta y seis.

Unit 15: **1 a** hora **b** tiempo **c** hora **d** tiempo **e** veces **f** vez
g veces **h** tiempo **2 a** la primera vez **b** por primera vez **c** dos veces
d ¿Qué hora es? **e** No tenemos tiempo. **f** algunas veces **g** a veces
h raras veces **3 a** I have been to Spain many times. **b** I haven't got the
time (i.e. no watch!). **c** I haven't got (the) time (i.e. too busy!). **d** I am
writing for the last time. **e** We are here for the second time. **f** We seldom
visit him.
4

```
      V       H
T I E M P O
      Z       R
              A
```

Unit 16: **1 a** roja **b** blanca **c** amarilla **d** purpúrea **e** rosada
f verde **g** gris **h** marrón **i** celeste **2 a** español **b** italiano **c** inglés
d ruso **e** griego **f** irlandés **g** alemán **h** japonés **i** americano
j australiano **3 a** negras **b** pequeñas **c** ricas **d** bonitas
e hermosas **f** celestes **g** pobres **h** fáciles **i** difíciles **j** diferentes
4 a los chicos italianos **b** las casas azules **c** las revistas inglesas
d los actores americanos **e** las chicas trabajadoras **f** las esposas mandonas
g las faldas grises **h** las botas marrones **i** los hombres diferentes
j las chicas tristes **5 a** una chica bonita **b** las chicas bonitas **c** La casa
es blanca. **d** Las casas son blancas. **e** Las mujeres son inglesas. **f** La
revista es española. **g** Ana es trabajadora. **h** Luisa y María son
trabajadoras. **i** Kylie es australiana. **j** Las chicas son españolas.

Unit 17: **1 a** muchos libros **b** pocas casas **c** mucho vino **d** algunas
chicas **e** la blanca nieve **f** ambos hombres **g** bastante/suficiente dinero
h bastantes/suficientes euros **i** varios chicos **j** poco dinero **2 a** Vivimos
en una casa pequeña. **b** Hay una buena película en la televisión. **c** Algún
general vive aquí. **d** Es un gran hombre. **e** Es un hombre grande. **f** Vivo
en Gran Bretaña. **g** El pobre chico no tiene amigos. **h** El hombre pobre no
tiene dinero. **i** El tercer libro/El libro tercero no es bueno. **j** El primer
capítulo/El capítulo primero es malo.

Unit 18: **1 a** una pequeña casa blanca. **b** muchos niños y niñas.
c faldas y blusas amarillas. **d** chicas y profesoras bonitas. **e** chicas y chicos
trabajadores. **f** periódicos y revistas alemanes. **g** revistas y películas
españolas. **h** un gran general importante. **i** un general grande e importante.
j un buen libro inglés. **2 a** unas botas verde oscuro **b** una camisa (de
color) naranja **c** una falda amarillo claro **d** unos calcetines gris oscuro
e unos vaqueros azul claro **f** una blusa café **g** la casa piloto **h** los coches
modelo **3 a** Quiero ver la casa piloto. **b** Lleva una falda verde oscuro.
c Vivimos en una pequeña casa azul. **d** Hay un pequeño coche

(de color) naranja en el garaje. e ¿Tiene usted algunos libros y revistas españoles? 4 a pequeño b bonito c muchas d viejas e grandes f bonitos g amarillas h azules i azul claro j raras k curiosos l diferente

Unit 19: 1 a diferentemente b difícilmente c fácilmente d formalmente e naturalmente f elegantemente g mayormente h principalmente i inteligentemente j cruelmente k evidentemente l responsablemente m raramente n rápidamente o claramente p estupendamente q lentamente r nerviosamente s calmadamente t tranquilamente u seriamente v francamente w divinamente x furiosamente **2** a sinceramente b bien c inteligentemente d puntualmente e mal f rápidamente g seriamente h sinceramente i cuidadosamente **3** a clara y tristemente b mal y lentamente c seria y profesionalmente d rápida y peligrosamente e poco y bajo f intensa y responsablemente g lenta e inteligentemente h mucho y bien i bien y elegantemente

Unit 20: 1 a Julia tiene más vestidos que Luisa. b Ignacio bebe más vino que Francisco. c Madrid tiene más habitantes que Granada. d Yo hablo más español que inglés. e Los españoles comen más carne que pescado. **2** a No como tanta carne como Luisa. b No escribo tantas cartas como mi madre. c No compro tanto pescado como tú. d No recibo tanto dinero como mi jefe. e No soy tan inteligente como el profesor. **3** a que b de lo que c de la que d que e de los que f de las que g del que h que i de

Unit 21: 1 a Barcelona es más grande que Sevilla pero menos grande que Madrid. b Carlos es más valiente que Federico pero menos valiente que Juan. c Luisa conduce más rápidamente que mi hermana pero menos rápidamente que Julia. d Paco canta mejor que Miguel pero peor que Julio. e La torre es más alta que la iglesia pero menos alta que la catedral. f El general es más importante que el ministro pero menos importante que el presidente. g El teatro es más caro que el cine pero menos caro que la ópera. h El actor es más famoso que la actriz pero menos famoso que el director. i El pescado es mejor que la carne pero peor que la fruta. j Mi novia es más guapa que mi hermana pero menos guapa que tu esposa. **2** a Barcelona es tan grande como Sevilla pero no es tan grande como Madrid. b Carlos es tan valiente como Federico pero no es tan valiente como Juan. c Luisa conduce tan rápidamente como mi hermana pero no conduce tan rápidamente como Julia. d Paco canta tan bien como Miguel pero no canta tan bien como Julio. e La torre es tan alta como la iglesia pero no es tan alta como la catedral. f El general es tan importante como el ministro pero no es tan importante como el presidente. g El teatro es tan caro como el cine pero no es tan caro como la ópera. h El actor es tan famoso como la actriz pero no es tan famoso como el director. i El pescado es tan bueno como la carne pero no es tan bueno como la fruta. j Mi novia es tan guapa como mi hermana pero no es tan guapa como tu esposa. **3** Individual answers.

Unit 22: 1 a el periódico más leído del mundo b la película más vista del año c el chocolate más rico de Europa d el coche más popular del continente e la piel más suave de todas f el banco más cooperativo de América g la música más vibrante de la capital h las playas más limpias de la costa i los precios más económicos de la ciudad j la selección más variada de la región **2** a Tengo el coche más viejo de la compañía. b Tengo el peor asiento del teatro. c Tengo la secretaria menos trabajadora de la oficina. d Tengo el colega más hablador del departamento. e Tengo la esposa más fea del mundo. f Tengo el dolor más terrible de todo. g Tengo el dentista menos simpático del pueblo. **h** Tengo el día más aburrido de la fábrica. **i** Tengo las vacaciones menos largas del colegio. **j** Tengo el plato más asqueroso del restaurante. **3** Suggested answers. **a** Es sabrosísimo. **b** Es rapidísimo. **c** Es comodísima. **d** Es elegantísimo. **e** Es buenísima. **f** Son riquísimas. **g** Son dulcísimos. **h** Son facilísimos. **i** Son guapísimas. **j** Son vivísimas.

Unit 23: **1 a** este **b** estas **c** esta **d** estos **e** estas **f** este **g** esta **h** estos **2 a** ese **b** esas **c** esa **d** esos **e** esas **f** ese **g** esa **h** esos **3 a** aquel **b** aquellas **c** aquella **d** aquellos **e** aquellas **f** aquel **g** aquella **h** aquellos **4 a** ésta **b** eso **c** aquéllas **d** éste **e** aquélla **5 a** ¿Ésa o ésta? **b** ¿Aquél o éste? **c** ¿Éstas o ésas? **d** ¿Éstos o aquéllos? **e** ¿Éstos o ésos? **6 a** Aquellos chicos son inteligentes. **b** ¿Qué estudiantes son aquéllos? **c** ¿Qué es aquello? ¿Es carne? **d** Esta chica es muy bonita. **e** Ésta es mi hermana. **f** Aquellas montañas son bonitas. **g** ¿Qué montañas son aquéllas? **h** ¿Qué es esto? **i** ¿Qué chica es ésa? **j** ¿De quién es aquella falda?

Unit 24: **1 a** nuestras hermanas **b** tus coches **c** sus habitaciones **d** vuestras universidades **e** mis clases **f** sus bicicletas **g** nuestros amigos **h** sus casas **i** mis revistas **j** tus periódicos **2 a** su casa de ellas **b** sus casas de ellos **c** su hermana de ella **d** sus hermanas de ella **e** su periódico de usted **f** su periódico de ustedes **g** su padre de él **h** su padre de ella **i** sus padres de ellas **j** sus padres de él **3 a** No, es mi coche. **b** No, es tu vino. **c** No, es su revista de ella. **d** No, son nuestras botas. **e** No, son sus periódicos de ellas. **4 a** Su periódico es interesante, señor. **b** Nuestra casa es pequeña y blanca. **c** ¿Tienes mis botas? **d** Su coche (de ellos) es verde. **e** Sus vaqueros (de ella) son azules. **f** Juanito, ¿quieres tu camisa? **g** Nuestro dinero está en el banco. **h** Mis padres viven en su casa de él. **i** Su casa de ellos está en Madrid. **j** Hijos, vuestros calcetines están aquí.

Unit 25: **1 a** ... pero el mío es más rápido. **b** ... pero la mía es más inteligente. **c** ... pero los míos son más trabajadores. **d** ... pero las mías son más estúpidas. **e** ... pero el mío es más difícil. **f** ... pero la mía es más bonita. **g** ... pero la mía es más hermosa. **h** ... pero las mías son más elegantes. **i** ... pero el mío es más famoso. **j** ... pero las mías son más ricas. **2 a** Tengo las mías pero las tuyas están en casa. **b** Tengo la mía pero la tuya está en casa. **c** Tengo el mío pero el tuyo está en casa. **d** Tengo los míos pero los tuyos están en casa. **e** Tengo los míos pero los tuyos están en casa. **3 a** mi casa y la de usted **b** mi coche y el de Julio **c** mis padres y los de ellos **d** mi dinero y el de ella **e** mis vaqueros y los de él **4 a** Esta casa es tuya. **b** Estos vaqueros son nuestros. **c** Estas faldas son vuestras. **d** Este dinero es (el) de usted. **e** Esta camisa es mía. **f** Este coche es de Julio. **g** Este vino es (el suyo) de ella. **h** Estos amigos son (los suyos) de él.

Unit 26: **1 a** yo **b** nosotros **c** vosotros **d** ustedes **e** Ella; él **f** usted **2 a** yo **b** nosotros **c** vosotros **d** vosotras **e** ustedes **f** usted **3 a** Tú vas a Madrid, pero yo voy a Barcelona. **b** Vosotros coméis carne, pero nosotros comemos pescado. **c** Nosotras somos profesoras, pero vosotras sois alumnas. **d** Ellas viven en el campo, pero ellos viven en la ciudad. **e** Yo prefiero vino, pero usted prefiere cerveza. **f** Ustedes escuchan música clásica, pero yo escucho música pop.

Unit 27: **1 a** ti **b** él **c** usted **d** ustedes **e** nosotros **f** vosotros **g** vosotras **h** nosotras **2 a** mí **b** conmigo **c** mí **d** mí **e** yo **f** yo **3 a** con él **b** consigo **c** consigo **d** con ella **e** con él **f** con ellos

Unit 28: **1 a** La tengo. **b** Los tengo. **c** Las tengo. **d** Lo tengo. **e** Lo tengo. **f** La tengo. **2 a** Te oigo. **b** Os oigo. **c** Lo oigo/Le oigo. **d** Te oigo. **e** Os oigo. **f** Los oigo. **g** Las oigo. **h** Os oigo. **3 a** No la he bebido, voy a beberla. **b** No la he limpiado, voy a limpiarla. **c** No me he duchado, voy a ducharme. **d** No lo he conducido, voy a conducirlo. **e** No los he visto, voy a verlos. **f** No las he lavado, voy a lavarlas.

Unit 29: **1 a** Te doy la limonada, hijo. **b** Nos entrega la limonada. **c** Me da la limonada. **d** Le digo la verdad. **e** Les entregamos el vino. **f** Le damos el libro. **g** Le doy un descuento, señor. **h** Les entrego el paquete, señor y señora. **2 a** Te doy a ti la limonada, hijo. **b** Nos entrega a nosotros la limonada. **c** Me da la limonada a mí. **d** Le digo a él la verdad. **e** Les entregamos a ellos el vino. **f** Le damos el libro a ella. **g** Le doy a usted un descuento, señor. **h** Les entrego a ustedes el paquete, señor y señora. **3 a** Me lo dice. **b** Quiero hablarle/Le quiero hablar **c** No puedo decírtelo./No te lo puedo decir. **d** Te las entregamos. **e** Te lo doy. **f** Nos lo presenta. **4 a** No puedo decirlo. **b** Quiero decírselo. **c** No quiero darles un descuento. **d** No quiero dárselo. **e** No queremos entregárselo. **f** ¿Por qué no quieres darme el vino? **g** ¿Por qué no quieres dármelo? **h** Voy a pagárselo. **i** No puedo confesártelo. **j** ¿No vas a preguntármelo?

Unit 30: **1 a** algunas **b** alguna **c** algún **d** algunos **e** algún **f** algunos **g** algunas **2 a** algo **b** alguien **c** Alguna **d** algo **e** alguna parte **f** alguna parte **g** Alguien **h** algunos **i** algún **j** algo **3 a** cualquier **b** cualquier **c** cualquier **d** Cualquiera **e** Cualesquiera **f** cualquiera **g** cualquier

Unit 31: **1 a** Yo no estudio mucho. **b** Luisa no tiene entradas. **c** Nosotros no nos levantamos tarde. **d** Usted no lo ha visto. **e** Ellos no se han levantado. **f** Esta paella no le gusta. **2 a** Tú nunca comes patatas. **b** Juan nunca llega tarde. **c** Nadie me ha ayudado en la casa. **d** Ningún español vive aquí. **e** Nada es interesante aquí. **f** Ninguna chica trabaja mucho. **3 a** Tú no comes patatas nunca. **b** Juan no llega tarde nunca. **c** No me ha ayudado nadie en la casa. **d** No vive aquí ningún español. **e** No es interesante aquí nada. **f** No trabaja mucho ninguna chica. **4 a** no **b** Nunca **c** ningunos **d** nadie **e** No **f** nunca **g** ningún **h** ningún **i** nada **5 a** No como patatas nunca./Nunca como patatas. **b** Julio habla español pero no habla portugués. **c** No quedan (ningunas) entradas para el cine. **d** Luisa nunca me ayuda./Luisa no me ayuda nunca. **e** Juan nunca se levanta tarde./Juan no se levanta tarde nunca. **f** Luisa no conoce a nadie aquí. **g** Tú nunca ayudas a nadie. **h** Nadie nunca bebe nada en este pueblo. **i** Aquí no me gusta nada. **j** No vuelvo nunca jamás.

Unit 32: **1 a** tampoco **b** ni; ni **c** tampoco **d** ni **e** tampoco **f** nada **g** nunca **h** ya no **2 a** todavía **b** Ya **c** ya **d** Todavía **e** Todavía **f** todavía; ya **g** ya; todavía **h** ya **3 a** Nada. **b** Nunca. **c** En absoluto. **d** Ya no. **e** Ningunos. **f** Nadie. **g** Nada. **h** En la vida. **i** Todavía/Aún no. **j** Tampoco.

Unit 33: **1 a** La chica que canta bien es la hermana de Luisa. **b** El vino que se hace aquí no me gusta. **c** La fruta que se vende en el mercado es mala. **d** El libro que me recomendaste fue interesante. **e** El hotel en que nos quedamos era muy caro. **f** El mecánico que repara mi coche trabaja bien. **2 a** Estos actores, quienes son los protagonistas principales, reciben mucho dinero. **b** Las actrices a quienes viste anoche son populares. **c** El inglés a quien conocimos en Londres es profesor de idiomas. **d** Los cantantes de quienes hablábamos han grabado un disco nuevo. **e** Julio, con quien salía Luisa, se ha marchado a América. **f** El niño a quien diste el dinero

lo ha perdido todo. **3 a** del cual **b** la cual **c** la cual **d** los cuales
e el cual **f** las cuales

Unit 34: 1 a Qué **b** Quién **c** Qué **d** Quiénes **e** Qué **f** Qué
g Quién **h** Quiénes **2 a** Quién **b** A quién **c** Quién **d** Quién
e A quién(es) **f** Con quién **g** Quién **h** A quién **i** De quién **j** Con
quién(es) **3 a** Cuáles/Cuál **b** Qué **c** Cuál **d** Cuál **e** Cuáles **f** Qué
g Cuál **h** Cuál

Unit 35: 1 a Dónde **b** qué **c** Cuántos **d** Quién **e** Cuál/Cuáles
f Por qué **g** Cuántas **h** Cómo **i** Qué **j** Adónde **2 a** ¿Quién?
b ¿Adónde? **c** ¿Cómo? **d** ¿Cuándo? **e** ¿Cuántos? **f** ¿Cuáles? **g** ¿Por
qué? **h** ¿(Para) Quiénes? **i** ¿Dónde? **j** ¿Por qué? **3 a** Cuáles **b** Qué
c Dónde **d** Quiénes **e** Cuánto **f** Cómo **g** Cuántos **h** Qué **i** Quién
j Cuál

Unit 36: 1 a Tengo una casa y un jardín. **b** Luisa habla inglés y español.
c Tenemos un coche y dos bicicletas. **d** Ana sale con Pedro y Julio.
e Muchos chicos y chicas estudian en el colegio. **2 a** Prefiero pescado o
carne. **b** Usted es alemán o inglés. **c** Bebo cerveza o vino. **d** Pasamos las
vacaciones en la playa o en la montaña. **e** Julio quiere ser profesor o
mecánico. **3 a** e **b** y **c** y **d** e **e** y **f** y **g** y **4 a** u **b** o **c** u
d u **e** o **f** u **g** u **h** o **i** u **j** o

Unit 37: 1 a Pedro vive en Madrid pero no es madrileño.
b Alberto vive en Lisboa pero no habla portugués. **c** Mi padre es mecánico
pero no tiene coche. **d** Vivimos en la costa pero no nos gusta la playa.
2 a No como patatas sino legumbres. **b** No es española sino americana.
c No estoy casado sino soltero. **d** No hablo italiano sino inglés. **3 a** pero
b sino **c** pero **d** pero **e** sino **f** pero **g** sino **h** sino **i** pero **j** sino
4 a Julio y Julia comen naranjas o uvas. **b** Héctor e Ignacio no comen
pescado ni fruta pero comen mucho. **c** ¿Su esposa es María u Octavia?
d Ni María ni Octavia sino Luisa. **e** No habla francés e italiano sino español
e inglés.

Unit 38: 1 a hablamos **b** comemos **c** vivimos **d** comes **e** vive
f comen **g** habla **h** como **i** vivís **j** hablan **2 a** bebo, bebes, bebe,
bebemos, bebéis, beben **b** fumo, fumas, fuma, fumamos, fumáis, fuman
c leo, lees, lee, leemos, leéis, leen **d** escribo, escribes, escribe, escribimos,
escribís, escriben **e** charlo, charlas, charla, charlamos, charláis, charlan
3 a bebe **b** Vivimos **c** Escribes **d** Fuman **e** Charlo **f** Lee
g Visitamos **h** Come **4 a** Comemos paella. **b** Fuman cigarrillos.
c Visito la catedral. **d** Juan lee un libro. **e** Charlamos con amigos.
f Beben vino. **g** Vive en Madrid. **h** Bebe/Beben vino.

Unit 39: 1 a salgo; salimos **b** pongo; ponemos **c** hago; hacemos
d traigo; traemos **e** caigo; caemos **2 a** doy; damos **b** voy; vamos **c** sé;
sabemos **d** conduzco; conducimos **e** conozco; conocemos **f** veo; vemos
3 a traduzco **b** produzco **c** parezco **d** aparezco **e** ofrezco
f introduzco **g** reduzco **h** obedezco **4 a** traducen **b** producen
c parecen **d** aparecen **e** ofrecen **f** introducen **g** reducen **h** obedecen
5 a Producimos el dinero. **b** Conozco Madrid. **c** Traduce el libro.
d Voy a Madrid. **e** Sé español. **f** Soy español. **g** Doy el vino. **h** Ve la
película. **i** Parece triste. **j** Aparezco en la televisión.

Unit 40: 1 a oigo; oyes **b** ofrezco; ofreces **c** sigo; sigues **d** cojo; coges
e conozco; conoces **f** huyo; huyes **g** río; ríes **h** escojo; escoges
i prohíbo; prohíbes **j** continúo; continúas **2 a** yerro; erramos **b** río;
reímos **c** envío; enviamos **d** continúo; continuamos **e** huelo; olemos

.

.

3 a ríe **b** cojo **c** escoge **d** conozco **e** huyen **f** oye **g** envías
h huele **i** continúan **j** prohíbe **4 a** Oímos la música. **b** Escojo un
regalo. **c** El niño huye. **d** Envía una carta. **e** Las patatas huelen bien.
f Seguimos el coche. **g** Julio y Luisa ríen en el cine. **h** ¿Reís, niños/hijos?
i Las chicas cogen flores. **j** Ofrezco el vino.

Unit 41: 1 a eres **b** es **c** son **d** soy **e** es **f** sois **g** es **2 a** están
b está **c** están **d** están **e** está **f** estamos **g** Está; está **h** estáis
i estoy **j** están **3 a** es **b** está **c** es **d** está **e** son **f** están **g** estás

Unit 42: 1 a es **b** somos **c** son **d** son **e** eres **f** soy **2 a** está
b están **c** estoy **d** estamos **e** estás **j** está **3 a** soy; **b** estoy; **c** es;
d es; **e** estoy; **f** estoy; **g** están; **h** están; **i** está; **j** es; **k** son; **l** es;
m es; **n** está; **o** está

Unit 43: 1 a hablando **b** fumando **c** buscando **d** viendo
e bebiendo **f** leyendo **g** escribiendo **h** viviendo **i** pidiendo
j durmiendo **2 a** estamos estudiando **b** estamos riendo **c** está muriendo
d están robando **e** estoy aprendiendo **f** estáis saliendo **g** estás
escribiendo **h** está esperando **i** estamos siguiendo **j** están repitiendo
3 a cantando **b** brillando **c** volando **d** haciendo **e** saltando
f preparando **g** leyendo **h** riendo **i** viendo **j** repitiendo **k** jugando
l corriendo **m** acercando

Unit 44: 1 a dicen **b** friegas **c** pierdo **d** vuelvo, vuelves; vuelve;
vuelven **e** ríes; ríe; ríen **2 a** visto **b** sirve **c** hierve **d** pienso
e tienen **f** sonríe **g** sigue **h** vienen **i** repiten **j** Dicen **k** quieren
l cuentan **m** reímos **n** ríen **o** divierten **p** puedo **q** pierdo **r** sonrío
s pido **t** vuelvo **u** siento **v** duermo **w** duerme **x** tiene

Unit 45: 1 a te lavas **b** nos levantamos **c** os ducháis **d** se bañan
e me baño **f** nos ponemos **g** se viste **h** te levantas **i** nos bañamos
2 a levantarse **b** ducharse **c** bañarse **d** vestirse **e** maquillarse
f lavarse **g** acostarse **h** ponerse **i** divertirse **3 a** Me lavo. **b** Lavo el
coche. **c** Nos bañamos en el mar. **d** Baño al bebé. **e** Nos levantamos.
f Levantamos la botella. **g** Ella se acuesta. **h** Ella acuesta al bebé.
i Se levantan. **j** Me pongo el pijama. **4 a** Me levanto. **b** Me ducho.
c Me visto. **d** Me acuesto.

Unit 46: 1 a tú te vas **b** yo me marcho **c** usted se pasea
d ellos se corren **e** él se cae **f** nosotros nos vamos **g** ellos se escapan
h tú te marchas **i** nosotros nos perdemos **j** ellas se pasean **2 a** se para
b para **c** pierdo **d** me pierdo **e** se cae **f** caen **g** detiene **h** se
detiene **i** mover **j** moverse **3 a** vas a bañarte; te vas a bañar **b** (usted)
va a perderse; (usted) se va a perder **c** vamos a ponernos; nos vamos a poner
d van a divertirse; se van a divertir **e** vais a lavaros; os vais a lavar **f** van a
vestirse; se van a vestir **g** va a escaparse; se va a escapar **h** vas a caerte; te
vas a caer

Unit 47: 1 a beben mucho vino **b** tienen una fiesta típica **c** toman el sol
d nadan en el mar **e** visitan la catedral **f** comen bien **g** no trabajan mucho
h ganan mucho dinero **2 a** se habla portugués. **b** se bebe mucho **c** Se
estudia mucho **d** Se sale por las escaleras **e** se fuma mucho **f** se come bien
g se trabaja mucho **h** se vive bien **3 a** uno se levanta tarde **b** uno se
acuesta a las dos **c** uno se siente mal **d** uno no se despierta hasta mediodía
e uno no se acuerda del trabajo **f** uno se duerme **4 a** ¿Se puede pagar con
dinero inglés? **b** ¿Se puede telefonear? **c** ¿Se puede comprar sellos? **d** ¿Se
puede sacar fotos? **e** ¿Se puede cambiar dinero? **f** ¿Se puede usar una tarjeta
de crédito? **g** ¿Se puede nadar? **h** ¿Se puede visitar la catedral?

Unit 48: **1** **a** A María no le gusta el vino blanco. **b** A Julio y Julia les gusta el teatro. **c** (A mí) no me gusta trabajar. **d** A Julia le gusta salir con Julio. **e** ¿(A ti) te gusta la paella? **f** (A nosotros) no nos gustan las novelas románticas. **g** Al padre le gusta su casa. **h** A los españoles no les gusta la comida inglesa. **i** A Julio le gusta beber y fumar. **j** A las inglesas les gusta ir a España. **2** **a** Me gustaban las tortillas antes, pero ya no. **b** Me gustaba estudiar antes, pero ya no. **c** Me gustaba nadar y tomar el sol antes, pero ya no. **d** Me gustaba beber los vinos dulces antes, pero ya no. **e** Me gustaban los vinos secos antes, pero ya no. **3** **a** Julio fue al cine y le gustó; Julia fue al cine pero no le gustó nada. **b** Yo probé el vino y me gustó; mi marido probó el vino pero no le gustó nada. **c** Julio y Julia visitaron el museo y les gustó; Juan y Juana visitaron el museo pero no les gustó nada. **d** Julia vio las películas y le gustaron; Julio vio las películas pero no le gustaron nada. **e** Julia y yo comimos en el restaurante y nos gustó; tú y María comisteis en el restaurante pero no os gustó nada.

Unit 49: **1** **a** 4 **b** 1 **c** 3 **d** 5 **e** 2 **2** **a** duele **b** hace falta **c** hacen falta; quedan **d** chifla **e** encanta **f** importa **g** toca **h** falta **i** conviene **j** sienta **3** **a** A Luisa le duele el diente. **b** Le hace falta ir al dentista. **c** Usted me hace daño, doctor. **d** A Julio le chiflan los coches. **e** A Julia no le importa un pepino. **f** A Juan le toca cantar. **g** Te queda un euro. **h** No te sienta bien el azul. **i** Me encantan las patatas. **j** ¿Te conviene mañana?

Unit 50: **1** **a** Es difícil alquilar un coche. **b** Está prohibido aparcar aquí. **c** Es más rápido ir en taxi. **d** Más vale ir al taller. **e** Es preferible comer temprano. **2** **a** A Julia le hace falta salir. **b** Nos es posible quedar aquí. **c** A Julia y Julio les es fácil hablar. **d** Te hace falta dormir. **e** Al profesor se le prohíbe entrar. **3** **a** Es preferible que Julio no cante. **b** Es inútil que nosotros rehusemos. **c** Es probable que mi padre visite Madrid. **d** Es preciso que los estudiantes estudien mucho. **e** Es injusto que tú pagues siempre.

Unit 51: **1** **a** saltó **b** abrimos **c** corrieron **d** cerré **e** escuchasteis **f** nos sentamos **g** volvieron **h** sentiste **i** contestaron **j** repetí **2** Suggested answers. **a** ¿A qué hora te levantaste? **b** ¿Cuántos años vivieron ustedes allí? **c** ¿Cuánto costó el libro? **d** ¿Qué bebiste? **e** ¿Te gustó la película? **f** ¿Dónde comiste? **g** ¿Cómo viajaron ustedes? **h** ¿Cómo pasaron ustedes el día? **i** ¿Qué decidiste comprar? **j** ¿A qué hora salió el tren? **3** **a** acosté **b** dormí **c** oí **d** desperté **e** senté **f** escuché **g** grité **h** contestó **i** sentí **j** volví **k** empecé **l** llamó **m** salté **n** corrí **o** abrí **p** descubrí **q** repetí **r** movió **s** acercó **t** reconocí **u** vi **v** cerré **w** decidí

Unit 52: **1** **a** dormí, dormiste **b** pidió, pedimos **c** sintió, sentisteis **d** durmió, durmieron **e** sentí, sintieron **f** murieron, murió **g** repetiste, repitió **h** me divertí, se divirtió **i** sirvió, servimos **j** seguí, siguieron **2** **a** pedí **b** sirvió **c** repetí **d** pidió **e** repetí **f** repitió **g** repetí **h** pidió **i** siguió **j** sirvió **k** pedí **3** **a** Fui **b** Fue **c** Fuisteis **d** Fueron **e** Fue **f** Fui **g** Fue **h** Fuimos **i** Fueron **j** Fue **k** Fue **l** Fui **m** Fue **n** Fuimos **o** Fue

Unit 53: **1** **a** Hice una tortilla ayer. **b** Estuve en el jardín ayer. **c** Dije la verdad ayer. **d** Conduje el coche ayer. **e** Puse la mesa ayer. **2** **a** Lo hicimos todos. **b** Lo tradujimos todos. **c** Estuvimos allí todos. **d** Condujimos todos. **e** Pusimos la mesa todos. **f** Pudimos comer todo el chocolate todos. **3** **a** quiso **b** dijo **c** produjo **d** hizo **e** puso **f** dijo **g** dijeron **h** dije **i** puse **j** dijo **k** supo **l** hicieron **m** pudo n conducjeron   o vinieron   p tuvieron   q pusieron.

Unit 54:   1 a Hablaba con Pedro.   **b** Íbamos a la ciudad.   **c** Bebía vino tinto.   **d** Cantaba una canción romántica.   **e** Eran las profesoras de mi hija.   **f** Pensábamos ir en coche.   **g** Jugaban al fútbol.   **h** Veía una telenovela.   **i** Solía comprar la fruta en el mercado.   **j** Solían fumar tabaco negro.   **2 a** Cantaba antes, pero ya no.   **b** Éramos estudiantes antes, pero ya no.   **c** Luisa nadaba antes, pero ya no.   **d** Practicabas deportes antes, pero ya no.   **e** Iba de paseo antes, pero ya no.   **f** Julio e Isabel escribían antes, pero ya no.   **g** Estudiábamos antes, pero ya no.   **h** Ustedes veían los partidos antes, pero ya no.   **i** Ayudabais antes, pero ya no.   **j** Leía mucho antes, pero ya no.   **3 a** éramos   **b** vivíamos   **c** vivían   **d** era   **e** trabajaba   **f** volvía   **g** comíamos   **h** jugábamos   **i** iba   **j** entraba   **k** estaba   **l** bebía   **m** veía   **n** dormía   **o** pasábamos   **p** acostábamos   **q** esperábamos

Unit 55:   1 a estabas; sonó   **b** preparaba; fui   **c** pasábamos; robó   **d** estaba; trató   **e** hacía; ocurrió   **f** éramos; fuimos   **g** veían; cogió   **h** era; llegaste   **2 a** Hacía frío cuando Luisa compró la fruta.   **b** El sol brillaba cuando mi madre fue a la ciudad.   **c** Llovía cuando nosotros entramos.   **d** Nevaba cuando mi padre fue a trabajar.   **e** Hacía viento cuando salí a nadar.   **f** Hacía sol cuando los estudiantes comenzaron a estudiar.   **3 a** Hacía   **b** decidimos   **c** Hacía   **d** pusimos   **e** quería   **f** persuadió   **g** venía   **h** cogimos   **i** llovía   **j** salimos   **k** Eran   **l** llegamos   **m** entramos   **n** Era   **o** estaba   **p** oyó   **q** Fue   **r** empezó   **s** tuvimos   **t** llegamos   **u** estábamos   **v** estaba   **w** movía   **x** podía

Unit 56:   1 a Pagaré la cuenta mañana.   **b** Contestará a la carta mañana.   **c** Repararán el coche mañana.   **d** Veremos la película mañana.   **e** Volverás a casa mañana.   **f** Escribirá la carta mañana.   **g** Irá a la ciudad mañana.   **h** Dormiremos aquí mañana.   **i** Me levantaré temprano mañana.   **j** Os bañaréis en el mar mañana.   **2 a** Tendré el dinero mañana.   **b** Dirán la verdad mañana.   **c** Harás una paella mañana.   **d** Saldrán mañana.   **e** Me pondré el traje mañana.   **f** Valdrá la pena mañana.   **g** Vendrá conmigo mañana.   **h** Podrá reparar el coche mañana.   **i** Sabré la dirección mañana.   **j** Compondrá la música mañana.   **3 a** Comeremos a solas.   **b** Nos acostaremos.   **c** Estaremos tristes.   **d** Saldremos al bar.   **e** Visitaremos a los vecinos.   **f** Veremos la televisión.   **g** Haremos mucho ruido.   **h** Pondremos la mesa.   **i** Sabremos la verdad.   **j** Diremos algo a su familia.

Unit 57:   1 a ¿Escribo la carta ahora?   **b** ¿Sirvo el café ahora?   **c** ¿Doblo a la izquierda ahora?   **d** ¿Lavo los platos ahora?   **e** ¿Corto el césped ahora?   **f** ¿Reparo el coche ahora?   **g** ¿Lleno el depósito ahora?   **h** ¿Enchufo la aspiradora ahora?   **i** ¿Les llamo ahora?   **j** ¿Salgo ahora?   **2 a** Vamos a comer mucho.   **b** Juan va a beber una cerveza.   **c** Luisa va a ir a la universidad.   **d** Tú vas a visitar América.   **e** Vas a tener problemas.   **f** Ustedes van a escribir muchas cartas.   **3 a** Sí, pienso lavar los platos.   **b** Sí, pienso salir con Julio.   **c** Sí, Juan piensa comer toda la paella.   **d** Sí, pienso pagar la cuenta.   **e** Sí, pienso servir la comida.   **f** Sí, pensamos hablar con el director.   **4 a** Sí, quiero lavar los platos.   **b** Sí, quiero salir con Julio.   **c** Sí, Juan quiere comer toda la paella.   **d** Sí, quiero pagar la cuenta.   **e** Sí, quiero servir la comida.   **f** Sí, queremos hablar con el director.

Unit 58:   1 a No comería calamares.   **b** No iría a pie.   **c** No vería la televisión.   **d** No saldría con Luisa.   **e** No hablaría con el médico.   **f** No trabajaría mucho.   **g** No diría la verdad.   **h** No escribiría una carta.   **i** No podría llegar a tiempo.   **j** No sabría la dirección.   **2 a** haría   **b** lavarías   **c** nadaría   **d** podrían   **e** escribiríamos   **f** jugaría   **g** tomaríais   **h** vendría   **i** diría   **j** trabajarías

Unit 59: **1** **a** He terminado la carta. **b** He hablado con el médico. **c** He salido con Julio. **d** He buscado el dinero. **e** He bebido el café. **f** He ido al mercado. **g** He limpiado las ventanas. **h** He leído el periódico. **i** He llamado a la policía. **j** He servido el té. **2** **a** Han comido. **b** ¿Has terminado? **c** Han creído. **d** Ha visto. **e** Hemos puesto. **f** Ha muerto. **g** Habéis roto. **h** He descrito. **3** **a** Porque no lo hemos bebido todavía. **b** Porque no la hemos escuchado todavía. **c** Porque no los hemos pintado todavía. **d** Porque no lo hemos comido todavía. **e** Porque no las hemos leído todavía. **f** Porque no nos hemos duchado todavía. **g** Porque no nos hemos dormido todavía. **h** Porque no nos hemos levantado todavía. **i** Porque no los hemos fumado todavía. **j** Porque no les hemos hablado todavía. **4** **a** Ya han dicho la verdad. **b** Ya han devuelto el dinero. **c** Ya han abierto la puerta. **d** Ya han frito el pescado. **e** Ya han puesto la mesa. **f** Ya han vuelto a casa. **g** Ya han hecho la paella. **h** Ya han descrito sus planes. **i** Ya han resuelto el problema. **j** Ya han muerto.

Unit 60: **1** **a** yo habré bebido **b** él habrá llegado **c** nosotros habremos comido **d** usted habrá leído **e** ellos habrán contestado **f** ustedes se habrán casado **g** tú habrás llamado **h** vosotros habréis dormido **i** yo habré dado **j** nosotros habremos ido **2** **a** tú habrás visto **b** nosotros habremos frito **c** yo habré puesto **d** ella habrá vuelto **e** ustedes habrán dicho **f** tú habrás hecho **g** nosotros habremos escrito **h** ellos habrán roto **i** yo habré devuelto **j** usted habrá muerto **3** **a** habrá vuelto **b** habrá salido **c** habrá decidido **d** se habrá casado **e** se habrá acostado **f** se habrá levantado **g** habrá resuelto el problema **h** habrá frito las patatas **i** habrá dicho la verdad **4** **a** Pedro habrá terminado su libro. **b** Yo habré pintado la casa. **c** Julio y Emilio se habrán casado. **d** Tú y Julio habréis frito el pescado. **e** El pobre hombre habrá muerto. **f** Tú y yo habremos recibido el dinero. **g** Usted habrá hecho la paella. **h** Tú habrás escrito la carta. **i** Ellos se habrán ido del pueblo. **j** Ustedes habrán visto la película.

Unit 61: **1** **a** yo había hablado **b** ellos habían comido **c** nosotros habíamos salido **d** ella había ido **e** vosotros habíais bebido **f** el ladrón se había escapado **g** la policía había venido **h** tú habías llamado **i** ellas habían contestado **j** usted había buscado **2** **a** Juan había escrito **b** nosotros habíamos puesto **c** ella había vuelto **d** vosotros habíais devuelto **e** ellos habían muerto **f** yo había visto **g** él había abierto **h** tú habías dicho **i** usted había roto **j** yo había hecho **3** **a** Nosotros no nos habíamos levantado. **b** Ellos nunca lo habían terminado puntualmente. **c** Nadie los había visto en el pueblo. **d** Yo nunca había querido comer nada. **e** Usted no se había levantado a las ocho. **f** Ustedes no los habían probado. **g** Tú no le habías escrito. **h** Ella nunca se había puesto nada. **i** Yo nunca me había acostado temprano. **j** Juan y María no se habían ido.

Unit 62: **1** **a** nosotros habríamos salido **b** ellos se habrían acostado **c** usted habría bebido **d** yo habría creído **e** ella habría leído **f** nosotros nos habríamos casado **g** tú habrías ido **h** yo habría dormido **i** ustedes habrían olvidado **j** vosotros habríais pensado **2** **a** ella habría muerto **b** tú habrías escrito **c** nosotros habríamos dicho **d** ustedes habrían frito **e** yo habría hecho **f** ellos habrían puesto **g** usted habría visto **h** vosotros habríais roto **i** tú habrías vuelto **j** él habría resuelto **3** **a** Yo no me habría acostado tarde. **b** Yo no los habría fumado. **c** Yo no me habría casado. **d** Yo no habría dormido toda la tarde. **e** Yo no lo habría estudiado. **f** Yo no lo habría creído. **g** Yo no me habría bañado en el mar. **h** Yo no la habría dicho. **i** Yo no me la habría puesto. **j** Yo no me habría vuelto loco. **4** **a** Nosotros no nos habríamos acostado tarde tampoco. **b** Nosotros no los habríamos fumado tampoco. **c** Nosotros no nos habríamos casado tampoco. **d** Nosotros no habríamos dormido toda la tarde tampoco.

e Nosotros no lo habríamos estudiado tampoco. f Nosotros no lo habríamos creído tampoco. g Nosotros no nos habríamos bañado en el mar tampoco. h Nosotros no la habríamos dicho tampoco. i Nosotros no la habríamos puesto tampoco. j Nosotros no nos habríamos vuelto locos tampoco. 5 a Habría viajado por el mundo. b Habría vivido en un país exótico. c Me habría casado con Julia. d Habría visitado a mi abuela en Perú.

Unit 63: 1 a El vino es bebido por Juan. b La carta fue escrita por Julio. c Luisa fue vista por los chicos en la calle. d La casa es pintada todos los años. e El ladrón fue cogido por la policía. f Las flores son cogidas por Luisa y Emilio. g La paella fue hecha por usted. h Esta revista es leída por todo el mundo. i Mi coche fue reparado por el mecánico. j La hierba es comida por los animales. 2 a Se come la paella/La paella se come por toda España. b Se habla inglés en muchos países. c Se fuman muchos cigarrillos en la calle. d El vino tinto se bebe con frecuencia. e Las cartas se escriben con lápiz. f Se abre la puerta lentamente. g Se lee mucho este periódico. h Se come la hierba en el verano. i Se cogen las flores en el campo. j Se conoce el pueblo. 3 a Juan López escribió el libro. b Las chicas hacen esta paella. c Un estudiante abre la puerta. d Las vacas comen la hierba. e Muchos turistas visitan la catedral. f Un ladrón robó mi dinero. g Un mecánico reparará su coche. h Un policía inspeccionó mi pasaporte.

Unit 64: 1 a tú comas b nosotros ganemos c usted grite d ellos contesten e vosotros bebáis f ella se lave g yo descanse h ustedes escriban i tú prometas j nosotros fumemos 2 a Julio prefiere que nosotros descansemos. b Julio espera que Luisa gane la lotería. c Julio quiere que usted coma. d Julio necesita que Juan y María contesten. e Julio no quiere que (tú) fumes. f Julio quiere que los niños se laven. g Julio necesita que vosotros trabajéis. h Julio no quiere que la gente grite. i Julio no quiere que yo escriba. j Julio insiste en que las chicas beban. 3 a No me gusta que usted fume. b No nos gusta que Luisa cante. c ¿No te gusta que yo descanse? d No les gusta que nosotros bebamos. e No le gusta a Luisa que Pedro escriba. f No me gusta que los niños griten. 4 a trabajemos b griten c escriban d fumes e cante f descanséis

Unit 65: 1 a tenga b salgamos c vengas d diga e hagamos f ponga g cuenten h nos divirtamos i durmamos j veamos 2 a Nosotros no queremos que los niños salgan. b Julio prefiere que Luisa se ponga el jersey azul. c Me gusta que digas la verdad. d Necesitan que hagamos una paella. e La madre espera que el niño no caiga. f Insisto (en) que usted pida permiso. g Espero que os divirtáis. h Al profesor no le gusta que durmamos en la clase. i Mando que cuentes el dinero. j No me gusta que haga frío. 3 a caiga b vea c tengamos d haga e pidas f diga g salgan h venga

Unit 66: 1 a vaya, vayas, vaya, vayamos, vayáis, vayan, b sepa, sepas, sepa, sepamos, sepáis, sepan 2 a siente b Es posible c Es necesario d Dudo e teme f impide g Estamos alegres de h Es importante i Es imposible j Es urgente.

3

Unit 67: **1** a gane b salga c vuelvan d empiece e digas
2 a lleguen b venga c llegue d reciba e podamos **3** a hasta que
b tan pronto como c tan pronto como d hasta que e hasta que f hasta
que **3** a hasta que b tan pronto como c tan pronto como e hasta
que e hasta que **4** a Vamos a cantar/Cantaremos hasta que salgan los
niños. b Luisa va a descansar hasta que Julio venga/llegue. c Compraré
una casa grande cuando gane la lotería. d Tan pronto como venga tu padre
comeremos. e Estarán contentos cuando digas la verdad. f Vamos a nadar
hasta que empiece a llover.

Unit 68: **1** a Si escribe Luisa, contestaremos en seguida. b Si tengo tiempo,
iré al médico. c Si te sientes mal, llamo al médico. d Si hay una película
buena, iremos al cine. e Si tú me invitas, iremos a un restaurante. f Si usted
tiene hambre, le invito a comer. g Si llueve, voy a leer un libro. h Si tú no
me quieres, me voy. **2** a Si tuviese/tuviera dinero... b Si viviese/viviera en
el campo... c Si supiese/supiera conducir... d Si viese/viera bien...
e Si visitase/visitara a mis amigos... f Si bebiese/bebiera menos...
3 a viene b tengo c tuviésemos d estuviera e estamos f tuviera
g llueve h lloviese

Unit 69: **1** a Es dudoso que tengamos bastante dinero. b Es posible que el
hombre comprenda. c No es cierto que haya un autobús. d Es probable
que hablemos con el profesor. e No es probable que encontremos una
habitación. **2** a Puede ser que visite al médico. b Puede ser que Juan
venga con nosotros. c Puede ser que puedan reparar el coche hoy. d Puede
ser que pueda ayudarle. e Puede ser que tengamos que ir. **3** a Quizás
b quizás c A lo mejor e Quizás e a lo mejor **4** a Es posible que llueva
hoy. b Es probable que no venga. c Puede ser que Pedro escriba pronto.
d Es dudoso que tengamos bastante dinero. e No es cierto que podamos ir.
f Quizá (etc.) llegue mañana. g Llegará mañana, quizás. h Tal vez el
hombre simpático pagará/pague. i Quizás comprenda/entienda español.
j A lo mejor pronto te sientes mejor.

Unit 70: **1** a Although Julio is coming we are not going to eat; Even if Julio
comes we are not going to eat. b Although it was raining hard we didn't
watch TV; Even if it rained hard we decided not to watch TV. c He wants to
study Spanish although it is difficult; He wants to study Spanish even if it is
difficult. d Luisa went to Madrid although she didn't like it; Luisa would go
to Madrid even if she didn't like it. e Although you are telling me the truth
I'm going to the police; Even if you tell me the truth I'm going to the police.
2 a hablas b gane c es d es e pidieses **3** a sea b hay
c haya d cambie e cambia **4** a Ojalá tuviese/tuviera dinero. b Ojalá
Julio me visitase/visitara. c Ojalá Elena me escribiese/escribiera. d Ojalá
mis padres fuesen/fueran ricos.

Unit 71: **1** a Speak Spanish. b Drink more water. c Pay the bill.
d Get on quickly. e Take care. f Tell the truth. **2** a No hable español.
b No beba más agua. c No pague la cuenta. d No suba rápidamente.
e No tenga cuidado. f No diga la verdad. **3** a No hables español.
b No bebas más agua. c No pagues la cuenta. d No subas rápidamente.
e No tengas cuidado. f No digas la verdad. **4** a Hablen español. b Beban
más agua. c Paguen la cuenta. d Suban rápidamente. e Tengan ciudado.
f Digan la verdad. **5** ¿Quiere usted...? a hablar despacio b abrir la ventana
c cerrar la puerta d lavar los platos e decir la verdad f pagar la cuenta
g salir conmigo h bajar rápidamente **6** a No se moleste. b No se lave.
c No la abra. d No la cierre e No me diga. f No me pague. g No se
sienten. h No se lo ponga. i No se lo quiten. **7** a Abran el paquete.
b Llenen el depósito con agua. c No aparquen. d Paguen la cuenta al salir.
e No pisen la hierba. f No canten en el bar.

Unit 72: **1** a bebe b habla c escribe d vive e corre **2** a bebed
b hablad c escribid d vivid e corred **3** a levántate b acuéstate
c vístete d duérmete e escóndete **4** a levantaos b acostaos c vestíos
d dormíos e escondeos **5** a di; decid b pon; poned c sal; salid
d ten; tened e ven; venid **6** a Poned la mesa, niños/hijos. b Di la
verdad, Julio. c Sal conmigo, Luisa. d Venid al cine, chicos. e Haz una
paella, mamá/madre. f Vestíos, niños/hijos. g Divertíos, chicas. h Idos,
chicos.

Unit 73: **1** a comiésemos; comiéramos b saliesen; salieran c escribiese;
escribiera d comieses; comieras e fuésemos; fuéramos f trabajase;
trabajara g estudiasen; estudiaran h hiciese; hiciera i hablaseis; hablarais
j dijesen; dijeran. **2** a hablaras b comieses c fuese d fuéramos
e saliese f bebieran g hablaseis h dijera i hicieras j bebieses
3 a hablásemos; habláramos b comiésemos; comiéramos c saliésemos;
saliéramos d dijésemos; dijéramos e hiciésemos; hiciéramos. **4** a que
Luisa comiese/comiera. b que los niños trabajasen/trabajaran. c que el
estudiante entrase/entrara. d que el profesor saliese/saliera. e que usted no
fumase/fumara. f que Julio llegase/llegara. g que cantase/cantara. h que
no bebieseis/bebierais.

Unit 74: **1** a Quiere comer. b Prefiero descansar. c Deciden comprar.
d No puedes salir hoy. e Debemos estudiar. f Olvidan escribir.
g ¿Piensas ir? **2** a Prefiero leer un libro. b Juan rehúsa comer pescado.
c Necesitamos visitar al médico. d Prometes lavar los platos. e Temes salir
por la noche. f Espero ir a Madrid. g Logré comprar un coche.
h Sabemos hablar portugués. i No pueden dormir bien. j He olvidado
pagar la cuenta. **3** a Los oímos jugar en el jardín. b Le oigo a Julio tocar
el piano. c Nos ven preparar la comida. d Te veo salir por la ventana.
e Sentimos al ladrón entrar por la noche. **4** a Te oigo llamar pero no
puedes entrar. b Rehusamos pagar la cuenta. c No sé hacer una paella.
d Me hace entrar por la ventana. e No logran/ consiguen dormir.

Unit 75: **1** a Vamos a tocar el piano. b Salgo a pasear en el parque.
c Mi madre baja a preparar la comida. d Suben a dormir. e Tú entras a
ver la televisión. f Corren a encontrar a papá. **2** a Comienza a leer.
b Empezamos a escribir. c Echan a reír. d Te pones a estudiar. e Ella
empieza a nadar. f Nos ponemos a correr. **3** a Luisa aprende a nadar.
b Julio estudia a ser mecánico. c Los niños aprenden a escribir. d Te
enseño a leer. e Aprendo a tocar el piano. f Estudian a hablar inglés.
4 a Nos obliga a descansar. b Te invitamos a comer. c Nos ayudan a
leer. d Me animas a nadar. e Le persuaden a hablar. f Ella se prepara a
salir.

Unit 76: **1** a Los niños terminan de jugar al fútbol. b Dejo de fumar
cigarrillos. c Julio termina de cantar canciones románticas. d El autor deja
de escribir novelas históricas. e Luisa quiere dejar de fumar. f Terminamos
de hablar. **2** a Ahora mismo termino de beber. b Ahora mismo Luisa
termina de preparar la comida. c Ahora mismo el mecánico termina de
reparar el coche. d Ahora mismo terminamos de comer. e Ahora mismo
termino de tomar la foto. f Ahora mismo los estudiantes terminan de escribir.
3 a No puedo dejar de comer chocolate. b Julio no puede dejar de beber
tanto. c No puedo dejar de hablar tanto. d No pueden dejar de fumar
mucho. e No puedo dejar de comprar billetes de lotería. f No puedo dejar
de reír. **4** a se encargó b se acordó c me arrepentí d trato e se
jactaron f presume g he dejado h Me he olvidado

Unit 77: **1 a** Los soldados luchan por ganar la batalla. **b** Me esfuerzo por llegar a tiempo. **c** Los estudiantes se esfuerzan por aprobar los exámenes. **d** El dictador lucha por ganar las elecciones. **2 a** Los padres consienten en comprar un coche. **b** Julio insiste en venir. **c** Luisa tarda dos horas en prepararse. **d** Nosotros quedamos en ir al cine. **e** Yo me intereso en ver la televisión. **f** Los estudiantes se empeñan en aprobar los exámenes. **g** Luisa y María vacilan en salir con Julio. **h** ¿Tú consientes en venir conmigo? **3 a** Los ladrones amenazaron con robar el dinero. **b** La chica sueña con salir con el chico. **c** Julio y Elena sueñan con ganar la lotería. **d** La policía cuenta con capturar a los criminales. **e** Nosotros contamos con encontrar un hotel. **f** El vecino amenaza con llamar a la policía. **4 a** en **b** por **c** por **d** en **e** con **f** en **g** en **h** con

Unit 78: **1 a** Tengo tres hijos. **b** No tienes tiempo. **c** No tenemos dinero. **d** ¿Tienes hijos o hijas? **2 a** He comprado un coche. **b** He bebido el vino. **c** ¿Habías comprado la casa? **d** Habían comprado un coche. **3 a** Hay vino en la mesa. **b** Hay niños en la playa. **c** ¿Hay servicios por aquí? **d** ¿Hay un hotel en la ciudad/el pueblo? **e** Hay una corrida hoy. **4 a** Había muchos burros en la playa. **b** Ha habido un accidente. **c** Va a haber una corrida. **d** Habrá muchos candidatos para el trabajo. **e** Sin dinero habría una huelga. **f** Había habido un coche en el garaje. **g** De repente hubo una llamada en la puerta. **h** No hay servicios en el bar.

Unit 79: **1 a** No, acabo de comer. **b** No, acabo de dormir. **c** No, acabo de tocar el disco. **d** No, acabo de hacer una tortilla. **e** No, acabo de llamar a Luisa. **f** No, acabo de salir con el perro. **g** No, acabo de ver la televisión. **h** No, acabo de trabajar en el jardín. **i** No, acabo de ir al cine. **j** No, acabo de lavar los platos. **2 a** Juan acababa de leer **b** Luisa y Pedro acababan de cantar **c** Yo acababa de levantarme **d** Sus padres acababan de salir **e** Vosotros acababais de recibir la carta **f** Nosotros acabábamos de servir el café **g** Tú acababas de dormir **h** Usted acababa de ver la televisión **i** Ellos acababan de hacer una paella **j** Yo acababa de telefonear **3 a** Yo acabo de comer pero vuelvo a comer en seguida. **b** Usted acaba de nadar pero vuelve a nadar en seguida. **c** Julio acaba de cantar pero vuelve a cantar en seguida. **d** Nosotros acabamos de leer pero volvemos a leer en seguida. **e** Ellos acaban de jugar al tenis pero vuelven a jugar al tenis en seguida. **f** Tú acabas de salir pero vuelves a salir en seguida. **g** Los señores García acaban de llamar pero vuelven a llamar en seguida. **h** Tú acabas de hacer una paella pero vuelves a hacer una paella en seguida. **i** Nosotros acabamos de ir a la ciudad pero volvemos a ir a la ciudad en seguida. **j** Ustedes acaban de escribir pero vuelven a escribir en seguida. **4 a** acaba de **b** vuelvo a **c** acaba de **d** volver a **e** volver a **f** acabo de **g** acaba de/vuelve a **h** vuelve a **i** acaba de **j** Vuelve a

Unit 80: **1 a** conoce **b** sabe **c** conoce **d** conozco **e** sé **f** conoces **2 a** Conozco bien Madrid. **b** Sabemos que Madrid es la capital de España. **c** ¿Sabes que Luisa es española? **d** ¿Conoces a Luisa? **e** La conocí en Barcelona. **f** La familia de Luisa es muy conocida en Barcelona. **3 a** podemos **b** conoces **c** conoce **d** sabéis **e** conoce **f** conoce **g** puedes **h** sé **i** saben **j** sabéis

S	P	O	C	E	S	A
C	O	N	O	C	E	S
O	D	E	N	O	D	A
N	E	B	O	N	E	B
O	M	A	C	O	U	E
C	O	S	E	C	P	I
E	S	A	B	E	I	S

Unit 81: **1 a** Puede **b** puedo **c** puedes **d** sé **e** puede **f** puedo **g** sé **h** sabe; puede; puede **2 a** ¿Sabe(s) nadar? **b** ¿Puedes nadar si te duele la pierna? **c** Sé hablar español. **d** Aquí (se) puede(s) hablar español o inglés. **e** ¿Se puede fumar aquí? **f** El pobre niño no puede leer sin sus gafas. **g** El pobre niño no sabe leer. **h** ¿Puedes leer un periódico? **i** ¿Sabes leer un periódico español? **j** No puedo salir hoy porque tengo que estudiar.

Unit 82: **1 a** Suggestioned answers. **a** Sí/no, (no) tengo (mucha) hambre. **b** No, no tengo tiempo./No, no tengo ganas. **c** Porque tengo (mucha) prisa. **d** Porque tiene (mucho) frío. **e** Sí/No, (no) tengo (mucha) suerte. **f** Mi problema no tiene nada que ver con Julio. **g** No, no tienes razón. **h** Porque tengo (mucho) sueño. **i** ¡Ay, tengo miedo! **j** Sí, tengo que estudiar. **2 a** 2 **b** 4 **c** 5 **d** 10 **e** 3 **f** 9 **g** 8 **h** 7 **i** 1 **j** 6 **3 a** mucha **b** muchas **c** mucha **d** mucha **e** mucho **f** mucho; mucho **g** mucho **h** mucho

Unit 83: **1 a** tomar **b** coger **c** sacar **d** tardar **e** tomar **f** sacar **g** tomar **h** llevar **i** sacar **j** tomar **2 a** cojo **b** tomé **c** llevar **d** sacamos **e** sacamos **f** tomamos **g** sacamos **h** cogimos **i** cogimos **j** tardamos **k** saqué **l** tomé

Unit 84: **1 a** Este regalo es para mi padre. **b** El tren sale para Barcelona. **c** ¿Es el vino para mí? **d** Necesito una pieza para mi radio. **e** ¿Tiene dos habitaciones para la noche? **f** Para mí, el libro es interesante. **g** Luisa estudia para médico. **h** Sólo vive para estudiar. **i** Para cantante tiene una voz terrible. **j** Somos amigos para siempre **2 a** ti **b** nosotros **c** mí **d** ellos **e** usted **3 a** For a father he does not play with the children very much. **b** As far as he is concerned this letter means nothing. **c** Juan is studying to be a mechanic. **d** Do you have a tyre for my car? **e** It is a great honour for us. **f** The plane had arrived by then. **g** I need the repair by tomorrow. **h** We bought a present for my mother. **i** We work hard in order to live well. **j** My brother has left for school.

Unit 85: **1 a** por mi madre **b** por mi tío **c** por mis vecinos **d** por el profesor enfermo **e** por el analfabeto **2 a** por Madrid **b** por una camisa **c** Por aquí **d** por el coche **e** por todas partes **f** por fax **g** por el sol **h** por los niños **i** por el regalo **j** por pan **3 a** Estudio para los exámenes. **b** Estudio por los exámenes. **c** Preparo la comida para mi madre. **d** Preparo la comida por mi madre. **e** Necesito esta reparación para hoy. **f** Eso es todo por hoy. **g** Quiero gasolina para mi coche. **h** Quiero una bicicleta por mi coche. **i** Trabaja para médico. **j** Trabaja por el médico.

Unit 86: **1 a** sin **b** sin **c** con **d** sin **e** sin **f** sin **g** con **h** con **i** con **j** Con **2 a** Do you have a room with a bath? **b** By pushing the button the door will open. **c** He went out without saying anything to his friends. **d** Why are you angry with me? **e** Do you want meat with potatoes or without? **f** He doesn't want to go with you, he prefers to go with her. **g** Is there unleaded petrol? **h** The box is locked. **3 a** Agua sin gas, por favor. **b** Té con limón pero sin azúcar. **c** Es muy amable/simpático con nosotros. **d** Parece/Está elegante con ese vestido negro. **e** Con todos sus problemas estudia mucho. **f** Tienes que atar el paquete con cuerda. **g** Siempre sale sin llave. **h** ¿Quiere usted una habitación con baño o sin baño? **i** Veinte litros de gasolina sin plomo, por favor. **j** Salió sin robar nada.

Unit 87: **1 a** en; en **b** a; en **c** de; a; a **d** En; al **e** en; a **2 a** por la mañana **b** en la playa **c** en el trabajo **d** en casa

e Voy a la iglesia. f Voy a casa. g Entro en la habitación.
h Llegan a la fábrica. i Salgo de la casa. j Sale de la oficina.
3 a en b al c en d de e en f en g de h a i de j en
k en l de m a n a o en p del q a r de s a

Unit 88: **1** a between you and me b from the balcony c in my room
d outside the restaurant e over the house f under the street g beyond the
horizon h inside the mine **2** a dentro del cine b fuera de la casa
c cerca del colegio d lejos de la ciudad e entre las casas f desde mi
ventana **3** a En b lejos c más allá d en e encima f dentro
g Fuera h al lado i debajo j entre

4

```
      D e
      E n
    e n T r e
d e n t R o
  d e l A n t e
    d e S d e
```

Unit 89: **1** a El hombre está/comparece ante el juez. b Julio está enfrente
de Julia. c El jardín está delante de la casa. d Ana va a llegar antes de las
diez. **2** a antes de b delante de c enfrente del d ante e ante
f delante de g enfrente h antes de i delante de j antes de **3** a Hay
un café enfrente de la farmacia. b Tenemos que llegar antes de las ocho.
c El cantante compareció ante su público. d Hay un coche delante de
nuestro garaje. e La parada está enfrente del/frente al colegio. f ¿Quiere
pagar la cuenta antes de salir? g ¿Qué puede hacer Pedro ante la cuenta?
h La plaza está delante del hotel. i Voy a España antes de septiembre.
j ¿Quiere usted reparar mi coche antes del sábado?

Unit 90: **1** a hasta mañana b desde ayer c desde agosto d hasta
entonces e un libro sobre Madrid f hacia el parque g según Luisa
h durante la semana i sobre/en la mesa j mi actitud hacia ti/para contigo
2 a hasta b desde c desde d hacia/para con e hacia
f menos/salvo/excepto g durante h Según i sobre j durante
3 a sobre b hacia c hacia d durante e durante f desde g Según
h salvo i hasta j desde **4** a debajo de la mesa b bajo la influencia del
vino c bajo los liberales d debajo del libro e bajo llave f debajo de la
casa **5** a día tras día b después de la guerra c detrás de la casa
d después de las clases e carta tras carta f detrás del colegio g después
del colegio h tras/después de tus problemas